# THE KING
## *AND*
# THE VICE QUEEN

## *GEORGE IV'S LAST SCANDALOUS AFFAIR*

## TOM AMBROSE

SUTTON PUBLISHING

First published in the United Kingdom in 2005 by
Sutton Publishing Limited · Phoenix Mill
Thrupp · Stroud · Gloucestershire · GL5 2BU

Copyright © Tom Ambrose, 2005

Tom Ambrose has asserted the moral right to be identified as the author
of this work.

British Library Cataloguing in Publication Data
A catalogue record for this book is available from the British Library.

ISBN 0-7509-3494-8

For Ann

Typeset in 11/14.5 Sabon.
Typesetting and origination by
Sutton Publishing Limited.
Printed and bound in England by
J.H. Haynes & Co. Ltd, Sparkford.

Read From 25th May 2009
Finish on 1st June 2009.

# Contents

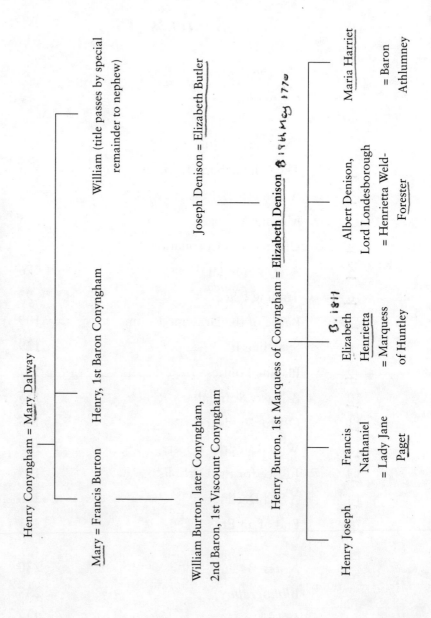

# Chronology

| | | |
|---|---|---|
| 1762 | 12 August | Birth of George Augustus Frederick, Prince of Wales |
| 1770 | 19 May | Elizabeth Denison born to Joseph Denison, banker |
| 1779 | December | George falls in love with Mary Robinson |
| 1783 | September | George visits Brighton |
| 1784 | March | Becomes obsessed with Maria Fitzherbert |
| 1785 | 15 December | Marries Mrs Fitzherbert in London |
| 1789 | April | Elizabeth Denison falls in love with John Ponsonby |
| 1794 | Spring | George begins an affair with Lady Jersey |
| | 5 July | Elizabeth Denison marries Henry, Lord Conyngham at St Martin-in-the-Fields, London |
| 1794 | August | George becomes engaged to Caroline of Brunswick |
| 1795 | 6 April | Birth of Henry Francis, Earl of Mount Charles |
| | 8 April | George marries Princess Caroline at St James's Palace |
| 1796 | January | Their daughter, Princess Charlotte, is born |
| 1797 | 11 June | Birth of Francis Nathaniel, 2nd Marquess of Conyngham |
| 1800 | July | Henry and Elizabeth Conyngham return to London |
| 1805 | 21 October | Albert Conyngham, 1st Baron Londesborough, born. Battle of Trafalgar |
| 1806 | Autumn | George begins an affair with Lady Hertford |
| 1811 | June | George finally breaks with Mrs Fitzherbert |
| | 24 August | Birth of Lady Elizabeth Conyngham |

| 1814 | July/August | Elizabeth Conyngham has an affair with Grand Duke Nicholas of Russia |
| | 14 August | Queen Caroline leaves England on her travels |
| 1815 | 18 June | Battle of Waterloo |
| 1816 | October | Henry, Viscount Conyngham elevated to Marquess |
| 1818 | 11 June | Milan Commission begins investigating the Queen's scandalous behaviour |
| 1819 | December | George separates from Lady Hertford and appears in public with Elizabeth Conyngham |
| 1820 | 29 January | George III dies at Kew and George IV is proclaimed King |
| | 5 June | Queen Caroline returns to London |
| | 17 August | The Queen goes on trial |
| 1821 | 17 April | The Sumner Affair |
| | 19 July | King George IV crowned in Westminster Abbey |
| | 8 August | Queen Caroline dies |
| | August/September | George and Elizabeth visit Ireland |
| | 24 September | George leaves for State Visit to Hanover |
| 1822 | 10 August | George visits Scotland |
| | 12 August | Lord Castlereagh cuts his throat |
| 1824 | 24 December | Earl of Mount Charles dies in France |
| 1825 | 2 August | George decides to live at Royal Lodge, Windsor |
| | 10 August | John Ponsonby returns to London |
| 1827 | 17 February | Lord Liverpool suffers stroke and resigns as Prime Minister |
| | | George Canning succeeds him |
| | 8 August | Canning dies suddenly |
| | 7 September | Lord Goderich becomes Prime Minister |
| | 20 September | Harriette Wilson attempts to blackmail the King and Lady Conyngham |
| 1828 | 17 January | Lord Goderich resigns the Premiership |
| | 18 January | Duke of Wellington becomes Prime Minister |

| | | |
|---|---|---|
| **1829** | 10 April | George gives assent to Catholic Emancipation Bill |
| **1830** | 26 June | King George IV dies at Windsor |
| | 27 November | Elizabeth returns the Stuart sapphire |
| **1832** | 18 May | Great Reform Bill passed |
| | 28 December | Henry Conyngham dies |
| **1834** | March | Isabella Hertford dies |
| **1835** | 17 February | Francis, 2nd Marquess of Conyngham, becomes Lord Chamberlain of England |
| **1844** | 7 July | Tsar Nicholas and Elizabeth Conyngham meet again |
| **1855** | 24 March | John Ponsonby dies |
| **1861** | 11 October | Elizabeth Conyngham dies at Bifrons in Kent at the age of ninety-one |

# Prologue: 19 July 1821

On the hottest day of the year King George IV set off for his coronation and, characteristically, arrived at Westminster Abbey thirty minutes late. He had decided to wear the newly fashionable Elizabethan style consisting of white satin knee breeches, a velvet jacket skilfully tailored to disguise his bulging corset and a crimson velvet robe, twenty-seven feet long and embroidered with golden stars. Perched on his brown wig was a vast, black Spanish hat decked with ostrich feathers and herons' plumes.

Shorn of his russet side-whiskers for the occasion he looked more the ruddy-faced farmer than the first gentleman of Europe. One female witness thought him a most unpleasant sight, saying 'anyone seeing this disgusting figure, with a wig the curls of which hung down his back, and quite bending beneath the weight of his robes and his sixty years would have been quite sick'.

Sweating profusely, the King, now weighing over seventeen and a half stone and suffering badly from gout, looked more the victim than the hero of the occasion. As he shuffled past the ranks of peers, peeresses, generals and bishops, all in sumptuous robes, he seemed to be searching for one face in particular. Then, as he passed the section reserved for the peeresses, he appeared to find it. Pausing, he nodded gravely then – to everyone's surprise – winked 'very indecently'. In guarded acknowledgement Elizabeth, the Marchioness of Conyngham, gently inclined her head.

Throughout the five hours of the coronation ceremony, even at the most solemn moments, the King continued to make eyes, nod and wink at Lady Conyngham. At one point he lifted a diamond brooch from his chest and, looking directly at her, kissed it. She, in reply, and to the disgust of many peers, removed her silk glove and kissed the huge diamond ring that he had given her. For Elizabeth

Conyngham was now the King's favourite, and to the chagrin of both the politicians and the aristocracy, a power in the land.

This English 'Madame Pompadour' had risen from middle class origins to become the wife of an Irish peer, the lover of the future Tsar of Russia and the last openly acknowledged mistress of a King of England. For the remaining ten years of his life she would influence many of his decisions both personal and political. She would bring him sexual passion combined with a settled domesticity that he had never before enjoyed. But this would come at the price of public ridicule and she would be portrayed as the greediest and most avaricious woman of her age. One name that would stick to her was coined that year by the diarist Thomas Creevey – he called her the 'Vice Queen'.[1]

# ONE

## *The Conyngham Trap*

Three years before that coronation – the most lavish and expensive in British history – George, Prince of Wales, had made two important changes in his personal life. He stopped powdering his natural hair in favour of a curly brown wig and he changed mistresses. Out went the portly 58-year-old Marchioness of Hertford and in came the even plumper 48-year-old Marchioness of Conyngham. Amused at the Prince's increasing predilection for overweight women the wits at White's Club laid bets with each other on which lady was the heavier. When asked, as a close friend and drinking companion of the Prince, for his expert opinion on the matter the playwright Richard Sheridan thought for a moment before replying, 'Hertford is heavy but the Conyngham outweighs her by stones!'

This new love, Elizabeth Conyngham, was the eldest daughter of a once illiterate Yorkshire farm worker who had risen by his own efforts to become an immensely wealthy London banker. She was also the wife of an Irish peer of no great distinction. The mother of four grown-up children, she had gained a reputation in society for her fashionable clothes and her dark good looks. Her best-known portrait, painted by Sir Thomas Lawrence a few weeks before the coronation and now at Slane Castle in Ireland, confirms her beauty. Lawrence, a notorious flatterer of his sitters, emphasised the unusual pale blue of her eyes that had inspired the diarist Grantley Berkeley to write effusively:

> Her eyes of the favourite colour, were extremely animated in their expression; her transparent complexion, of the favourite roses and lilies, was always bright with the most winning smiles; and a sweetly musical voice, low and tender, as her august friend liked the feminine tones to be.[1]

What had caused the Prince to split with his current mistress Isabella Hertford after a twelve-year relationship and take up with Elizabeth was rumoured to have been a violent incident that occurred at the Hertford's town house in Manchester Square, London. One evening Isabella's son, the dissolute Earl of Yarmouth, was said to have awoken from his customary drunken slumber at the dinner table to discover that his mother and her royal guest were missing. Yarmouth, known as 'Bloater' for his red hair and florid face, eventually found them together in a side room sprawled on a sofa 'in a very peculiar situation'. Enraged at the Prince's liberties with his mother Yarmouth was supposed to have flown at him and 'treated him to as handsome a pair of black eyes as his soul could wish for'. So violent was the assault, it was claimed, that the Prince kept to his bed for a month.[2] News of this supposed event spread throughout London and inspired a best-selling cartoon, 'Royal Stripes or Kick from Yarmouth' and a poem from the satirist Peter Pindar, who offered this sound advice:

> Ye Princes, as you love your lives,
> Ne'er meddle with your neighbours wives,
> But keep your brittle hearts from tripping:
> Lest some rude lord, to scare beholders,
> Should compliment your princely shoulders,
> With such another royal whipping.

The truth was far less dramatic. George had indeed injured himself that evening but in an incident wholly unconnected with Lady Hertford or Manchester House. The Prince had merely twisted his ankle demonstrating the Highland fling to his daughter Princess Charlotte at his London residence, Carlton House. Yet the public preferred to believe the more sensational rumour because it corresponded with their image of the errant Prince whose misdeeds and mishaps had been chronicled for decades. Hardly a week had passed in the previous two decades without some new cartoon depicting the Prince of Wales as a hard drinking, gormandising womaniser appearing in the windows of the Fleet Street print shops. Brilliantly drawn by such artists as James Gillray, George Cruikshank and William Heath, these satirical cartoons were a uniquely British institution of the time. In no other European country could the follies and mendacity of politicians, aristocrats and royalty be so openly mocked without fear of prosecution.

For years the cartoonists had mocked Isabella Hertford as a lofty dominatrix towering over and bullying her wretched royal lover. Soon her successor, Lady Conyngham, would have to bear the same public ridicule that had so distressed Isabella. Throughout the decade of their relationship until the King's death in 1830, George IV and Elizabeth Conyngham would be the subject of over 300 satirical cartoons. Without exception they depicted Elizabeth as a fat, greedy woman and the Prince as a salacious, gullible fool. One of the first of the anonymous satires warned the Prince of Elizabeth's cunning designs on his person and purse through the use of the deadly 'Conyngham Trap':

> A most ingenious contrivance (in horn-work) for taking the largest animals alive . . . it opens easily, receives its prey with security and will work equally well in all weathers . . . it will supersede the use of the celebrated Hertford Snap. It is rather clumsy in its construction and not new in its principles, being very similar to the Robinson and Fitzherbert Catches formerly in vogue.[3]

These 'catches' were two of the Prince's best-known former mistresses, the actress Mary Robinson, the great love of his youth, and his morganatic wife, the Catholic widow Maria Fitzherbert. Both were supposed to have inveigled the disingenuous Prince into dangerous and compromising relationships. Nor had his judgement of women improved by 1795 when, in return for having his mounting debts paid off, he allowed his father George III to dragoon him into a disastrous marriage to Princess Caroline of Brunswick – a woman who, he claimed, physically revolted him.

After the torments of this ludicrous misalliance his next serious relationship, with Isabella Hertford, had appeared almost sensible. Although he had been friendly with the Marquess of Hertford and his wife for many years, suddenly in the autumn of 1806 and for no apparent good reason, George convinced himself that he was desperately in love with Isabella. So consumed with desire was he for this large and formidable woman that, according to his friend

Lady Bessborough, 'he frets himself into a fever . . . to persuade Lady Hertford to live with him – publickly!! This sudden passion astonished everyone at court not least the lady herself.'[4] Other courtiers were equally amused. 'She must be scarcely able to believe', wrote Sir George Jackson, 'that charms she had not been aware of possessing – at least for many a year – should now prove . . . so irresistibly attractive.' Yet after a short period of hesitation, for the sake of propriety, Lady Hertford succumbed to the Prince's importunings. His canary-yellow carriage soon became a common sight parked outside her London home and was immortalised by Tom Moore in his poem *Diary of a Politician*:

> Through Manchester Square took a canter just now –
> Met the old yellow chariot, and made a low bow.
> This I did, of course, thinking 'twas loyal and civil.
> But got such a look – oh 'twas black as the devil!
> How unlucky! – incog. he was travelling about
> And I, like a noodle, must go find him out.

Now the Prince became an even more frequent guest at Manchester Square and at the Hertfords' fine country houses of Sudbourne in Suffolk and Ragley Hall in Warwickshire. As he was living apart from his own wife Princess Caroline he seemed to find family life with the Hertfords highly congenial. Their son, the Earl of Yarmouth, delighted the Prince and became his constant companion. In spite of his reputation as a violent and unpleasant alcoholic, Yarmouth was one of the most astute and knowledgeable art collectors of the age and helped George acquire many important works for Carlton House and the Brighton Pavilion.

Isabella Hertford's relationship with the Prince gave her unrivalled power over him, which she used ruthlessly to further her own interests and those of her family. Throughout her twelve-year reign as royal favourite Isabella never once lost an opportunity, as Elizabeth Conyngham would later do, to profit from the relationship. Nor was her husband ever known to complain of his wife's open infidelity. He maintained a discreet silence as the Earl of Jersey had done before him and the Marquess of Conyngham would do after when their wives became the Prince's intimate companions.

That Lord Hertford clearly condoned the compromising relationship for personal gain only confirmed the widely held belief that the Hertfords, in spite of their vast income of over £100,000 a year, were no more than an unprincipled bunch of money-grabbers. One of their severest critics at Court, Lady Blessington, considered that love of money pervaded the whole family and that Isabella Hertford was so fond of diamonds that even the Prince's wealth would not be sufficient to satisfy her greed.[5] The satirist William Combe shared this poor opinion of the Hertfords, believing that avarice was the hereditary taint of the entire family.

Soon, Isabella's blatant nepotism and supposed interference in political matters drew down on her the wrath of satirists and politicians alike. The Fleet Street cartoonists began lampooning her as 'the Sultana', 'the old Lady of Manchester Square' or the Prince's 'matured enchantress'. One cartoon showed her as a gigantic puppeteer manipulating the strings of tiny ministerial marionettes and declaring, 'I can make them do anything . . . Why, I have had the honour of performing before the Regent!' A more serious political attack on Isabella's supposed interference in politics was launched by the Whig opposition when their leader Lord Grey denounced in Parliament 'the unseen and separate influence that lurked behind the throne . . . leading to consequences the most pestilential and disgusting'.[6]

The Radicals were even bolder in their attacks on Isabella Hertford, openly castigating the Prince's relationship with her and condemning his own dissolute lifestyle in unambiguous terms. Without the accepted protection of a humorous context the radical journalist Leigh Hunt risked all when he launched an assault on the Prince in *The Morning Post*. 'Who would imagine that this Glory of the People,' he wrote, 'this Adonis in Loveliness, was a corpulent gentleman of fifty! A violator of his word, a libertine over head and ears in debt and disgrace, a despiser of domestic ties, a man who has just closed half a century without one single claim on the gratitude of his country or the respect of posterity!'[7] But Hunt had gone too far and for this unequivocal attack on the Prince he was jailed for two years and given an exemplary fine of £1,000.

Yet in spite of the scandal and embarrassment Isabella Hertford proved to be a thick-skinned survivor. With their vast estates, great wealth and powerful political connections the Hertfords were far too grand to be troubled by mere public opinion. When London was celebrating the defeat and first exile of Napoleon in April 1814 Isabella defied her critics by proudly draping a huge banner proclaiming 'The Prince's Peace' across the front of Manchester House. The Prince, too, generally ignored the ridicule, Hunt apart, and remained devoted to Isabella – who might well have survived as royal favourite for many more years had she not by 1818 begun to lose her looks. Now at 59 this once beautiful woman could best be described as 'merely handsome'. The diarist Mrs Calvert thought her 'still beautiful but on a very large scale', but then added contemptuously, 'I think her, without exception the most forbidding, haughty, unpleasant woman I ever saw'.[8] Isabella was no more popular with the Prince's other friends, who were delighted when they noticed that he appeared to be looking around for a suitable replacement.

Until 1819 all of the Prince's relationships with women had been marred by his frantic insecurity and recklessness. After a series of wild, youthful infatuations he pursued Maria Fitzherbert, a woman six years older than himself, threatening to commit suicide if she did not submit immediately to his sexual demands. Maria was wary at first but having obtained certain assurances from him, the most important being his agreement to marry her in the eyes of the Catholic Church, she eventually gave in. Yet a stable, almost domestic relationship with Maria Fitzherbert proved such a disappointment for George that his attention soon wandered. He became obsessed with the Countess of Jersey and the Marchioness of Hertford in turn. These three key emotional relationships in his life were interspersed with many short-lived affairs with much younger women. But as he grew older it became apparent to observers that he was clearly and consistently drawn to older women. What he appeared to be groping for since adolescence was a relationship with a woman who combined emotional maternity with physical sensuality. In the end, he did not have to look far to find such a being, for Elizabeth Conyngham met both requirements. She and her husband Henry were already known to George, having been introduced, ironically, by Isabella Hertford herself. They had attached themselves to the Hertford circle on arriving from Ireland where Henry Conyngham had a large estate at Slane, County Meath.

Many sharp-eyed women at Court had suspected for years that Elizabeth had designs on the Prince. Lady Charlotte Bury, daughter of the Duchess of Argyle, one of the beautiful Gunning sisters, had been told by her mother as early as 1815 that Lady Conyngham had openly declared that she 'would arrive at that goal one day or another'. Now, said the Duchess in a letter to her daughter in January 1820, 'she has reached it and may it prove all she thinks it worth! But what a false notion of happiness and honour . . . may Lady C need only behold Mrs Fitzherbert and Lady Hertford and tremble lest such should be her own fate.'[9] The Hertford family became aware too late of the danger that the attractive Elizabeth Conyngham posed to their interests. The Tory MP Charles Greville recalled Isabella's grandson Lord Beauchamp's horror when he witnessed the Prince and Elizabeth Conyngham riding together in Hyde Park one morning. 'By God', he exclaimed, 'our grandmother must learn to ride or it is all over with us!'[10] A month later the Prince's old friend Joseph Jekyll confirmed the arrival of Elizabeth Conyngham as royal mistress but thought that she would be merely a short-lived infatuation for the fickle Prince when he wrote in his diary, 'tomorrow I dine with a rural queen, Lady Conyngham who will not triumph. Tis l'esprit faible contre l'esprit fort of Lady Hertford.'[11]

When Isabella Hertford discovered that the Prince had found a new love she went straight to her friend Princess Lieven, the wife of the Austrian ambassador to London, complaining of the shabby treatment she had received. Dorothea Lieven, a friend of both parties, reminded her of the fickleness of princes and urged her to dry her tears. Rather than rail against the inevitable, the Princess advised, Isabella should accept her fate and be content with all the royal gifts and patrimony that already she had already received. That evening, more amused by than sympathetic to her friend's predicament, the Princess wrote to her lover Prince Metternich in Vienna. Her letter mocked Isabella's outrage and she declared herself astonished that Lady Hertford had the gall to complain that she found 'the new love ridiculous in view of the age of the contracting parties. I had to keep a straight face at this point of the story', wrote the Princess, for 'she is sixty three and Lady Conyngham forty eight!'[12]

In the first decades of the nineteenth century Dorothea Lieven was a shrewd observer of English society and politics, sending a daily report to Vienna chronicling events at Brighton, Windsor and Westminster. In spite of being both an intellectual and a foreigner Princess Lieven had managed to ingratiate herself into English society. Such was her determination that she managed to get herself elected as one of the three all-powerful committee members of Almacks, the most exclusive social club of the day. Throughout the 1820s she was an intimate witness of the progress of the affair between the King and Elizabeth. As a regular guest of the King she was one of the first to see them together in public. As she told Prince Metternich in a letter five months after the tearful encounter with Lady Hertford:

> The new favourite appeared yesterday in society for the first time since her accession; and I enjoyed a new light on the English character. Everyone seemed embarrassed. Nobody wanted to be the first to greet her; there was at least five minutes' suspense, painful for her and for the others. She is a nice enough woman and, as such, welcome, so that after a few minutes she secured a few 'How do you do's' – but she was not received cordially, as she was last year.[13]

Within a year the whole of London had come to accept that Elizabeth Conyngham was now the King's intimate and inseparable companion. He confirmed her new status in his customary fashion by presenting her with a miniature portrait of himself. George's demeanour was now so cheerful and good humoured that many thought the new relationship a vast improvement on the old. As Lady Holland put it, 'the reign of the Loves and Graces is better than his former reign of Terror; for . . . her predecessor, certainly ruled with the instruments of inspiring him with hatred and suspicion of all about him, not a good mechanism for a King's mistress.'[14]

Now that the Prince's final rejection of Lady Hertford was common knowledge, a rash of valedictory cartoons appeared mocking the unfortunate woman's fate. But a month later a rumour spread through London that Isabella was determined to make one last desperate attempt to regain George's affections. An anonymous story appeared purporting to be an account of Lady Hertford's clandestine visit to Brighton where, disguised as one of the sea-bathing attendants, she was said to have lain in wait for her ex-lover to emerge from the waves:

> When he came out of the water she began giving him a rubbing with a flesh brush . . . in a rather more familiar manner than he was accustomed to. But this expression of pleasure was only momentary, and far from succeeding . . . all the eloquence and alluring smiles had no effect.[15]

But to Elizabeth Conyngham the lingering threat of Isabella Hertford was no joke. She remained convinced that the rejected mistress still posed a threat to her interests and took every precaution to keep her away from the King. Anyone too friendly with the Hertfords was treated with suspicion and removed from the royal guest list. Most galling of all was the King's refusal, in spite of Elizabeth's constant entreaties, to dismiss his old friend Lord Hertford from his post as Lord Chamberlain of the Royal Household. To the King's amusement the Hertford threat continued to occupy Elizabeth's mind and he could not resist teasing her from time to time.

His greatest success came in February 1823 when Elizabeth left London for a short holiday in Ireland, leaving George at Windsor and desperately lonely. No sooner had she arrived at Slane Castle than she received a letter from George telling her of a strange visitor to the Royal Pavilion. It appeared that Isabella, hearing a rumour that the Conynghams had fallen out of favour with the Prince, had sent her nephew down to Brighton to enquire after the King's health and to let him know that she was more beautiful than ever. Of course, the King assured Elizabeth, he had refused to see the young man personally and had asked his old friend, Admiral Nagle, to stand in for him. The crusty old sailor had, according to George, told the nephew in blunt nautical terms to tell his aunt that she should 'sheer another way'.[16] Although the whole story had been made up by the King to alarm Elizabeth and get her to return early, he was surprised by the degree of success he achieved. Elizabeth immediately left Slane and, returning to London a few days later, ordered her carriage to take her post-haste down to Brighton. There she found him in unusually good humour as he guiltily confessed to her that he had made up the whole story just to get her to return to him.

In spite of Joseph Jekyll's prediction that George's fascination with Lady Conyngham would be short-lived, she had by late 1820 completely captured his heart. Her unusual combination of sensual attraction and motherly charm now provided him with all that Maria Fitzherbert, over twenty years earlier, had tantalisingly promised but failed to deliver. Moreover, unlike the widowed Mrs Fitzherbert, Elizabeth Conyngham had the advantage of a living and compliant husband and would make no demands for a marriage. Whatever her apparent avarice she was also clearly untroubled by either moral or religious scruples and would certainly not drag George into another begrudging and politically compromising marriage.

But there was a price to pay for this compliancy. Like Isabella Hertford before her, Elizabeth would make sure that her husband was rewarded with a prestigious and lucrative office in the royal household. As Francis, Marquess of Hertford, had been made Lord Chamberlain with a salary of £3,000 a year so Henry, Marquess of Conyngham, was soon be appointed to the equally lucrative post of Lord Steward of the Royal Household. Elizabeth herself would receive from her lover the greatest treasure trove of jewels ever given to a royal mistress in England – much of it paid for by money purloined, on George's orders, from the public purse.

# TWO

## A London Heiress

The Duke of Wellington was known to have disliked the new royal mistress from the moment he set eyes on her and was as dismissive of her character as he was of her middle-class origins. A consistent champion of aristocratic privilege and a critic of vulgarity in any form, Wellington often complained that Lady Conyngham's voice gave him 'a revulsion of the blood' whenever he heard it, knowing that he was about to hear 'some fresh vulgarity'.[1] In complete contrast to the patrician Duke, George, Prince of Wales was a man who could chat as easily to a common page as to a fellow prince. A democrat in everything but political views, George was the first British monarch to make friends with the emergent members of the mercantile class. The best known of these self-made men was the sea-biscuit manufacturer turned banker Sir William Curtis, a genial character who returned the Prince's lavish hospitality at the Brighton Pavilion with his own less sophisticated pleasures at his splendidly vulgar villa near Ramsgate. Although totally dissimilar in character and tastes, Curtis's rise to riches had much in common with that of Elizabeth Conyngham's own father, Joseph Denison.

Born to a family of poor country labourers in Yorkshire in 1726, Joseph Denison was to become even wealthier that William Curtis. At the age of fourteen he decided to leave the land and, like so many before him, set out to make his fortune in London. Arriving in the capital illiterate and penniless he only survived in the first years by working as an ill-paid casual labourer. Showing a determination that his daughter would one day inherit, each evening Denison set about teaching himself to read and write by the light of a candle that he could ill afford. Once he had mastered literacy he went looking for a position as a clerk. Good fortune took him to the counting house of a Mr Dillon, an Irish banker with a drink problem. By hard work

13

and his own natural acumen Joseph Denison so prospered in his post that within a few years roles were curiously reversed and Dillon was the clerk and Denison became the banker.[2]

His timing was perfect, for there was no better time or place to acquire wealth than London in the booming economy of the mid-eighteenth century. British trade was expanding in India and America and threatening the Dutch monopoly in the Far East. Funding this commerce was the City of London, which provided venture capital for every almost every imaginable enterprise. Joseph Denison's bank played its small part in all this, driven by its proprietor's 'unabated industry and rigid frugality'. By 1754 Denison had become an important figure in the booming London money market and had accrued sufficient funds to be able to form the financial alliance that was to make him one of the richest men in England.

Realising that the new industries developing in the north of England lacked local funding, Denison decided to give them access to London capital. What he needed was a partner in the north, and after much searching he put a proposition to the small bank owned by the Heywood family in Liverpool. Together they formed a London-based company with unprecedented contacts throughout the north of England. This new company, Messrs Denison, Heywood and Kennard, gave Joseph Denison unprecedented access to the new manufacturing companies as well as to the long established and highly profitable slave trade based in Liverpool. Denison's was the first bank to make the abundant venture capital of London directly available to the embryonic industrial revolution in the north which, with the coming of steam in the early nineteenth century, would give Great Britain the most powerful economy in the world.[3]

This new venture soon proved so successful that within a decade of its inception Denison had accumulated enough money to be accepted as an established member of the new British mercantile elite known as 'the monied interest'. Now he regularly attended meetings with London's leading merchants, overseas traders, bankers and financiers. All shared a buccaneering enthusiasm for commerce and a near-total disregard for even the primitive rules and regulations that existed at the time. These entrepreneurs flourished on insider trading and the privileged information passed on by their placemen in the government and revenue services. As the country prospered internally and Britain gained complete dominance over the French in India, huge fortunes like Denison's were made, many as a consequence of the quick profits that could be made from provisioning the army and navy.

Driven by ambition and favoured by circumstance Joseph Denison had by 1771 outshone most of his rivals and had become one of the twenty celebrated millionaire merchant princes of London. His personal life had changed no less radically. When his first wife, who shared his humble origins, died, he remarried into the London middle class, choosing as wife one Elizabeth Butler, 'a well-educated and very amiable woman' and the daughter of a hat maker from Tooley Street, Southwark. Within four years she too was dead, having borne him, in quick succession, three children: Elizabeth, the eldest, a son William and a second daughter, Maria. To celebrate his new prosperity and the birth of his eldest daughter Denison in 1770 moved his family from their modest home in Prince's Street near the Bank of England to a large mansion in the newly fashionable St Mary Axe.[4]

Now Joseph Denison set about consolidating his newly acquired fortune by buying vast tracts of land in the Home Counties. He began by purchasing the large Denbies estate in the Surrey hills from the bankrupt entrepreneur Jonathan Tyers, the man who had once owned the most famous entertainment venue in London, the Vauxhall Pleasure Gardens. Then in 1787, in what must have been a triumphant vindication of his once-humble status, Denison paid the enormous sum of £111,000 for the 160,000-acre estate of the Duke of Leeds.[5] This purchase, 47 years after he had left the county, now made him the largest single landowner in Yorkshire. But in character Denison had changed little from the hard-working, God-fearing young Yorkshireman who had walked all the way to London sixty years earlier. Yet, in spite of his new-found wealth, Joseph Denison, like the cotton mill owner Richard Arkwright or the road builder Thomas Telford, was unable to rise to the highest ranks of society himself. He did, however, make sure that both his girls acquired the education and social polish that he lacked in the expectation that they would, with good fortune, eventually marry into society.

Again Denison was fortunate in his timing, for in late eighteenth-century England such marriages between trade and high society had become possible for the first time. Being in trade was no longer considered as disreputable as it had once been and there was a dawning recognition among the aristocracy that new money could help preserve their estates as readily as old. Consequently many landed families had begun encouraging their offspring, the younger sons in particular, to marry wealthy heiresses from rich, middle-class families like the Denisons. The result was to raise the status of those in trade rather than to lower that of the aristocracy. To the rest of Europe it was seen as the profoundest folly that could only lead to unrest and discontent. Ironically it was France, where the greatest social upheaval in history would take place, that was most critical of English inter-class fraternisation. Although the French aristocracy enjoyed similar benefits to the English aristocracy, derived from colonial trade made possible by entrepreneurial merchants, the French elite shunned their country's middle classes, even forbidding them by law from displaying their new-found wealth in public.

Growing up in London, Elizabeth Denison and her sister Maria enjoyed a freedom of behaviour denied earlier generations of English girls. In the early years of the eighteenth century respectable young women had been virtually confined to their fathers' houses and forbidden to venture out unless closely chaperoned. But by 1780 the new social liberalism that had begun to permeate society permitted such young women, once they had 'come out', to attend private balls and parties together, often without their parents. What every middle-class family desired was to find their daughter a husband from a respectable, wealthy and preferably aristocratic family. This resulted in a refined human cattle market, bitterly condemned by such pioneering feminists as Mary Wollstonecraft, who wrote:

> What can be more indelicate than a girl's coming out in the fashionable world? Which, in other words, is to bring to market a marriageable miss, whose person is taken from one public place to another, richly caparisoned.[6]

What every respectable family feared most was that their cherished daughters might fall into the hands of the unscrupulous adventurers who were known to haunt such venues as public balls and assemblies. These men would attempt to persuade young heiresses to elope with them and then, after compromising the girl's honour, agree to marry only in return for a large dowry. Rich merchant families like the Denisons were prime targets for such predators and they made sure that their vulnerable offspring were kept under discreet but careful observation. Although Elizabeth and Maria would have been permitted to go shopping together they were closely chaperoned at all other times. London was then unequalled in Europe for the range and the quality of goods on display and Elizabeth would have been familiar with the stylish shops of the Strand, Pall Mall and Bond Street. It was while driving back with her sister in her father's carriage after such a shopping trip that Elizabeth Denison, now an attractive nineteen-year-old, made a fatal encounter that was to affect her emotionally for the rest of her life.

Having decided to return through Hyde Park she joined the late afternoon cavalcade that gathered in Rotten Row where members of fashionable society would promenade to see and be seen. Captain Gronow, a European visitor to England, later described the scene with the keen eye of a foreigner:

> The men were mounted on such horses as England alone could then produce, and the carriage company consisted of the most celebrated beauties . . . you did not see in those days any of the lower or middle classes of Londoner intruding themselves . . . it was given up exclusively to persons of rank and fashion.[7]

That fatal afternoon in 1789 Elizabeth noticed an unusually attractive young man riding beside her carriage. As he came closer she was so struck by his fine looks that she fell instantly in love with him. Later that evening, in great excitement, she told her friend Julia Storer that she had met a mysterious stranger in the park. From his description, Julia recognised him as the Honourable John Ponsonby, the eccentric son of Lord Ponsonby. Born in the same year as Elizabeth, he had grown up in Ireland and was now generally considered the handsomest young man in England, and possibly in France too, for when trapped in Paris at the time of the Terror, a few years later, he was mistaken for a French aristocrat and strung up on a lamp-post. He was only saved by the intervention of a crowd of local women who, struck by his exceptional good looks, insisted that he be cut down immediately.[8] An easygoing wastrel by nature, Ponsonby had squandered almost every opportunity that his father, the irascible Irish peer Lord Ponsonby, had given him. Provided with a safe seat in the Irish parliament he complained that the routine business of politics bored him to death. Moreover, he claimed to be so nervous in the House that he could only summon up the courage to speak in debates if he made himself half-drunk first. But in spite of being opinionated, unreliable and lazy, Ponsonby was redeemed by having an unusually keen sense of humour that entertained his many friends.

One of his many later conquests, in a long-running affair that began in May 1806, was the famous courtesan Harriette Wilson, who thought him 'a very god' and was much enthralled by his 'pale expressive beauty'. In her memoirs, written long after she had parted from him, Harriette relates a story that perfectly demonstrates Ponsonby's famously endearing quick wits. When appointed British Ambassador to Turkey he was summoned to deliver a formal address to the Sultan in front of his entire court. Knowing that none of the Turks could understand English Ponsonby produced a piece of paper from his pocket and began reading slowly and dramatically the numbers, 'one, two, three, four, five', until he reached fifty, putting particular emphasis on an occasional number. When thanked by the Sultan for his impressive speech, Ponsonby bowed gravely and continued with an encore, counting from sixty upwards. Later that day, when ordered by the Sultan to enter his private chamber by crawling under a low wall on all fours – a routine frequently used to humiliate European diplomats – Ponsonby, with great presence of mind and considerable courage, turned round and crawled in backward, presenting his backside to the astonished Sultan.[9] It is easy to see why Elizabeth Denison and Harriette Wilson should both have fallen for such an endearing character. Both saw him as the perfect man and Harriette's opinion, at least, should be respected in view of the dozens of lovers she had in a long career of professional romance.

But in 1789 Elizabeth Denison's family was shocked by the dramatic effect that Ponsonby had upon her. Soon an engagement was announced and the impecunious Ponsonby seemed delighted by the prospect of marriage to such a rich and attractive heiress. One of

Elizabeth's closest friends at the time was the aristocratically born Julia Storer, later to become the courtesan Julia Johnstone and destined to fall in society as spectacularly as Elizabeth was to rise. Julia was certain that a marriage between Ponsonby and Elizabeth must soon take place and she later told Harriette Wilson that Elizabeth's wedding clothes were already made and that Elizabeth 'used to sleep in my room, with his picture round her neck. She adored him beyond all that could be imagined of love and devotion.'[10]

Although Joseph Denison had no objections to the marriage John's father, Lord Ponsonby, certainly did and, according to his son, refused point blank to agree to the match. Ponsonby then broke off the engagement claiming that as he was so financially dependent on his father that he had little choice but to obey. This seems a lame excuse, for Ponsonby would surely have soon received a handsome dowry from his father-in-law, one of the wealthiest men in England. It seems far more likely that the other side of Ponsonby's character, 'sly, voluptuous and most luxurious', as he was described by a contemporary, prevailed and he had spotted an equally wealthy and far more socially desirable catch in Frances, the youngest daughter of the Prince of Wales's future mistress the Countess of Jersey. Within a few months of abandoning Elizabeth, Ponsonby had married Frances with full parental approval. The effect of this abrupt rejection on Elizabeth was catastrophic and, according to Julia Storer, the poor girl's sufferings were so severe that her parents 'trembled for her reason'. For the next two years no one was permitted to mention Ponsonby's name in Elizabeth's presence.[11]

As time passed Elizabeth slowly recovered from her bitter disappointment over John Ponsonby and her family began to hope that he would soon be replaced in her affections by a more reliable, if less attractive, member of the aristocracy. But it was nine years before a new suitor finally appeared in the form of another Irishman, the little-known peer Viscount Conyngham. Ironically Elizabeth, having been frustrated in her attempt to marry the handsomest man in England, now settled for one of the ugliest in Ireland. Henry Conyngham was a long, lean man with a distinctive set of protruding teeth rather like a comb, a 'thin lean parboiled looking sort of gentleman'. His odd appearance would later be a godsend to the London cartoonists, who portrayed him in numerous works as a tall, skinny buffoon. Although poor in looks, Lord Conyngham was theoretically rich in land and should have been a suitable, if uninspiring, catch for Elizabeth. Henry was descended from a Scottish clergyman, the Reverend Alexander Conyngham, who had left Scotland in 1611 to take part in the plantation of Ulster, an English attempt to pacify the rebellious Irish. Conyngham became Dean of Raphoe, and prospered in spite of the harsh conditions and the hostility of the local Catholic population. His son consolidated the Conyngham presence in Donegal as well as proving to be a highly successful soldier, rising to become Lieutenant General of the Ordnance in Ireland. In this capacity he commanded the artillery under King William at the Battle of the Boyne and survived to enjoy the spoils of the victory – a large estate at Slane in County Meath. This land together with its castle had been seized by the Crown from the Jacobite Fleming family, which had chosen to fight on the wrong side in the battle. Throughout the eighteenth century the Conyngham family continued to increase their wealth by developing their lands in Meath, Donegal and Clare. By the time Henry, the first Viscount Conyngham, married Elizabeth Denison in 1798 he was the second-largest landowner in the whole of Ireland with estates totalling 166,000 acres that were said to yield over £70,000 a year in rents.[12]

A frequent visitor to London, Henry met first Joseph Denison's attractive daughter when he became a customer of her father's bank. Denison clearly introduced the young Irish peer to his elder daughter as a likely prospect for marriage and encouraged the relationship between them, believing that Lord Conyngham would make a far more reliable husband for her than John Ponsonby could ever have done. Henry's arrival was fortunate for Elizabeth too as she was now in her mid-twenties and the need to find a husband would soon become pressing. His looks may have been unprepossessing, but Henry Conyngham at least had a title and large estates in Ireland so Elizabeth wisely decided that this time she must allow her head to rule her heart and accept his proposal of marriage.

It was certainly not a whirlwind romance, although one of the scandal sheets of the time claimed that Lord Conyngham, who it described quite erroneously as 'a dashing colonel of the guards', insinuated himself into Elizabeth's good graces and 'after a courtship of just three weeks they were married'.[13] This, at least, was true for on 5 July 1794 Elizabeth Denison married the 28-year-old Viscount Conyngham at one of the most fashionable churches in London, St Martin-in-the-Fields.

A month later the newlywed Conynghams made the tedious journey by road and sea back to Henry's estate in Ireland. They must have appeared an odd couple: he tall, thin and ugly and she short, fat and pretty. Impressed by the new French revolutionary fashions that he had seen in London, Henry Conyngham had undertaken a complete makeover of his appearance, abandoning the powdered wig and tricorn hat of his youth for short hair and a low-crowned topper in the French fashion. But there was little he could do to alter the strident voice for which he had become notorious. While Elizabeth's was soft and attractive, his was said to be un-pleasantly high-pitched and gratingly harsh. Henry appeared unaware of this and had developed a fondness for the sound of his own ill-favoured voice. 'He could talk, ye gods how he could talk', lamented the anonymous author of the scurrilous novella *The Secrets of the Castle*. Yet the compiler of a more respectable work, the *Sketches of Irish Political Characters*, published in 1799, gives a more sympathetic and generous description of Lord Conyngham. It praises his debating skills in the Irish parliament, noting that his arguments were 'condensed, pointed and powerful', while regretting that he had an almost fatal tendency to lisp.[14] What this ill-matched couple thought of each other is now impossible to discover but within a year of their arrival in Ireland Elizabeth gave birth to a son named Henry Joseph, the heir to the Conyngham inheritance. Two years later in 1797 a second son, Francis, was born followed by a daughter named Elizabeth after her mother. Two more children would be born to the Conynghams, a third son Albert and a second daughter Maria.

Born and brought up in the urban prosperity of the City of London, Elizabeth would have found Ireland an alarmingly pro-vincial and a potentially extremely dangerous place in 1794. Just three years earlier, inspired by the Republican principles of the French Revolution, the Society of United Irishmen had been formed under the leadership of the lawyer Theobald Wolfe Tone and Lord

Edward Fitzgerald to unite Catholics, Protestants and Dissenters to remove English control from Irish affairs. By the time that the Conynghams arrived at Slane much of the country had already witnessed attacks on Ascendancy property by small bands of early Republicans known as the Defenders. In 1792, in one fortnight alone, nearly forty Protestant houses in the counties of Meath and Louth had been broken into by Defenders looking for arms. Just a dozen miles from Slane even the property of the Catholic peer Lord Bellew had been attacked by over 1,500 rioters who had only dispersed when a large troop of cavalry arrived. Many similar attacks had taken place in the nearby town of Drogheda, where the trial of seven Defender ringleaders had opened just before the Conynghams' return.[15]

As Colonel of the local Drogheda Militia, Lord Conyngham had been much involved in policing the local countryside before his marriage. Now with the political situation fast deteriorating he returned immediately to his duties with the army, leaving his new bride to cope with the unfamiliar servants at Slane Castle. When the security situation allowed Henry would travel to Dublin to attend sittings at the Irish House of Lords, where the threat of Catholic insurrection was constantly debated. When she did not accompany him Elizabeth was left to her own devices at Slane where, given that her son was looked after by servants and there was a limited availability of stimulating company in the area, she became increasingly bored. Another of the anonymous and salacious biographies of her, *The Amatory Life of the Marchioness of C—ny—m*, claims that, neglected by her husband, she now took to amusing herself with one of the estate servants:

> A farmer's son by name of Bishop was taken into the house as a kind of superior servant. He was all in all with my lady. He had the happiness of driving her around the plantation in a sociable kind of carriage made to hold two persons side by side. His lordship never enjoyed good health and was never able to exercise his filly as much as necessary and therefore the duty was taken off his hands by the trusty Bishop.[16]

This version of events that were supposed to have happened 35 years earlier was typical of the scurrilous rumours that beset Elizabeth in the 1820s and 1830s. It is almost certainly wishful thinking by a progandist out to blacken her name for Elizabeth was far more likely to have looked to Dublin for such diversion, as Slane was less than two hours' carriage drive from the Irish capital. Then at the height of its prosperity, the elegant second city of the growing British Empire offered a social life only marginally less glittering than London's. As members of the Protestant Ascendancy the Conyng-hams would have received many invitations to receptions and balls there. Although a stranger to the city Elizabeth was quick to make friends with the Dublin ladies and one in particular, the Countess of Glengall, niece of one of Ireland's senior peers, the Earl of Clare, was credited by the diarist Thomas Creevey with introducing her to the more boisterous side of Dublin social life.[17] It was apparent that even as a young bride Elizabeth was beginning to develop the repu-tation of an adventuress.

Then in June 1798 the rebellion that would change the fortunes of the Irish Ascendancy for ever broke out in County Wexford. The original plan of the United Irishmen had been to start the rising in Dublin but the leaders, through good British intelligence, had been swiftly arrested. Without word from their leadership the peasants in the south-east of the country pressed on with the revolt, and after several victorious encounters with British troops reached the hills overlooking Dublin. The city was plunged into a panic as its Protestant community prepared to flee or risk massacre. The Conynghams too must have feared an attack when the United Irishmen in County Down, just two counties distant, rose under the command of Henry Monro, a shopkeeper from Newtownards. But the rebels, greatly outnumbered, were soon routed in an engagement at Ballynahinch suffering several hundred casualties. Monro was arrested, tried and promptly hanged outside his own front door.

The Wexford rebels were also driven back from Dublin by a British army hastily assembled by the Prince of Wales's old friend General Lake, who on 21 June with 20,000 men finally surrounded them on Vinegar Hill and slaughtered the great majority. Two months later a body of experienced French troops landed near Killala in County Mayo in the west of Ireland, but they were too late and, outnumbered, were forced to surrender at Ballinamuck in County Longford. As was customary in dealing with the Irish, the captured French were treated as prisoners of war and returned to France while the unfortunate Irish who had joined them were slaughtered on the spot.[18]

The Great Rising of 1798 had been crushed, but the very act of insurrection itself and the initial success of the rebels had caused a crisis of confidence throughout the Protestant Ascendancy. Its members now realised that their future lay not in an independent Irish parliament but in total political integration with Britain. Consequently an Act of Union with England was introduced into the Irish parliament and Henry Conyngham was among those Irish peers who voted for it in the Lords. The incentive was the offer by the British government of bribes and peerages. As William Carpenter wrote in his bitter tract of the time *A Peerage for the People*, 'a man is created an Irish peer for servility, oppression and bigotry in his own country . . . when a man is made a peer by corruption in Ireland he is glad to take the next step in England'.[19] Many wealthy Protestants were to follow this route to England and the effect of their departure on the Irish economy and above all on Dublin society was catastrophic. Within a few years many landlords had become near-permanent absentees, abandoning their large estates and fine Dublin houses for the safety of London.

Among the first to leave were the Conynghams, who for the next twenty years would spend most of their time in or near London. Apart from the deteriorating political situation there may well have been another reason why the Conynghams, in particular, made such an early departure from Ireland. Although Lord Conyngham was known to be the second-largest landowner in Ireland, much of his holding was in the counties of Donegal and Clare where the land was poor and the tenantry lived on the edge of subsistence. In these years of bad harvest they would have been unable to pay even their nominal rents and the Conynghams' income would consequently have been drastically reduced. This may well have happened for, according to local gossip, their finances had become much depleted and Lord Conyngham needed desperately to restore them. It was certainly rumoured in Dublin that it was because of his depleted fortunes that Conyngham had gone to London in the first place in the hope of finding himself a rich English heiress. Elizabeth's friend Lady Glengall would probably have known the truth and she told the English diarist Thomas Creevey that she was sure Lord Conyngham had serious financial problems.[20] Creevey may well have spread this story in London for it was picked up by the satirists, ever eager to embarrass any members of the ruling class. Consequently the anonymous author of *Secrets of the Castle* repeated the claims that Lord Conyngham had deliberately brought his wife and son over to England in the hope of improving his prospects. It was even suggested that he had been forced to let out 'the very gardens of Slanes [*sic*] Castle' to local farmers and the house to be used as a hospital.[21]

Whatever the reason for the sudden departure to London the prospect of a return to the great city after several years of provincial life in Ireland would certainly have appealed to Elizabeth. Although Lord Conyngham would, in the years to come, make regular visits back to manage his estates in Meath and Donegal his wife preferred to remain in London at the centre of the social and political events that were about to unfold. But if the Conynghams really were in financial difficulties they showed little sign of penury when they arrived in London in the summer of 1800. As Elizabeth was determined to establish herself immediately in English society she realised that the first requirement was a large house in the right part of London. So with the help of her father and his financial resources she found a property commensurate with her new social status. This property, 5 Hamilton Place, was a large mansion located at the lower end of Park Lane – then, as now, one of the most fashionable addresses in London. This street had certainly been good enough for the hero of Waterloo, the Duke of Wellington, who had taken a house there while the renovations to his official residence, Apsley House at Hyde Park Corner, were completed.

As soon as she was established in Hamilton Place Elizabeth set the tone for her future actions by secretly contacting her old love John Ponsonby, who was living in nearby Curzon Street. Already bored with his marriage, Ponsonby responded immediately and the two met and began an illicit affair that would continue until May 1806 when he became involved with the courtesan Harriette Wilson. In the course of their secret liaison Elizabeth and Ponsonby wrote each other dozens of passionate love letters. These highly compromising documents would fall into the hands of Harriette Wilson, probably stolen by her from among Ponsonby's possessions, and were used twenty years later by Harriette in the most outrageous attempt in British history to blackmail a king.[22]

When not consorting with Ponsonby, Elizabeth set about establishing the Conynghams at the centre of London society. Hamilton Place was less than half a mile from Manchester Square, where the Marquess of Hertford and his wife lived in splendour. This was fortunate because Isabella Hertford was the aunt of the Conynghams' old neighbour in Ireland, Lord Castlereagh. Not only had they lived in the same part of the country but Henry Conyngham and Robert Castlereagh had attended the Irish House of Lords together and both had commanded neighbouring militia regiments prior to the Rising in 1798. There any similarity ended for whereas Lord Conyngham was politically insignificant, Lord Castlereagh was now the rising star in the Tory party and destined for great things. Such a man would be an invaluable contact in London high society.

When introduced to Lady Conyngham, Isabella Hertford was naturally unaware of the threat that this attractive newcomer would pose. Instead she was struck by the charm of this new addition to the London scene and took to her immediately. Soon the Conynghams were regular guests at Manchester House and would have met all the Hertfords' friends including the Prince of Wales himself. When in town George dined regularly with the Hertfords as well as calling round most afternoons, in the absence of Lord Hertford, for an intimate tête-à-tête with Isabella. As the friendship developed the Conynghams too became part of the Prince's intimate circle. Evidence of their increasing proximity is revealed on a paper fan discovered at the Theatre Royal, Drury Lane. It shows a seating plan for the 1802 season with the name 'Lady Conyngham' appearing as stallholder for a seat directly behind that of His Royal Highness the Prince of Wales.

There can be little doubt that George found both Conynghams good company and Elizabeth, with her dark good looks and voluptuous figure, particularly attractive. The author of the scandal sheet *The Secrets of the Castle* claims that the Prince fell for Elizabeth the moment he set eyes on her. The fateful meeting was supposed to have occurred one evening after dinner at Manchester House when she approached a table where the Prince was playing cards with other guests and sat quietly down beside him. Struck by her beauty George turned and engaged her in 'a long and delightful conversation which in the conclusion made one lady perfectly happy, and another perfectly miserable' – a reference to the supposedly jealous Isabella. The next morning, the story continues, the Prince asked his secretary, John McMahon, if he knew the identity of this mysterious woman. Colonel McMahon confessed that he knew her very well indeed for her name was Elizabeth Conyngham and she was his very own 'privy companion'. With characteristic opportunism McMahon is said to have added, 'but she is very much at your service'.[23]

Although this story appears in an anonymous scandal sheet it may, in essence, be an accurate account of the first meeting between George and his future mistress. A formal dinner at Manchester House would have consisted of up to 100 guests. The party would have assembled to await the arrival of the Prince of Wales who, after a formal greeting en masse, would have led them all into dinner. Only after the meal was completed would the party retire to the drawing room and mix with the Prince. That Elizabeth should have approached him so boldly is quite compatible with her known character. This, after all, was a forceful, ambitious and determined woman who had already embarked on an illicit affair with her old love John Ponsonby. That she had also become Colonel McMahon's mistress is quite believable, for not only was he one of the most charming men at Court but he was also the most intimate conduit to the Prince of Wales himself.

John McMahon was a fascinating character. As far as the Prince of Wales was concerned he had the great advantage of being Irish, for George was never happier than in the company of an easygoing Irishman. Indeed, two of the closest friends of his youth, Richard Brinsley Sheridan and the dissolute George Hanger, heir to Lord Coleraine, were both Irish. Hanger, the prototype for the caricature of a dissolute Irishmen, was the most outrageous of all the Prince's early companions and was invariably depicted in cartoons with a bright red drunkard's nose. Bankrupted and wrecked by drink, Hanger had long passed out of George's intimate circle when the Prince's political adviser, the Whig peer Lord Moira, suggested to him that one of his officers, Colonel McMahon, would make him an excellent royal secretary.[24]

Born the illegitimate son of Lord Leitrim's butler in Ireland, John McMahon had escaped the poverty of rural Ireland by enlisting in the British army at the time of the War of American Independence. By good fortune he had chosen the regiment commanded by Lord Moira and whatever his military abilities, McMahon soon discovered that he possessed a unique talent as a 'fixer' for his dissolute colonel. Armed with Moira's purse he would procure locally anything his master required, from good wine to accommodating women. Soon Moira had him performing the same services for his fellow officers and McMahon's remarkable success in this vital area of campaign life ensured his rapid promotion from private soldier to commissioned rank of ensign.[25] Poncing for his superiors in America proved so profitable that when the war ended and the army returned to Britain McMahon arrived back with a full purse and ready-made career. Maintaining the useful contacts he had made in the army he continued his profitable career as procurer-in-chief to the aristocracy. Soon he had accumulated enough money to marry one of his own attractive protégées and settle with her in rural comfort at Richmond in Surrey. It was this lady, according to the scandal sheets, who would enable McMahon to take his final step up the ladder of society.

One day, it was alleged, 'a certain illustrious individual' was riding with Lord Moira near Richmond when he noticed a dark, mysterious beauty at a cottage window. When the Prince pointed her out Moira claimed to recognise her as the wife of his old friend John McMahon, adding that he was sure she would be only too delighted to meet the Prince. Without more ado, the story continues, they called at the house and the lady found George so charming that she invited him to drop by at any time. The Prince took her at her word but whenever he called McMahon was invariably away on business, leaving his wife to entertain her royal guest alone in a manner she thought appropriate.[26] Again, there must have been an element of truth in this story for the public was soon made aware of the Prince's amatory excursions to Bushey Park. A cartoon entitled 'Princely Predilections' by George Cruikshank depicted George and Mrs McMahon romping together in rural bliss. The story was given further credence when McMahon, on the Prince's personal direction, was, for no good military reason, suddenly promoted first to Brevet

Major and then to Lieutenant Colonel – a commission worth thousands of pounds. These appointments appeared to be handsome rewards for McMahon's generosity with his wife's favours and his own well-mannered discretion.

Clearly such a man could go far in the Prince's service and McMahon was promptly offered a minor post that he filled with 'diligence and affability'. Then, to the indignation of the Prince's more established advisers, George offered him the important and highly sensitive position of Royal Secretary. McMahon accepted immediately, relishing the challenge, and with energy and efficiency set about relieving his master of most of the tedious bureaucratic duties that George found so irksome. Behind the scenes McMahon used his unrivalled experience as a procurer of exceptional talent to add even more colour to the Prince's private life. One of his many clandestine duties was to smuggle Isabella Hertford in and out of the Brighton Pavilion through a secret passageway. Even the dynamic McMahon soon found himself fully employed by the Prince's varied and energetic sex life. He would have to pay off an angry, cuckolded husband one day then hurry down to Fleet Street to bribe a cartoonist into suppressing yet another scurrilous cartoon the next.[27]

George IV's first biographer, Robert Huish, a proponent of the moral rectitude that was to characterise the reign of the Prince's niece Queen Victoria, discovered factual evidence of McMahon's nefarious activities. He quotes a highly compromising letter written by McMahon to his royal master in which the secretary, 'ever alive to obtaining the possession of any object which may contribute to your royal pleasure', claims to have picked up two attractive young girls while travelling through Wiltshire in a public coach. When a local clergyman and his daughters got on at Marlborough McMahon was struck by their beauty, considering them ideal fodder for his master. The letter describes their 'apparent simplicity and ignorance of the world', making it clear that, with McMahon's help, the unfortunate girls could soon 'be brought to comply with the wishes of your Royal Highness'. The first step, McMahon suggested, was to lure them to London by offering their father a lucrative living at a parish in the city. The Prince thought this an excellent scheme and told McMahon to proceed with the plan at once.

According to Huish the unwary girls duly arrived a few weeks later and McMahon persuaded their father to allow them to lodge with his old friend, a certain Mrs Duff, in the ominous sounding Fops Alley. Unknown to their ingenuous father, Mrs Duff was a fashionable courtesan whose box at the opera was always full of such notorious libertines as the Prince's own chaplain at Carlton House, the Reverend Knight. After a few weeks of careful grooming by Mrs Duff the girls were taken by McMahon to the house of a Mrs Hamilton where both he and the Prince, in the guise of a 'Colonel Fox', seduced them. Huish ends this sad story with a bitter condemnation of the moral depravity of both McMahon and the Prince. 'The heart sinks,' he writes, 'at such cold blooded, systematic destruction of female innocence'.[28]

Adventures like these made McMahon the custodian of George's most intimate secrets which, as a hazard against fortune, he carefully and systematically documented. But he appears to have been even more intimately involved with the Prince than many contemporaries suspected, for McMahon not only procured attractive ingénues for his master but also kept a lookout for older society ladies with compliant husbands – men who would be prepared to turn a blind eye to their own wives' infidelity in return for a lucrative royal appointment. This was the path already taken by both the Earl of Jersey and the Marquess of Hertford, who had clearly condoned their wives' activities with the Prince and received prestigious offices in the royal household in return.

McMahon's duties may well have included playing a much more active role himself for he appears to have at times assumed the role of 'woman tester' for the Prince, checking out amenable women before passing them on to his master. This would have involved having a brief liaison with the lady himself to ascertain her suitability, but above all to test her discretion and, indeed, that of her husband. It seems likely that Elizabeth Conyngham was 'checked out' in this manner by John McMahon. The author of *The Secrets of the Castle* has no doubt that this was the case and that Elizabeth and John McMahon were indeed lovers before she embarked on her affair with the Prince. The Colonel, it claims, paid her such 'assiduous attention' that one Sunday they were 'found by the fond husband . . . preparing to be particularly intimate'. Henry Conyngham was said to have been so outraged that he challenged

McMahon to a duel and only withdrew the challenge when the secretary 'offered a purse in lieu of a bullet to the noble lord'.[29] This aggressive defence of his wife's honour does seem uncharacteristic of Henry Conyngham, particularly as the author goes on to suggest that when McMahon recommended her to his master 'the lady did not hold out long . . . priding herself on the conquest she had made. Her first connection with the Prince produced her a present of £1,000 and her husband received something equal to £600.'[30]

Yet the assertion that Elizabeth Conyngham and John McMahon were lovers may not only depend on the word of an anonymous author, for in Thomas de Quincey's *Autobiographical Sketches* he recalls travelling with a school friend to Ireland one summer in the first years of the nineteenth century. On board ship they noticed a dark, attractive woman in a carriage on deck – at the time people of quality remained in their coaches on deck during short sea voyages. The lady was obviously an aristocrat and became so amused by their admiring glances that she invited them to her carriage to talk. The night was sweltering and the boys decided to sleep on deck. In the early hours of the morning when the ship was quiet they noticed 'a certain Colonel' whom they had seen earlier creep up from below and slip quietly into the lady's carriage. It appeared to them that these goings on were 'not entirely a secret even among the lady's servants'. Years later De Quincey realised that the amorous lady he had seen was none other than the King's notorious mistress Lady Conyngham and the mysterious Colonel, John McMahon.[31]

De Quincey's observation that Elizabeth's servants were aware of her relationship with McMahon shows the difficulty a member of the aristocracy had in pursuing a sexual affair in a society that depended so heavily on servant labour. Footmen opened front doors, maids came virtually unannounced into bedrooms and coachmen were needed to take ladies to their assignations. It was impossible to keep secrets from these people, who were prone to gossip among themselves and to members of their family. In London there was the added temptation of the cartoonists and satirical press, who would pay handsomely for titbits of salacious information. It is remarkable how much the public knew of the foibles of public figures. Becoming part of fashionable London society as the Conynghams did in 1800 and, above all, being on the fringe of the Prince of Wales's circle,

31

would have left them open to such scrutiny. Elizabeth, in particular, was quickly marked down as a ruthless sexual predator working her way, like a professional courtesan, through the British aristocracy. The author of the *Memoirs of the Celebrated Lady C\*\*\*\*\*m* depicts her supposed progress in lurid detail:

> The Earl of W came into the course and was soon the acknowledged 'riding postilion' of Lady C. The noble peer became a politician. He called out Viscount M—d—n who did not respond. Then the son called out the Viscount who replied that he had fought too often. The Marquess now became an indifferent husband and upon his promotion (to General?) abandoned his wife to her ways. Sir Harry Vane 'in a short chace ran her down to cover'. The consequence was a duel and Sir Harry fell, a trial took place and the M was acquitted.[32]

This item of gossip is again typical of the confusion that existed at the time between real events and scurrilous speculation. The supposed duel referred to by the author is, in fact, a later quarrel that occurred between Elizabeth's second son Lord Francis Conyngham and the then Foreign Secretary, Lord Castlereagh. In 1821, at the time of the royal marriage crisis, Lord Francis challenged Castlereagh to a duel for criticising his mother's relationship with the King. Although these spurious *Memoirs* appear to be malicious fantasy they do contain intriguing suggestions that can in part be corroborated by recorded events. *The Secrets of the Castle* even suggests that Elizabeth Conygham had a child by the Prince in 1805 for, 'after a connection of three years, her ladyship sojourned for a while on the continent where she brought forth a child which many said was very little like her husband and exceedingly like somebody else'.[33] The facts do seem to endorse the story that became common gossip in London, for Elizabeth did leave London in the spring of 1805 and return to Ireland for a confinement. To be absent from London for a period of months was, at this time, often an indication of an illicit pregnancy and the need for a secret confinement. Some at Court certainly believed that Lady Conyngham had become pregnant by the Prince, the diarist Thomas Creevey among them. He frequently refers to Elizabeth's youngest son Lord Albert Conyngham, born in that same year 1805, as 'The Great Infant of England', clearly implying that the Prince was Albert's natural father.[34] Yet apart from Creevey, a notorious gossip and scandalmonger, there is no corroboration of the rumour and photographs of Lord Albert, when an adult, show a striking resemblance to his lean and angular father rather than to the distinctly Hanoverian features of George IV. But what all these allegations, true or false, have in common is the assertion that Elizabeth Conyngham became the Prince's mistress long before she appeared in public with him in 1819.

Nine years after the birth of Lord Albert and when the Prince was still openly involved with Lady Hertford, Elizabeth certainly embarked on a short but high-profile love affair with a far younger man. To celebrate the first overthrow of Napoleon, the victorious European monarchs visited London in June 1814. As official host the Prince Regent had invited the Tsar to stay with him at either Carlton House or St James's Palace. To the Prince's chagrin Tsar Alexander informed his host that he would prefer to join the rest of his party at the Pulteney Hotel in Mayfair. None of the Russians appeared to like London and, according to Creevey, were soon 'sick to death of the way they were followed about' by the London mob. The Tsar, in particular, grumbled about the interminable drunken dinners he had to endure at Carlton House. As a protest, he decided to annoy his host by flirting with the Prince's current mistress, Lady Jersey. The Tsar's twenty-year-old son, the Grand Duke Nicholas, appears to have used his time in London far more constructively for according to the diarist Thomas Creevey he took a great fancy to the 46-year-old Lady Conyngham and was encouraged by her to begin a short but passionate affair.[35] Lady Emily Cowper, Lord Castlereagh's niece, also met Nicholas at the time and had the pleasure of being taken in to dinner by him one evening. She described him as 'a tall stripling, his fine line of features giving promise of the splendidly handsome man he became'. Lady Emily clearly shared Elizabeth's opinion, describing Nicholas as her 'beau ideal of a young Prince, so handsome, so well mannered, and so gay'.[36] It is not difficult to see why Nicholas, a bored young man in a foreign city, would have welcomed what would have been little more than a holiday affair with a mature and attractive woman. Two years later their relationship resumed when the Russians returned to London for more celebrations after

Napoleon's defeat at Waterloo and final exile to St Helena. This time Grand Duke Nicholas managed to excuse himself from engagements in London and slipped down to Brighton alone. Conveniently, Elizabeth too was at the Conynghams' house in Brighton that week, just around the corner from the Pavilion. For the next four days, according to Creevey, they resumed their passionate affair while his father and her husband were detained by their official duties in London.[37]

As Elizabeth was entertaining the Grand Duke in Brighton, the Prince's longstanding mistress, Isabella Hertford, was making her own contribution to the celebrations by draping the front of Manchester House in a gigantic banner proclaiming 'The Prince's Peace'. More importantly, she also acted as the Prince's hostess for a number of celebratory dinners which the Tsar found even more boring than those he had to endure at Carlton House.[38] Perhaps Isabella had already begun to lose her looks, for the Tsar confessed to an aide that he found Lady Hertford most unattractive and 'mighty old'. The Prince might well have begun to share the Tsar's opinion, for a few months later it was noticed that he was becoming ever more flirtatious with Lady Conyngham. An understanding between the Prince and Elizabeth might well have come about at this time, for Henry Conyngham was suddenly – and to almost universal surprise in both London and Dublin – created Viscount Slane, Earl of Mount Charles and Marquess of Conyngham – the second highest rank in the peerage. Elizabeth accordingly became a marchioness – the same rank as the Prince's current mistress Isabella Hertford. Perhaps she had made this her condition for embarking upon a public affair with George and facing the lampooning and hostility that she knew would inevitably follow.

# THREE

## *Ménage à Trois*

By 1819 it was apparent to everyone at Court that the Prince's new favourite was Lady Conyngham and that Isabella Hertford had been finally rejected. Since the Russian visit of 1816 the Prince had paid Isabella increasingly less attention. In the intervening three years he pursued a discreet but flirtatious courtship of Elizabeth in London and particularly at Brighton. Once a modest fishing village, Brighton had by end of the eighteenth century replaced Bath as the summer capital of fashionable England. The Conynghams had taken a house there in 1805 in order to join the fashionable *haut ton* that made up the Prince's guests at the Royal Pavilion. Intriguingly, their house in Marlborough Row was close to the vast, glass-domed stables of the Royal Pavilion where a secret passage led directly into the Pavilion itself.[1] As regular guests of the Prince their comings and goings were recorded in the social columns of the local Brighton newspapers. With Lord Conyngham making regular visits to his estates in Ireland, Elizabeth was often invited by the Hertfords to Ragley Hall or Sudbourne, where she had every opportunity of developing a closer friendship with the Prince. This must have been achieved with a degree of secrecy unparalleled in any of the Prince's earlier liaisons, for the London cartoonists were completely unaware of it and continued ridiculing the unfortunate Lady Hertford. Consequently they were as surprised as the great majority of the Prince's friends when in the summer of 1819 it became obvious that Lady Conyngham was the new favourite.

Their first public appearance together was at the annual St Carlo Ball in December 1819 when George entered the room with a smiling Lady Conyngham on his arm. Close friends such as Princess Lieven and Charles Greville were astonished to see his undisguised passion for her and both noted that he spent the entire evening at her side.[2]

Greville noted that the Prince gazed constantly at his new love, frequently touching her arm as if to reassure himself that she was still there. This behaviour was all the more surprising for never once throughout the long relationship with Lady Hertford had he behaved in such an attentive and adoring manner. Soon the lovers were appearing together at balls and assemblies. George was clearly in the grip of a youthful passion that appeared, to many, amusingly incongruous in a portly 57-year-old. This new passion had a visibly dramatic effect on him too for, ashamed of his vast seventeen-stone figure and a ballooning stomach scarcely contained by a mighty whalebone corset, he had decided that he must lose weight immediately. For the next few months he was seen, to the amazement of friends and servants alike, to refuse the rich foods that he so much enjoyed. So thorough was this new slimming regime that he even adopted an alarming but short-lived routine of regular daily exercise. The whole Court was both astonished and impressed by this unsuspected display of willpower and self-discipline in a man notorious for the lack of both. It was as if he had rediscovered his own physicality by constantly touching Elizabeth, which he did even in the presence of strangers. Some found his behaviour touching, others thought it amusing – but most were simply embarrassed by his behaviour, feeling it totally inappropriate for a man of his age and status. One of his most outspoken critics was the Duke of Wellington's strait-laced confidante, the censorious Harriet Arbuthnot, who complained that:

> Lady Conyngham spends every evening at Carlton House, when Lady Haggerstone (sister to Mrs FitzHerbert) is invited as chaperone. They spend the evening sitting on a sofa together, holding each other's hands, whispering and kissing, Lord Conyngham being present.[3]

More shocked than most was the elderly courtier Lord Burghersh, who thought such amorous behaviour ludicrous in a prince and noted sourly that George now 'never drank wine without touching her glass with his, holding her hand under the table all the time he was drinking'. Burghersh was further appalled when witnessing their flirtatious behaviour together at Carlton House a few days later and felt moved to complain to the Duke of Wellington that:

The King made himself ridiculous with Lady Conyngham . . . he was devoted to her the whole night and at last retired to one of the rooms with her and placed a page at the door to prevent anyone going in . . . as the King can see Lady Conyngham every day and all day long, I really think he might control his passion and not behave so indecently in public.[4]

Many witnessing this curious passion naturally felt concerned and embarrassed for the unfortunate Henry Conyngham, but he seemed curiously oblivious to it all. Gradually it dawned on the King's friends that Lord Conyngham was not only tolerating his wife's behaviour but positively condoning it. A daily routine was now evolving as the Conynghams became a constant presence at both Carlton House and the Brighton Pavilion. As was his custom with all past lovers, George would retire with his mistress most afternoons into the royal bedroom that contained a splendid couch on a dais draped in gold brocade and a vast bed, lined with green and white checked satin sheets. Lord Conyngham meanwhile would occupy himself downstairs in the drawing room with the newspapers or a book. Each evening all three would meet up again at dinner without any apparent sign of tension or hostility. After the meal, George and Elizabeth would leave the table and cuddle up together on a sofa in the drawing room, 'whispering and kissing like young lovers', as Princess Lieven caustically observed.[5] The rest of the embarrassed dinner party would then join them, sitting a discreet distance away, and either play cards or read while down at the far end of the room the Marquess of Conyngham would sit alone, his head buried in a newspaper, ignoring the giggles and whispered endearments. Another witness of these embarrassing occasions was Elizabeth, Lady Stewart, the sister-in-law of Lord Castlereagh, who was astonished one evening to see that the King, unable to rise from his chair through gout, was dragged to his feet by Elizabeth with 'a good hard tug'. Only the closest intimate of a monarch, she thought, would have been permitted such liberties.[6]

However, no one who witnessed these scenes could doubt the sincerity of the King's feelings towards Elizabeth nor deny the powerful sexual chemistry that existed between them. Proof of their passion at this stage was contained in hundreds of explicit and highly erotic love letters, which shocked the Duke of Wellington when he discovered them shortly after George's death in 1830.[7] Yet some of the King's friends still doubted, in spite of all the visual evidence, that the relationship could be as physical as it appeared. How, they asked, could a gouty, vastly overweight elderly man, half-inebriated and dosed with the powerful sedative laudanum, manage the basic mechanics of sexual congress? Certainly his descendant Edward VII – equally overweight and possessed of a similarly powerful libido – managed it well enough, as the recent discovery in a Paris brothel of his specially constructed 'intercourse chair' has proved. Perhaps the physical side of their relationship was confined to oral sex, a not uncommon practice in relationships between elderly men and younger women. Certainly it would explain why the King gave Elizabeth expensive gifts that would seem excessive if just platonic friendship was involved. On the other hand the constant kissing and touching he indulged in may have been merely a demonstration of harmless affection, for what clearly mattered most to him was the proximity of a woman who reassured and comforted him in an almost maternal manner.

Yet confirmation that they were, indeed, lovers appeared to come from the King's own lips in 1821 as he was preparing for a state visit to Hanover. Asked by Princess Lieven, perhaps his closest female friend, why he was not taking Elizabeth with him, he told her injudiciously that he and Elizabeth both feared that the rigours of the journey might make her miscarry. The Princess was convinced that George was implying that he was the cause of her pregnancy. Certainly it unlikely that Henry Conyngham would have been involved, considering Elizabeth's cool demeanour towards her husband. The most probable explanation, however, is that the King was teasing the Princess – knowing her reputation as the arch gossip at Court – and deliberately feeding her false information in the hope that she would make a fool of herself.[8]

However it was not solely Elizabeth's physical charms that attracted George, for she provided him with something that he had never experienced in any previous relationship – an almost domestic contentment and the simple enjoyment of a woman's company for its own sake. It was as if Lord Conyngham had become merely a ghostly presence and George had taken over his role as Elizabeth's husband. Princess Lieven was astonished to see such tranquillity in a man of his notorious predilection for emotional mayhem. She first noticed this unaccustomed serenity, she later told the Duke of Wellington, one evening when the King motioned her to sit down beside him on one side of a sofa with Elizabeth on the other. He turned to the Princess and whispered a confession in her ear that he now realised that he had never known what it was like to be truly in love before. He admitted that he was 'quite surprised at the degree to which he was in love, that he did nothing from morning to night but think what he could do to please Lady Conyngham and make her happy, that he would do anything on earth for her, that he owed his life to her . . . and that she was an angel sent from heaven for him'. Even the cynical Princess claimed to be genuinely moved by these touching words. 'He cried,' she wrote, 'Lady Conyngham cried and I cried. And all this passed in a crowded drawing room. One never did hear such folly!! from a man, too, of fifty eight!'[9]

While openly responsive to George's affectionate behaviour in private or among close friends, on public occasions Elizabeth remained cool and detached. Whenever she accompanied the King to the races or attended a ball or reception she made sure that her husband, or at least one of her two daughters, was always present and close by her side. The very openness of her behaviour was meant to convince bystanders that, in spite of the gossip they may have heard, the King and Lady Conyngham were merely the best of friends. Spectators were meant to ask themselves the question: surely even the most brazen adulteress could not go about with her lover on her arm and her husband a pace or two behind? But as with many women who become involved with a royal personage, Elizabeth had deluded herself into believing that the normal rules of behaviour did not apply. What made their affair unique in modern British history was that for the first time a king's mistress had virtually moved into his household, albeit with a husband and family in tow.

Naturally Elizabeth's close family, apart from her husband, found her intimacy with George highly embarrassing and difficult to condone. The worst affected was her brother, William Denison, a pious Nonconformist MP who felt scandalised by the rumours that had begun circulating in London. Thomas Creevey's great friend Mrs Angelo Taylor confided to him that poor William Denison was broken-hearted by his sister's disgraceful conduct in living openly under the King's roof. He said that he went in constant fear that the subject might come up before Parliament. Consequently, he told Mrs Taylor, he and his sister Lady Strathaven (Elizabeth's younger sister, Maria) and Elizabeth's eldest son, the Earl of Mount Charles, had all implored her to leave 'her fat and fair friend and go abroad'. Yet Denison insisted that in his opinion and contrary to all the evidence, there could never be 'anything criminal between persons of their age'.[10]

When William Denison finally plucked up courage to confront Elizabeth personally she was immediately defiant, defending herself vigorously and telling her brother, with tears streaming convincingly down her cheeks, that the King was merely 'a dear friend' and that she was innocent of all these vile accusations. Moreover, she told a now startled William, she had done no more in friendship than Lady Hertford, who was considered by the whole world to be the most virtuous of women. In spite of these passionate protestations of innocence William Denison remained unconvinced by Elizabeth's denials and in 1827 he spoke to her again on the matter, threatening to cut his sister out of his will unless she ended her compromising relationship with the King. As William was still the senior partner of Messrs Denison, Heywood and Kennard and had managed to greatly increase the fortune left by his father, this was not a threat to be taken lightly. Luckily for Elizabeth she now had little need of the Denison family fortune and is reported to have responded to his threats with more 'bursts of passion and defiance'. William Denison made good his threat and when he died in 1849 he left nothing to his elder sister, instead bequeathing the bulk of his vast wealth, well over £2 million, entirely to his nephew, Elizabeth's third son Lord Albert Conyngham. But there was one condition: Albert was required to change his name from Conyngham to Denison. Clearly William had not heard, or preferred to ignore, the scandalous rumour still circulating that Lord Albert was the love child of his sister and the King.[11]

Other members of Elizabeth's family, with the notable exception of her second son Lord Francis, also disapproved of her behaviour but were less outspoken in their criticism. Almost as concerned as his uncle was the Conyngham heir, Henry Joseph, Earl of Mount

Charles. Unlike his brothers and sisters he refused all offers of help and preferment from the King. Finally, unable to endure the constant embarrassment, he left England in 1821 and went to live on the Continent. Nor, according to the diarist Thomas Creevey, were these the only family members to resent the situation. Creevey claims that both of Elizabeth's daughters, in spite of their smiling demeanour, were bitterly opposed to their mother's intimacy with the King.[12] The elder, Lady Elizabeth, was a younger and equally attractive version of her mother with the same dark hair and blue eyes. Nevertheless, in spite of her private objections she appears to have performed the role of unofficial chaperone to her mother without complaint, standing close to her whenever the King was in the room. Always responsive to a pretty face, George found the young woman a charming companion and grew increasingly fond of her.

The person presumed to be most concerned by the scandal simply ignored it all. By 1820 the Marquess of Conyngham was the most famous cuckold in England, if not in the whole of Europe, and the object of constant jibes and derision from every section of society. Although he pursued his role with unusual amiability Henry Conyngham was merely treading the well-worn path of his predecessors, the Marquess of Hertford and the Earl of Jersey, who had both laid down their wives for the Prince. The latter's appointment as Master of the Horse for his compliance had been brilliantly lampooned by James Gillray in 1796 in a cartoon showing Lord Jersey as a scrawny midget being ridden to his own marital bed by a vast and triumphant Prince of Wales. Now it was Lord Conyngham's turn and it seemed that the whole of Britain was making fun of him. But thick-skinned or brass-necked Henry Conyngham appears to have taken it all with good grace and there is no record of him once responding in anger to the jibes or even attempting to distance himself from what must have been the most compromising of situations.

Why did Henry tolerate what appeared to be his wife's blatant adultery if, as the scandal sheets claimed, he had in the past twice fought a duel over his wife's honour? Perhaps, like her, he had brainwashed himself into believing that nothing untoward was going on and that the King was rewarding him with titles and honours for his own abilities rather than for condoning a sordid and adulterous affair. That these rewards had been given for Lord Conyngham's personal achievements would have been hard for even the most optimistic of self-deceivers to believe. His career as either soldier or politician had been far from spectacular. In Ireland he had played little part in the political life of the House of Lords and his military experience had been confined to a policing role in the militia at the very time Wellington was carving out a spectacular career for himself in India.[13] Consequently Henry's sudden elevation to a marquessate in 1816 appeared to be for no other reason than his wife's relationship with the heir to the throne. Some of his more cynical contemporaries repeated the old rumour that Lord Conyngham was hard up and had only endured the ignominy of cuckoldry so that he could restore his finances and rebuild his ancestral home, Slane Castle.

Whatever the speculation, one thing is certain: for the next decade Henry Conyngham accepted, without demur, anything the King cared to give him. In spite of his limited military experience he was made a general in the army and appointed a member of the noble Order of St Patrick. Whatever his apparent insouciance Henry Conyngham paid a heavy price in public mockery for these honours. The author of the anonymous *The Secrets of the Castle* wrote scathingly that 'although her lord got most heartily laughed at, still as the speculation was profitable he managed to overlook an inconvenience which did not prey upon his purse'.[14] Another anonymous tract was even blunter, declaring that Lord Conyngham lived under the same roof and received emoluments 'from the very person whom he knew was daily dishonouring him'.[15]

In spite of the derision that she and her husband received at the hands of the contemporary media Elizabeth continued to act with her customary confidence and determination. So regal was her manner that the courtier Lord Cowper found himself wanting to address her as 'your Majesty'. It was the sheer effrontery of her performance that served as a shield against political criticism if not against public ridicule. Not for Lady Conyngham the late-night visits via secret passages and blacked out coaches: unlike her predecessors she would come and go from George's various palaces openly and in broad daylight. In her view, as she and her family were clearly the King's dearest friends and closest companions, it was only natural that they should be constantly by his side in London, Brighton or Windsor. It was already apparent that the greatest threat to her relationship with the King would not be the political or social opposition of his subjects but her own fatal tendency to become bored rather easily.

Elizabeth had soon discovered the price she had to pay for her elevation to royal mistress. The whole of England appeared to be discussing her in the most intimate and familiar way, from the slums of Soho to the exclusive clubs of St James's. Charles Greville noted that his fellow members of White's were openly discussing Lady Conyngham's physical attributes. When one member suggested that she had a leg like a post, the wit John Copley added, 'a poste Royale'. The lovers' obvious physical enjoyment of each other had also begun to provoke scorn and contempt among the courtiers. Lord Berkeley wrote scathingly that 'the happy pair were talked of as Romeo and Juliet, then as Oberon and Titania; sometimes they were Hamlet and Ophelia, at other times Ferdinand and Miranda; and – alas, for the devotion of the courtiers! – not infrequently they were referred to as Falstaff and Dame Quickly'.[16]

The King now spent much of his time with Elizabeth and her family at the Pavilion in Brighton. With his customary generosity he had allowed them use of his own horses and carriages from the royal stables. Elizabeth could come and go as she pleased but she was always careful to do it discreetly and not flaunt herself publicly as Brighton remained the home of Maria Fitzherbert, a lady widely admired and much respected in the town. For this reason Elizabeth never drove out alone, always insisting that one of her daughters accompany her. Again, at dinner with the King each evening she would insist on entering the room with Lady Elizabeth on one arm and Lady Maria on the other. But Elizabeth now had every excuse for being a constant presence at the Pavilion, for at the behest of the Duke of Wellington the King in the autumn of 1820 had appointed her Lady Steward of his Household. As his official chatelaine she could now run his household, manage his servants and even act as hostess at dinners and receptions. Soon she was exercising her new authority with total confidence. One evening in May 1821 Charles Greville was present when Elizabeth ordered the hundreds of candles that illuminated the great saloon of the Pavilion to be lit ahead of the King's appearance. When he entered, Charles Greville reports, Lady Conyngham curtsied then said, 'Sir, I told them to light up the saloon, as Lady Bath is coming this evening'. The King seized her arm and replied with the greatest tenderness, 'thank you, thank you, my dear; you always do what is right; you cannot please me so much as by doing everything you please, everything to show you are mistress here'.[17]

In spite of the cautionary presence of Maria Fitzherbert in the town George continued to love Brighton and above all the architectural exuberance of the Pavilion. It was his pleasure dome and a constant refuge from his responsibilities in London. He had first discovered the town in 1783 when, against his father's wishes, he went to stay with his uncle William Augustus, Duke of Cumberland, victor of Culloden and a notorious debauchee. Encouraged to drink, gamble and woman-ise by his uncle, the Prince found the town much to his liking and within a year had bought a house there himself on the newly fashion-able Steine. When in Brighton he felt, as his first biographer, Robert Huish, put it 'a prisoner released from confinement and plunged at once into the joys of Society with all the avidity of the fainting traveller who hastens to the gushing spring to allay the torments of his thirst'.[18] Soon George had persuaded his younger brother, Frederick, Duke of York to join him there and together they enjoyed, according to Thomas Creevey, 'all the extravagances and debaucheries of this most virtuous metropolis'.[19] George encouraged his brother to drink to excess while Frederick persuaded the Prince to indulge in his own particular vice, gambling at cards. But what George enjoyed most over the next thirty years was the architectural adventure of transforming his modest house into one of the most ambitious building projects in all Europe. The result was the splendid creation known as the Royal Pavilion. Decorated throughout in various oriental styles, it also contained the latest modern domestic technology including gas lighting and central heating. To the dismay of George's many guests the heating was invariably turned full on regardless of season. Visitors more familiar with draughty English country houses sweltered in the heat of the vast dining room where 'the inmates are nearly baked or encrusted'.[20] To the amazement of their guests George and Elizabeth always appeared, in spite of their supposed mutual passion, cool and relaxed in spite of the insufferable heat.

The Prince had taken a personal interest in the plumbing arrangements too. Always obsessed with personal hygiene, as his unfortunate wife Queen Caroline found to her cost, he had an ingenious pipe system installed that conducted sea water via a boiler directly to his own bathrooms. George had no fewer than five of these, ranging from a vast seawater plunge bath lined with veined marble to a modest douche bath. Hundreds of workmen were involved in these projects but only a handful were entrusted with constructing the notorious secret tunnel to the stables that had, according to the diarist Charles Greville, cost more than £3,000.[21]

Although George expressed himself wholly delighted with the completed Pavilion most of his friends shared John Wilson Croker's opinion that it was 'an absurd waste of money, and will be a ruin in half a century or sooner'[22] – a prediction that almost came true. When George boasted to Princess Lieven that the chandeliers alone had cost nearly £11,000 she was shocked by the wanton extravagance. 'I do not believe that, since the days of Heliogabalus,' she wrote, 'there has been such magnificence and such luxury. There is something effeminate in it, which is disgusting. One spends the evening half-lying on cushions; the lights are dazzling; there are perfumes, music, liqueurs . . . to light the three rooms used when the family is alone, costs 150 guineas an evening.'[23]

In the economic depression that followed the Napoleonic Wars the Pavilion attracted savage criticism as an example of almost obscene extravagance and the London cartoonists mocked it mercilessly. To them it was a godsend but to the Prince it became an architectural albatross hung around his neck so that whenever he was ridiculed over a new misdemeanour this oriental folly was shown accusingly in the background. Robert Seymour mocked it perfectly when he wrote.

> The outside – huge teapots all drilled round with holes
> Relieved by extinguishers sticking on poles
> The inside – all tea things and dragons, and bells,
> The show rooms – all show, the sleeping rooms cells.
> But the grand Curiosity's not to be seen –
> The owner himself an old fat MANDARIN;
> A patron of painters who copy designs,
> That grocers and tea dealers hang up for signs;[24]

But it was not just the cost of the building that so enraged radical opinion, for the daily running expenses were known to be enormous. George stinted on nothing; the food bill alone was colossal, for he never dined without company and there were seldom fewer than thirty guests each evening. Regarded as Britain's leading gastronome, he was obsessed by the quality of his dinners, employing at various times two of the finest chefs in Europe, Marie-Antoine Carême and Jean-Baptiste Wattier. He enticed Carême to Brighton for an unprecedented salary of £2,000 a year to preside over the best-equipped kitchen in Europe. Over £6,000 was spent on such items as an ingenious ventilation system and a clockwork mechanism for roasting and basting meat joints. No expense was spared and no fewer than three rooms were dedicated to preparing the puddings and confectionery of which George and Elizabeth were particularly fond. The result was the finest catering establishment in England. George was so delighted with the result that he would occasionally take his guests on a conducted tour, even putting on an apron to serve dinner himself.

The amounts of food consumed were staggering. One dinner alone consisted of over 100 hot dishes. Turbot was served with lobster sauce, pike with oysters, and eel with quenelles, truffles and cock's combs. Even a modest family dinner with the Conynghams included turtle or jardinière, a choice of two soups, then turbot, lobsters and trout à la genevoise. This was followed by no fewer than fourteen entrees including two sorts of capon, game, veal in béchamel sauce, lamb cutlets, two sorts of sweetbreads, quenelles of whiting, peafowl, roast hare, mutton, crayfish and lobster. Finally a vast array of puddings appeared to accompany George's favourite Nesselrode pudding, created in his honour by Carême and consisting of a sweet, iced purée of chestnuts beaten with eggs covered in a mass of whipped cream, laced with maraschino and then topped with cherries and dried fruit.[25]

Such feasting was not uncommon among the aristocracy in England and neither George nor Elizabeth was vastly overweight by the standards of their time. But it was no wonder that by the time the King was fifty he weighed over seventeen stone. His corset eventually became so uncomfortable that he abandoned it altogether and his friends noticed that his stomach now reached almost to his knees. Charles Lamb's anonymously published poem depicted him as a human whale:

Not a fatter fish than he
Flounders round the polar sea.
See his blubbers – at his gills
What a world of drink he swills . . .
. . . By his bulk and by his size,
By his oily qualities,
This (or else my eyesight fails)
This should be the Prince of Whales.

The gormandising at Brighton was common knowledge in London and it was assumed that Elizabeth Conyngham was an enthusiastic participant. As the years passed she was shown in cartoons as ever more bloated from the good life. Together she and her lover became the Tweedledum and Tweedledee of high society. One scandal sheet, clearly aimed at Elizabeth, appealed for a nursemaid for 'The Great Babe of England' who 'must be able to hold her nose at any offensive smell, for the Babe having a glorious appetite, devours rare quantities of soups and other sweetmeats and needs to be well-washed behind and before three or four times a day!' Another scurrilous cartoon shows a vast-bottomed Elizabeth perched on the King's equally fat knees.[26]

Accompanying these prodigious quantities of food were copious volumes of alcohol. George had spent his youth in the company of drunkards and had long been one himself. Even in 1811 Charles Greville had noted in his diary that 'the Regent was very near dying in consequence of a disgraceful debauch, about ten days ago. He sent for Mr Colman of the Little Theatre . . . and sat up the whole night with him, and others of his Friends drinking, until he was literally dead drunk.'[27] As with food, George's over-indulgence in alcohol was typical of his age. Captain Gronow was astounded by the amount the English drank. 'A three-bottle man was not an unusual guest at a fashionable table,' he wrote, 'and the night was invariably spent in drinking bad port-wine to an enormous extent.'[28] At the Pavilion George resolutely maintained the tradition, commencing the day with a breakfast accompanied by ale or claret followed by a mid-morning tipple of Madeira or sherry. Should a guest need anything more between meals, a flask of brandy was left ready on the sideboard. In the evening, champagne would precede dinner followed by wine, port and brandy. Serious drinkers, like George and his companions, considered even expensive table wines rather too anaemic and preferred the full-bodied punch 'Brown Brandy', called by the King *diabolino*, or his own particular favourite 'maraschino' – a fortified but sickly cherry brandy.

But there was another, gentler, side to life at the Brighton Pavilion for, although the high living continued it became increasingly tempered by George's new domesticity as the Conyngham family became the dominant group and the more racy characters from his past receded into the background. Although one of thirteen surviving children, the largest royal family in English history, George did not enjoy a happy childhood. His father George III was a domestic bully and a tyrant and as the oldest son the Prince of Wales bore the brunt of his father's disdain and his mother's cold formality. As Lord Melbourne told the young Queen Victoria, young George was 'monstrously afraid' of his father.[29] His children's education was left to a succession of near nonentities, and the King only occasionally intervened to give one of his eldest sons a sound thrashing. A wayward but intelligent child, George was harangued by both parents for the most minor transgressions of behaviour. At the age of eleven he and his younger brother Frederick, Duke of York, were separated from their siblings and sent to live on their own at Kew Palace where their heartless exile was an exact reprise of George III's own. Thrown together for mutual support, they remained unusually close until York's death in 1827. The result of this deprivation of normal maternal love in childhood was that both George and Frederick made disastrous formal marriages and only found real affection in the arms of mistresses.

In consequence of this spartan childhood George, when he was eventually released from parental bondage at the age of twenty-one, embarked upon a spree of wild living that lasted for over thirty years. Yet no matter how ephemeral his lifestyle became the Prince pursued a determined quest for the emotional stability that a home of his own would bring. It began with the constant renovations at Carlton House before he became obsessed with the Brighton Pavilion and then the Royal Lodge at Windsor. This search for a symbolic stability was complemented after 1785 by a similar quest for a motherly companion who could provide him with a combination of sexual excitement and emotional support. None of his early mistresses proved capable of this and his official wife Queen Caroline, a wilful German princess, was quite irrelevant to his needs. The only serious candidate for the role had been Maria Fitzherbert, but she demanded too many concessions from him and their relationship deteriorated into mutual acrimony. There is no doubt that the attraction of Elizabeth Conyngham was enhanced by her ability to fulfil this important role. Having a compliant husband and a good-natured family in tow also helped to create the much-needed illusion of domestic content. George found that he liked the Conyngham family enormously and enjoyed playing the role of an affectionate uncle or even a second father to them. Whatever his proven inadequacies as a real father he had sincerely loved his own daughter Princess Charlotte, and had been heartbroken by her tragic death in 1817. Now the presence of the Conyngham girls in his household allowed him to show the open affection that he had been denied with Charlotte after she became the object of an emotional tug-of-war between himself and Queen Caroline.

The presence of the young Lord Francis Conyngham also provided him with the novelty of having a surrogate son, for Francis took the place in George's affection of Isabella Hertford's eldest, the Earl of Yarmouth, a man once alarmingly described by the art historian John Ingamells as 'a wayward son, a wretched husband, a feckless Irish landlord, a Tory autocrat abusive of reform, and an example . . . of undisguised debauchery'.[30] George became exceptionally fond of Francis, 'dearest Frank', who often performed the duties of a second, unofficial secretary for him when he could no longer bear listening to the recriminations of the official occupant of the post, Sir Benjamin Bloomfield. As a reward George nominated Lord Francis for the Grand Cross of the Guelphic Order, telling him that he wanted the world to know how much he loved and respected him. It was easy to like Lord Francis, for he was a particularly handsome and charming young man. In 1824 he married Lady Jane Paget, daughter of the Marquess of Anglesea, who had famously lost a leg on the field of Waterloo. As a token of his attachment to Frank and the Conyngham family George gave the bridal couple a splendid wedding present of a fine silver candelabra bearing his own arms and those of the Conynghams. What Elizabeth did not know was that her son and her lover had a common interest in the courtesan Harriette Wilson, both having had relationships with her.

When State commitments allowed, the Conynghams had the run of the house in either Brighton or London, providing George with a normal domestic ritual such as he had never experienced as a child. The high point of the day would be the family dinner when everyone gathered together in the presence of the King. Princess Lieven described to Metternich the unvarying ritual of such occasions when Elizabeth would enter and seat herself at the King's right hand with Lady Elizabeth on his left and Lord Francis at one end of the table and his father at the other. As Charles Greville put it, 'the honours are done by the Father on one side and the son on the other'.[31] Occasionally Elizabeth's eldest son, the cold and censorious Earl of Mount Charles, would deign to be present but his visits were mere acts of filial duty. But the Conyngham girls more than made up for their absent brother and George found them both high-spirited, intelligent and amusing. The elder daughter in particular combined good looks with a vivacious personality and the King enjoyed treating her with mock gallantry to which she responded with such flirtatiousness that observers sometimes wondered if it were the daughter rather than the mother that the King really loved. Thomas Creevey noted in his diary in December 1822 when Lady Elizabeth was twenty-three that 'many are perfectly convinced of the truth of the report that dear Prinny is really to marry Lady Elizabeth'.[32] Yet it was the younger daughter Maria, always referred to as 'Darling Ri', who most delighted the King. His letters to her are unusually affectionate and paternal, revealing a natural sensitivity and concern that had never been apparent in his relationship with his own unfortunate daughter. His fatherly concern for Maria appears delightful if almost comic at times, as when he wrote inviting her to join them at Windsor:

Dearest Mater mentioned to me . . . that you complained of being tormented to the greatest degree with chilblains. I instantly sent off to our little friend Barrett at Brighton for his lotion . . . I need not say how much I have missed you and how long I have wished to see you . . . and it is therefore with a delight I have not words to express that I announce to you that upon the arrival of a Knight Errant, who will suddenly arrive, seize upon you, and as suddenly convey to the old Castle at Windsor when you may be sure, my beloved child, you will be received with open arms by its old Possessor.[33]

Lady Melbourne once said that George IV was unusually fond of children and Queen Victoria, in spite of condemning her late uncle's morals, always praised his kindness and that of Lady Conyngham towards her. 'He always took notice of me,' she wrote in middle age. Nor was his fascination with the young Conynghams and his generosity to them anything new. A decade earlier, when involved with Lady Hertford, he had shown a similar affection for her young ward, the eight-year-old Minny Seymour. A typical letter from her to the Prince is preserved in the Royal Archives at Windsor:

My dear Prinny,
How kind you were to remember my birthday, and send me such a beautiful present; I have placed it in a very conspicuous situation, and it is very much admired, pray accept my grateful thanks for it. I must not omit thanking you, for the piece of paper, I found inclosed [sic] in Colonel McMahon's letter, it is very acceptable, as sometimes I am rather an extravagant personage. I ride almost every day, and Adonis is as great a favourite as ever, dear little Sancho, is rather neglected, for I fancy myself almost to [sic] idle on him. I hope my dear Prinny that you enjoy good health, and that you will ever believe me to remain

Your most grateful and affectionate, MINNY[34]

Minny's brother George Seymour revealed in old age just how generous the Prince had been to Minny, always sending her an expensive birthday present. On her twenty-first birthday he wrote to tell her that he had secretly invested a small fortune of £10,000 on her behalf. Now he 'was happy to find the interest had increased to make it nearly £20,000' and was enclosing a draft on Messrs Coutts in her favour for that sum.[35] This generosity and genuine concern for children was a side of George IV not widely known in his lifetime and contrasts strongly with his public image as a selfish, uncaring debauchee who despised his wife and neglected his own daughter.

What made him so unusual among his contemporaries was his ability to relate intuitively to children and young people and to write and converse with them about their own little concerns and interests. In another letter to Maria Conyngham he tells her of the 'pretty pranks' of his favourite puppy which ran to and fro across the room from Maria's father to himself before 'sitting up on its hind legs and doing everything but speak'. In reply Maria wrote 'how can I express my delight and thanks for your affectionate letter. I kissed it as I could not kiss the dear person that wrote it. I am overjoyed at the thought of seeing you soon.'[36]

The Conynghams were now at the heart of the King's daily routine, sharing the duties and responsibilities of the royal household. Lady Holland thought Elizabeth's presence, in particular, had made the Pavilion a far more appealing place even though she had begun, as befitted her middle-class origins, to exercise a far tighter control on the household budget:

> Lady C. has certainly the merit of inviting society befitting the King to see; and there is a very moderate degree of form, great attention to expense, much abridgement in wax candles and fires; the whole denoting an attention to economy.[37]

The main event of the day was dinner, after which the entire company would retire to the Music Room where the King would often sing to his guests accompanied by his resident orchestra, the King's Band. With over seventy musicians this was as large as any modern symphony orchestra. His favourite numbers were. 'A Friar of Orders Gray' and appropriately 'Life's a Bumper'. His voice, according to Thomas Croker, was a bass 'not good . . . but with the force, gaiety and spirit of the glee in a superior style to the professional men'.[38]

Elizabeth's role had broadened too, for now she was not only the King's lover but also an intimate friend with whom he could discuss his domestic arrangements and, increasingly, matters of state. In the autumn of his life he had found comfort in the companionship of Elizabeth Conyngham and her family. As a contemporary ballad put it:

> 'Tis pleasant at seasons to see how they sit,
> First cracking their nuts, then cracking their wit;
> Then quaffing their claret – then mingling their lips,
> Or tickling the fat about each other's hips.

# FOUR

## Divorce and Coronation

With the long-awaited death of his father in January 1820 George became King and, relieved of any constitutional inhibitions, hurried forward his plans to end the debacle of his marriage to Caroline of Brunswick. For him his involvement with Caroline had been a long and wearying penance but to the British public it was an entertaining long-running farce to be enjoyed at George's expense. Now that he was King the prospect of having Caroline as his queen was too awful for him to contemplate, for she would certainly return to claim her rights and privileges as consort. George decided that now was the time to expunge Caroline from his life, from her titular position in the Church of England and preferably from Britain altogether. How to bring this about was a problem that had long concerned him, for as early as January 1818, perhaps as a consequence of his growing intimacy with Elizabeth Conyngham, he had written to the Lord Chancellor telling him that his intention was to:

> Turn my whole thoughts to the endeavouring to extricate myself from the cruellest, as well as the most unjust predicament that ever even the lowest individual, much more a Prince, ever was placed in by unshackling myself from a woman who . . . is suffered to continue to bear my name, to belong to me and to the country.[1]

The Prince had only agreed to marry Caroline in the first place in a rare and ill-advised attempt to please his father. George had been led to believe that if he agreed to marry and settle down with a suitable German princess his father would make a substantial contribution to reducing his son's colossal debts. He had been encouraged in this risky stratagem by his then mistress, Lady Jersey, who saw the match as an opportunity to consolidate her own position. Her plan was to befriend the new bride and make herself indispensable to her while continuing her own affair with the Prince. Lady Jersey was so persuasive in her argument that the Prince allowed her to travel down to Dover to meet Caroline on his behalf. A foretaste of coming events occurred on the journey back to London when Lady Jersey grabbed the best seat in the carriage and waved to the cheering crowd as regally as Caroline herself.

Misled as to both the character and looks of his intended bride, George was appalled when confronted by the reality. Not only was Caroline short, fat, coarse and unattractive but she was also dirty and malodorous as he discovered, to his horror, on the first and only night they spent together. At the wedding ceremony supported, literally, by his friends George Brummel and Lord Moira, George was almost footless with drink having spent the drive to the church tearfully declaiming his undying love for Maria Fitzherbert. At the climax of the ceremony when asked to make his wedding oath George was seen to gaze soulfully at Lady Jersey for a moment or two before he 'hiccupped out his vows of fidelity'. When the Archbishop of Canterbury asked if anyone knew of any just impediment to the marriage the Prince, to the amusement of his friends, gazed hopefully round at the congregation before bursting into tears.[2] Later that evening, fortified by drink and with the house packed full of his dissolute cronies 'drunk and filthy, sleeping and snoring in boots on the sofas', as Caroline recalled, he stumbled to the marriage bed like a prisoner going to the scaffold. Yet so successfully did he perform his duty to the country that Caroline was found to be pregnant a month later. She always maintained that they did not actually have sex until the following day as the Prince was too drunk to perform on the wedding night. Instead of getting into bed, Caroline insisted, he staggered across the room and collapsed into the fireplace where he passed out in a drunken stupor.[3]

Again, the embarrassing details of this disastrous wedding night were soon public knowledge in London and a cartoon appeared suggesting that George's sexual performance had only been made possible by the use of the powerful aphrodisiac cantharides. The Prince was not the only one who found Caroline personally disgusting. His friend Lord Malmesbury, who was designated to take care of her, had previously been impressed by Caroline's 'good bust and tolerable teeth' but was horrified when she presented him with a tooth that had just fallen out when he came to collect her a month later. It made the Prince's own account of the worst aspects of that appalling wedding night only too credible for he had confided in Malmesbury that Caroline had 'such marks of filth both in the fore and hind parts of her . . . that she turned my stomach and from that moment I made a vow never to touch her again'. Taking upon himself the role of personal adviser Malmesbury began lecturing Caroline 'on the toilette, on cleanliness and on the delicacy of speaking'.[4] The obstinate woman totally ignored all his advice and continued to smell horribly, mainly as a consequence of the supposedly Germanic custom of refusing to 'wash all over'. Such was Caroline's reputation for poor personal hygiene that when her lover Pergami was later said to have shared her bath Thomas Creevey noted sarcastically that it was an event that would have occurred most infrequently.

Until the birth of their daughter in January 1796 Caroline divided her time between Carlton House and the Brighton Pavilion, but received little more than frigid courtesy from her husband who continued to consort openly with Lady Jersey. Each day the lovers teased Caroline remorselessly, competing with each other in getting her drunk. When that diversion palled the Prince lost interest in her altogether, finding it almost impossible to disguise his contempt and boredom. Soon they were living in separate establishments. Caroline, a woman of robust if coarse tastes, saw no reason to deny herself a sex life while in London, and embarked upon a series of short but vigorous relationships with some of the most prominent celebrities of the time. These included her lodger Admiral Sir Sidney Smith, a brother of the Irish patriot Lord Edward Fitzgerald, and the society painter Sir Thomas Lawrence, whom she skilfully seduced while sitting for him.[5] Although the government always considered her sympathetic to the Whig opposition Caroline demonstrated her true impartiality by inviting the rising star of the Tory party, George Canning, round to dinner and promptly ravished him on the sofa afterwards. When she inevitably became pregnant by one of her lovers in 1801, she put about a story that she had gone back and spent a night or two at Carlton House. By the time the child was born she had abandoned the idea of persuading the country that the Prince was the father, and made out instead that she had adopted a baby born to a poor couple.[6]

After years of incessant bickering with her husband over finance and the upbringing of their high-spirited daughter Princess Charlotte, born in 1796, Caroline left England with her 'adopted' son and embarked on a bizarre progress through Europe. Arriving in Italy in August 1814 she swiftly gained herself a handsome consort and general factotum in one Bartolomeo Pergami, a swarthy Italian who had served in the French army and then mysteriously acquired the title of Baron della Francina. Hired as Caroline's *valet de place* he soon became her lover and was promoted to chamberlain, presiding over a household that consisted mainly of his own family and friends. Caroline's outrageous behaviour with her chamberlain soon scandalised the whole of European society and deeply embarrassed her husband back in England. The people of Genoa, for instance, were startled to witness her entrance to their city travelling in a gilt and mother-of-pearl phaeton, resembling a sea-shell, drawn through the streets by two piebald horses, a child dressed in flesh-coloured tights like an operatic cherub acting as coachman. Sprawled across the seat was Caroline, now a fat woman of fifty, wearing a pink hat with several pink feathers floating in the wind, a pink bodice cut very low and a short white skirt beneath which showed two stout legs in a pair of top-boots. Preceding the phaeton on a small piebald horse was the flamboyantly moustached Pergami, dressed to resemble King Murat. Soon stories of her eccentric behaviour were being reported back to her resentful husband in London.[7]

Ignoring any criticisms that filtered back to her, Caroline continued on her travels. When she reached Germany the Margravine of Baden, considering it her duty to entertain a fellow royal, invited her to join the royal box at the Opera. When Caroline failed to appear the Margravine gave orders for the opera to commence, but the theatre door was suddenly flung open and with a great, coarse laugh Caroline strode in decked out in an enormous headdress, as worn by the local Oberlander peasants, and decorated with flying ribbons and glittering spangles. The elderly and sedate

Margravine was seen to nearly swoon in her box at the sight of this strange apparition. A month later Caroline capped even this performance by appearing at a public ball in Geneva dressed as Venus and naked to the waist.[8]

This outrageous behaviour clearly shamed and embarrassed her husband back in England but in a perverse way it caught the imagination of the public. With Caroline anything seemed possible, so that a country clergyman living in Devonshire was capable of noting in his diary that he had heard 'the Princess of Wales has been brought to bed of a fine boy in the harem of the Bey of Algiers'.[9]

The only good thing to have come out of George's brief union with this extraordinary woman was their daughter, Princess Charlotte, but when she died tragically in childbirth in 1817 the single tenuous link between them was gone. With the coronation approaching George decided that the termination of their relationship was imperative, particularly as his relationship with Elizabeth Conyngham was proving to be far more than a passing infatuation. He had even begun to speculate on the future they might have together. What would be the constitutional position if the Marquess of Conyngham, who never appeared to be in robust health, suddenly died? Could he not then marry Elizabeth and make her his queen? The first step towards any kind of optimistic future, George decided, must be to free himself of his current encumbrance by divorcing Caroline. Princess Lieven confirms that this was indeed how his mind was working when she writes to Metternich of one particular evening at Brighton:

> Here is one of the scenes between the trio – King, Favourite and Myself: The King pointing to Lady Conyngham, 'Ah heavens, if she were what I am!' I was at a loss to understand what this meant. Ought Lady Conyngham to be a man? The King stopped and sighed, and then went on: 'If she were a widow, she would not be one for long'. Lady C: 'Ah, my dear King, how good you are'. The King: 'Yes, I have taken an oath', then turning to me, he added in a low voice, 'patience; everything in good time'.[10]

Had he known of this conversation with its ominous reference to 'widows' Lord Conyngham might well have felt uneasy. But the

## The King and the Vice Queen

King had already begun the process of laying plans for divorce, for in the summer of 1818 his constant appeals to the Lord Chancellor to do something had led to the establishment of the Milan Commission to investigate Caroline's adultery. For the next two years three government-appointed commissioners followed in her wake as she progressed through Europe, questioning dozens of servants, sailors, innkeepers, postilions and gardeners about her bad behaviour. Much of the testimony, scandalous in the extreme, was collected together under the title 'Delicate Investigation' and housed in two large green bags of evidence. Samuel Roberts, her footman, for instance told the investigators that his mistress was 'very fond of fucking' and other servants agreed that their buxom mistress had an unusually voracious appetite for sex.[11] Few of the men who crossed her path, it appeared, managed to escape being dragged off to bed. Now in 1820 with the volumes of evidence collected by the commissioners in hand the King proposed to bring his unruly Queen to trial. But here he encountered the unexpected opposition of the Prime Minister Lord Liverpool and the Lord Chancellor Lord Eldon, who were both hesitant to bring the monarchy into further disrepute by revealing the evidence in public. Their reluctance to support his cause wholeheartedly confirmed the King's resentment at what he saw as constant and unnecessary foot-dragging by ministers. The acrimony that developed at this time would affect their relationship for the next five years, for George maintained that if the divorce proceedings had been brought earlier, when he and Caroline were still Prince and Princess of Wales, then the whole business would have been far simpler to deal with.[12]

His first step in cutting Caroline adrift was to insist, the moment he became King, that the words 'our most gracious majesty, Queen Caroline' be removed from the Church of England liturgy. Soon there must be a coronation and he was determined that Caroline would neither be crowned Queen nor play any part whatsoever in the ceremony. To his delight the Archbishop of Canterbury agreed without protest, but persuading Caroline to accept this obvious humiliation would be a far more difficult business.[13] A suggestion from his ministers was that Caroline be generously compensated for her removal. An annuity of £50,000 a year for life was suggested, provided that she agreed to co-operate, relinquish the title of Queen and finally remove herself from England altogether. Faced with total ignominy Caroline predictably refused the government's offer without hesitation and decided instead to return immediately to England.

Princess Lieven was among the guests at the Brighton Pavilion in June 1820 when the royal secretary Sir Benjamin Bloomfield rushed into the dining room and announced that Queen Caroline was on her way to London. To the Princess's surprise, Elizabeth Conyngham of all people seemed delighted by the news, claiming that the Queen's return 'will decide the affair'.[14] It appeared to others, however, that an involvement in what was bound to be a bitter and protracted confrontation must be detrimental to the favourite's interests. At the king's instigation a last-ditch effort was made to placate Caroline. The lawyer Henry Brougham, a leading Whig and another of Caroline's past conquests, agreed to travel over to her lodgings at St Omer on the French coast, where she was waiting to invade England. He pleaded with her to see reason and accept what amounted to a generous annuity. True to character Caroline remained obstinate and again curtly refused his offer, demanding instead that a British naval yacht be sent to carry her over from Calais. When Brougham told her that this was impossible she dismissed him abruptly and immediately boarded a public packet boat, arriving defiantly at Dover on 5 June 1820.

There began Caroline's triumphal progress to London to face her divorce trial at Westminster. For the journey she chose, with faultless vulgarity, a puce-coloured sarcanet pelisse lined with ermine, and a white willow hat. The first crowd she met was in Canterbury where a cheering mob, delighted by her arrival in the town, unhitched the horses and dragged her carriage through the streets. Her triumphal progress continued all the way to London and in every town and village she received the same enthusiastic cheers, the same pealing bells. When her entourage reached the Thames at Gravesend the local mob held a rope across the road, forcing the carriage to stop. Dozens of young ruffians then leapt forward and took up the shafts, pulling her carriage through the town. As they climbed Shooters Hill on the outskirts of London, the mob still pushing from behind, carriages of all sorts arrived to join the boisterous cavalcade. At Blackheath the atmosphere had become that of a continental fair and at Deptford and Greenwich the equally large crowds were swollen to 'an indiscriminate concourse, by all ranks and conditions of the inhabitants'.[15]

The return of Queen Caroline had demonstrated a remarkable outpouring of support for her cause by the ordinary people and national disgust at the King's treatment of her. It also proved that in the matter of the forthcoming divorce he now had a bitter fight on his hands. Later that same week, when reviewing a body of troops on Hounslow Common, George was greeted with jeers and shouts of support for Queen Caroline. Further proof of the damage Caroline was doing to George's popularity with his people occurred a few weeks later when he and the Conynghams were driving together down the course at the Ascot races. The crowd was uncharacteristically silent so that George could not have failed to hear a coarse male voice bellowing from the crowd 'where's the Queen, Georgie?'[16] Elizabeth, however, appeared determined that a mere ruffian would not spoil her enjoyment of the occasion and an eyewitness described her as smiling serenely and 'looking remarkably well in the morning, her complexion being so fine'.[17] But by the Friday of Ascot week she had become as bored with the races as she was with the issue of the wronged Queen. Significantly, when she refused to accompany him that day the King announced to the assembled party that if Lady Conyngham did not go, then neither would he.

Meanwhile Caroline continued her flirtation with the London mob. A few days after her arrival she set off from the Hammersmith home of Alderman Wood, her most ardent supporter, on a provocative drive to Carlton House. As her elderly carriage trundled past the door the sentries outside, reported to be near-mutiny themselves, were so confused that they presented arms 'but in a manner indicating some embarrassment'. Next day an unruly mob appeared outside Lady Hertford's house in Manchester Square and smashed all the windows. Now the King, his ministers and royal mistresses past and present were the targets of public wrath and Queen Caroline their blameless hero. As she made her way to the trial at the House of Lords on 17 August 1820 the mob ran alongside her carriage shouting their loyalty and declaring 'we'll give our blood for you'. Arriving at the House she entered the great chamber dressed completely in black and wearing a girlish coal-black wig looking, according to Thomas Creevey, like a 'wooden Dutch doll with a the kind of lead-weighted base that always sprang upright no matter in what position it was laid down'. Creevey found her behaviour that day as odd as her appearance for 'she popped all at once into the House, made a duck at the throne, another to the Peers, and a concluding jump into the chair which was placed for her'.[18] Within minutes of her arrival all present realised the terrible mistake the King had made in bringing her to trial.

As Caroline returned, later that day, to her temporary lodging at St James's Square, an even larger mob ran beside her carriage demanding that anyone passing give a hearty cheer for the Queen. What most outraged public opinion was the sheer hypocrisy of a monarch prepared to put his wife on trial for adultery while openly consorting with the latest in a long string of mistresses himself. The next day the first of dozens of cartoons revelling in the King's discomfiture appeared. It showed him dressed in Chinese costume, waiting in terror at the Pavilion for the arrival of the Queen. In a vain attempt to stem the flow of such ridicule his secretary, Sir Benjamin Bloomfield, set out to visit the artists and publishers with tempting offers of cash to suppress their work, even suggesting to the more discreet of them that they might publish some scurrilous items, which he would provide, about the Queen instead. One of those sorely tempted by the offer was the most illustrious of the cartoonists, George Cruikshank, who was deep in his own financial difficulties at the time. That month Cruikshank is recorded as having accepted £100 'in consideration of a pledge not to caricature His Majesty in any immoral situation'.[19] A year later his brother Isaac would accept £60 from Bloomfield for withdrawing a savage caricature of the King sneeringly entitled 'The Dandy at Sixty'. Yet George Cruikshank, against the spirit of the agreement, continued to provide illustrations for other satirists' work, such as William Hone's merciless lampoon 'The Queen's Matrimonial Ladder'.

As the trial continued few close to the King escaped the attentions of the mob. When the Duke of Wellington returned from the House later that first week he was accosted by a mob urging him to give a shout for the Queen. 'Yes, yes,' he growled 'very well, the Queen, then, and may all your daughters be like her!'[20] For the next three months the government of the country ground to a virtual halt as almost the entire peerage of England and most of the King's ministers sat listening to the trial. The prosecution, led by the Lord Chancellor Lord Eldon, began by calling dozens of witnesses to testify against the Queen. These were invariably of the servant class and were memorably described by her defence counsel, Henry Brougham, as 'pimps of hideous aspect, whose prurient glance could penetrate through the keyholes of rooms, where the rat shared with the bug the silence of the deserted place'.[21] Brougham, together with the Whig opposition, the London mob and most of England thought the King a hypocrite and a bully to have brought the action in the first place. Then as the trial approached its climax Brougham announced dramatically to his colleagues that he proposed to call an important new witness – the Marchioness of Conyngham. This was clearly his trump card, as subpoenaing Elizabeth would result in the maximum of embarrassment for the King.[22] Even the opposition were alarmed at the prospect and their leader Lord Grey immediately implored Brougham to withdraw his threat or be prepared to face an apocalyptic clash with the sovereign.

Throughout the long hot summer of 1820 the public enjoyed the almost daily revelations of scandal and one phrase in particular, 'Non mi ricordo', meaning 'I can't remember' – the reply repeatedly given by one of Caroline's more colourful Italian servants under cross-examination – became the catchphrase of the year. As the balance of evidence inclined one way then the other Brougham attempted to bring the King into the debate by hinting that he, not the government, was the real plaintiff in the case. In one speech quoting Milton's description of Satan he described George as a 'vast shapeless and shadowy mass'. This reference to his figure outraged the King far more than any of Brougham's other allegations and he refused to speak to him for years. 'He said that I might at least have spared him the attack on his shape,' Brougham wrote later, 'whatever faults he might have, his legs were not as I described them.'[23] Sharing the King's humiliation, Elizabeth Conyngham now became the target for many of the lampoons. One of the first pamphlets in which she features as 'Old Q' went immediately to two editions and, as with the King, it was her plump appearance that presented the satirists with an unmissable target:

Give the devil his due, she's a prime bit of stuff,
And for flesh she has got in all conscience enough.
He'll never need pillows to keep up his head,
Whilst old Q and himself sleep and snore in one bed.

Finally, when the Lords came to vote on the Divorce Bill on 6 November the majority for it was so small that the government thought it not even worth putting to the Commons. When called on for his vote, the King's brother, the Duke of Clarence, had leant over the rail of the gallery and yelled his 'Content!' like a savage.[24] On the night that the government capitulated the London mob carried Henry Brougham in triumph on their shoulders all the way to Brook's Club. Yet the collapse of the bill was perhaps fortunate for the King, as Brougham later revealed that he had in his possession a copy of the King's will in which he referred to Maria Fitzherbert as his 'dear wife'. If the Queen had been convicted, Brougham asserted, then he would then have introduced a parliamentary motion seeking to impeach the King for treason for secretly marrying a Roman Catholic. Brougham had other damaging evidence, too, including a mysterious witness who claimed to have seen the King's sexual exploits with dozens of women including the daughters of a turnpike keeper named Hyfield, a French courtesan called Mme de Meyer, a lodging-house keeper called Mary Lewis, a widow named Mrs Crowe, by whom it was claimed he had a child, and many more.[25] None of this much impressed the Duke of Wellington, however; when told of Brougham's secret witness he replied nonchalantly that he thought it of little matter, for the King was 'degraded as low as he could be already'.[26]

As far as George was concerned, the whole affair had been a debacle completely mishandled by his ministers and he repeated his perennial threat to resign the throne and to retire to Hanover. Still seething with anger, at the next Privy Council he abused them all, according to Charles Arbuthnot, in the language of a 'Bedlamite'.[27] Even his guest at the Brighton Pavilion that weekend, Mrs Wellesley-Pole, left early complaining that the King's coarse language was 'beyond anything indiscreet and improper'. The collapse of the King's faith in his ministers was so comprehensive that it marked a fundamental change in his attitude towards them. From now on he put more store by Elizabeth Conyngham's advice, even on political issues, than he did on theirs. A state of thinly disguised warfare now existed between Brighton and Westminster.

Throughout the trial the Queen had enjoyed the discreet support of the parliamentary opposition and now that the divorce bill had been abandoned even respectable Whig ladies began calling on her. Their behaviour outraged the Tory Harriet Arbuthnot, who marvelled that they should 'condescend to notice a person who had been proved to have slept for five weeks with her menial servant'.[28] Princess Lieven was equally contemptuous of anyone fraternising with Caroline, particularly as her own carriage had recently been stopped by the mob and her servants ordered to take off their hats as the Queen's carriage approached from the opposite direction. As it passed, according to the Princess, the Queen threw her a withering glance and 'I saw two enormous black eyebrows, as big as two of my fingers put together; the contents of two pots of rouge on her cheeks: a veil over everything'.[29] To the King's disgust the whole nation appeared united in joy at the Queen's triumph and bells rang throughout the land as towns and cities were illuminated in her honour in what became the greatest national celebration since the victory at Waterloo. Ominously the Peterborough magistrates were forced to call in troops to control the rioting crowd and Wellington was booed in the street while Lord Castlereagh, the Foreign Secretary, was roughly handled at Covent Garden. Brougham in contrast was now the hero of the hour and offered the freedoms of many cities, together with the greatest accolade that the English can bestow – public houses were named after him.[30]

But the Queen's apparent triumph was to prove little more than a nine-day wonder. Within a few weeks her cause seemed to have all but evaporated as politicians lost interest and even the London mob appeared to suddenly grow weary of their idol. With characteristic fickleness it changed its cries of support to catcalls and insults and began to chant a new rhyme as she passed:

> Gracious Queen, we thee implore,
> Go away and sin no more;
> Or if that effort be too great,
> Go away at any rate.

Past experience had taught the King not to trust the volatile public mood and he sensibly kept out of their way until the excitement died down. For the whole of the following winter he remained in near-seclusion with Elizabeth and the Conyghams at Brighton. Not until the following February did he finally pluck up the courage to appear again in public when, accompanied by Elizabeth, he went to his favourite theatre, Drury Lane, to watch a performance of Handel's opera *Artaxerxes*. Expecting little more than public indifference at best he was surprised and delighted when the entire audience rose to greet him with a three-minute standing ovation as he entered. Clearly affected by their cheers, he responded by standing in his box and bowing repeatedly to the audience. Even when a coarse voice shouted an insult from the gallery the King remained unconcerned.[31] As was customary at the time, the opera was followed by the performance of a farce which that evening was the highly successful *Who's Who*. The King was seen to enjoy it immensely, throwing himself back in his seat beside Elizabeth and roaring with laughter. On the way down from his box he stopped Lady Bessborough and told her that he had never enjoyed an evening more in his life. Both Princess Lieven, who was present, and the remorselessly critical correspondent of *The Times* were astonished by the enthusiastic reception George had received. As Lady Cowper wrote, 'the King is as popular as possible. Not only in the theatres he is received with the greatest applause but also in the avenues to the theatres where he has been hissed before.'[32]

This sudden and dramatic reversal of public opinion in his favour was further confirmed by the poor attendance at later public meetings in support of the Queen's cause. When a well-publicised service of thanksgiving for the abandonment of the Divorce Bill was held at St Paul's Cathedral it was also poorly attended. A month later Queen Caroline herself ventured to the rival Convent Garden theatre to watch a performance of the farce *Tom Thumb*. At first the audience appeared to ignore her presence but when an actor uttered the words, 'the Queen is drunk' and the reply was 'Damn the Queen!' the whole audience erupted into frenzied applause. Her second public appearance, this time at Drury Lane, was even more disastrous. At the interval a drunken member of the audience staggered up to her and bellowed 'damned whore!' in her face.[33]

London society too was now heartily sick of the Queen and her troubles and had decided that she was a liability to herself and an embarrassment to the country. This opinion was confirmed when news spread that after she had left Brandenburg House, which she had rented during the trial, it was found to be in an appalling condition with expensive carpets ruined by wax, ink and oil, curtains ripped, the silver 'much bruised and damaged' and, worst of all, all the bedding and blankets had to be 'sent to the scourers from total neglect'. No wonder that the Lord Chancellor, the pompous Lord Eldon, was so alarmed by rumours that Caroline was considering the purchase of a vacant house next to his own that he immediately rushed out and bought it for £3,000 more than the asking price.[34]

Now in 1821 for virtually the first time in his adult life the King found himself content in his domestic life and popular with his people. The time was right, he decided, to make preparations for his coronation postponed from the previous year. Predictably he planned it as a great extravaganza to rival Napoleon's own spectacular coronation in Paris in 1804. The government, eager to distract the London mob from more violence with a diverting spectacle, agreed in principle that the nation would foot the bill. But when the detailed estimates were revealed they were appalled by the cost of it all. Even Sir Walter Scott, the most committed of royalists, was moved to complain to his daughter that the vast ermine-trimmed robes would cost a whole £400 apiece! Scott consoled himself with the thought that it would, at least, give work to British manufacturers, and ended his letter by reprimanding those 'who sneer coldly at this solemn festival and are disposed to dwell on the expense which attends it, than on the generous feelings which it ought to awaken'.[35]

As the great day approached a temporary wooden floor covered in blue cloth was laid over the flagstones of Westminster Abbey and continued out of the Abbey along a covered raised walkway into Westminster Hall, where the coronation banquet would be held. As a token of changing taste the chairs chosen to line the route were designed in the newly fashionably gothic style and upholstered in scarlet cloth. To offset the mounting cost of the ceremony someone had come up with the novel idea of charging spectators a fee and the best seats in the stands were soon on offer at twenty guineas each. When it came to his own appearance George stinted on nothing, ordering no fewer than nine wigs, each costing fifteen guineas – then half a year's wages for a working man. Still obsessed by the need to outshine Napoleon he spent hours with Elizabeth gazing at the pictures of the 1804 coronation before deciding to send an aide off to Paris to find the exact cloth used by Napoleon.[36]

But when the Earl Marshal went to collect the most important artefact in the coronation regalia – the Crown of England – he found to his astonishment that it was missing. At the restoration of the monarchy in 1660 a copy of the original Crown of St Edmund had been made but had bizarrely passed out of royal ownership into private hands. When told that it was needed for the imminent ceremony the current owner decided to cash in on his good luck and demanded the colossal sum of £10,000 for the one-day hire. The embarrassed government reluctantly agreed, realising they had little alternative other than to pay the ransom and the crown was duly handed over. After the ceremony the King tossed it nonchalantly into the back of a cupboard and it was lost again. By the time it was found and restored to its legal owners the accumulated rental costs were so high that the government quietly agreed to purchase it out-right for £54,000.[37] The rest of the regalia was hired more econom-ically from the King's old favourites, Messrs Rundell, Bridge and Co. Never before or since has a coronation cost the nation so much. The final bill for the extravaganza amounted to £243,000 – almost ten times that of his brother William's coronation nine years later.

For the King it would be money well spent, a celebration of the restoration of his popularity with the people; for Elizabeth the coronation would be a public confirmation of her assured relation-ship with the King and a demonstration of her new influence at Court. As part of this assertion of her role she had insisted upon sending out the invitations herself. George had also allowed her to choose the pages as well and, to the fury of Tory ministers, she had selected them exclusively from the children of Whig families. This was tantamount to a challenge to the ruling party and a declaration that Lady Conyngham intended to meddle with the King's political as well as his domestic affairs. Many aristocratic recipients were so outraged by her presumption that they refused to respond. One who did, Lord Manvers, replied indignantly that although he considered his son highly honoured he 'would not listen for an instant to such a proposal from any woman whatsoever' and furthermore 'rejected her offer with the utmost indignation'.[38] There were further complaints when it became known that the King had also allowed Lady Conyngham to design the costumes for the Privy Councillors. The result demonstrated that the King was not alone in his taste for garish and unsuitable clothes. So inappropriate was her choice of blue and white satin, Elizabethan-style doublets and hose that the unfortunate Councillors would, on the day, cringe with embarrassment as they emerged. When shown the proposed designs a month before the ceremony Lady Cowper told her friends that she thought the spectacle would surely 'convulse the whole of Westminster Abbey with laughter'.[39] Even the loyal Sir Walter Scott, who had come down from Leith on one of the first steamships for the occasion, was forced to admit when he saw it that 'so gay a garb had an odd effect on the persons of elderly or ill-made men'.[40]

In the days preceding the ceremony George and Elizabeth spent much time closeted together at Carlton House, where the King took particular pleasure in displaying his coronation robe. One foreign dignitary who called in was the Polish Count Joseph Boruwlaski, a dwarf less than three feet in height, who presented the king with a copy of his memoirs and received in return a miniature watch. Standing incongruously beside the portly figure of King George, Boruwlaski expressed particular admiration of his majesty's 27-foot-long coronation train.[41] Yet there were few other visitors that week for in spite of the enthusiastic reception at Drury Lane, George remained wary of meeting anyone outside his intimate circle. In preparation for the great day he had decided to move his household into Buckingham Palace, his latest renovation project. At dinner in the Palace two days before the coronation Princess Lieven's sharp eye spotted Elizabeth wearing a new string of pearls of enormous value – even finer, she thought, than those of any Prussian Princess or Russian Grand Duchess. She suspected, correctly, that the King had bought them for his mistress as a gift and had simply added the cost to the coronation bill.[42]

As a further reward for her emotional support during the stress of the divorce trial the King had commissioned the eminent portraitist

Sir Thomas Lawrence to paint Elizabeth's picture. The sittings were held at Buckingham Palace and on the eve of the coronation George sat with her for three hours as Lawrence completed the portrait that now hangs in Slane Castle. The tranquillity of the sitting seemed to calm the King's nerves for he had been much agitated by the stress of it all and was constantly arguing about costs with his secretary, Sir Benjamin Bloomfield. But his greatest fear was that the Queen would make an appearance at the Abbey even though he had given specific instructions that she must be admitted to neither the ceremony nor the coronation banquet afterwards. Caroline had stayed on in London in a rented house and drove out every day in her shabby carriage. Although her popularity had declined many thought she was still capable, with the help of the mob, of ruining the great day. Lord Temple reported that the public were aware of this and it was proving difficult to sell some seats along the procession route because of the fear of rioting. Among the most pessimistic was Lady Sarah Lyttelton, who wrote:

> The mob is rather too cross, and too fond of the Queen to permit a ceremony in which she is not to take part . . . every day there is a gathering on some account or other. And her Gracious Majesty takes care to keep it up, by showing herself all about London in a shabby post-chaise and pair of post-horses and living in the scruffiest house she could think of, to show she is kept out of the palace.[43]

That evening when the sitting with Lawrence was completed the King left Elizabeth at Buckingham Palace and drove quietly across London to the Speaker's residence at the House of Commons. Still apprehensive of the London mob, he had decided to spend the night there and so avoid having to travel across the city on the morning of the coronation. He shared a quiet dinner with the Speaker and then retired alone to the comfortable new state bed that had been purchased specially for the occasion. But to his consternation he was kept awake by the bells of St Margaret's Church nearby, which pealed every half hour throughout the night. At dawn the warships moored on the Thames outside his windows added to his discomfort with a loud cannonade.

Later that morning, 19 July, tired and irritable from lack of sleep, the King put on his finery and set off to join the procession assembled in Westminster Hall. Spectators had been warned to be in their seats by 7 a.m. sharp and the temporary galleries built between the Hall and the Abbey were already crammed to capacity. Each section had been given a name, reminiscent to some of London public houses. There was 'The Royal George', 'The Royal Cambridge' and bizarrely but perhaps appropriately, 'The Ladies' Fancy'. There was no sign of trouble from the huge crowds for everyone seemed determined to enjoy themselves at this most spectacular of coronations. Even foreign guests such as Prince Esterhazy, the Austrian ambassador, had dressed up for the occasion. His choice was a hussar uniform but decorated with fabulous jewels reputed to be worth over £100,000.[44] The boisterous atmosphere that morning was further heightened by the presence of a group of famous English pugilists hired for the day as 'bouncers' and eager to eject anyone foolish enough to try and enter without a valid ticket. Such was the demand for these that a black market had existed for over a month. One speculator hoping to make a killing secured four adjoining houses in Palace Yard and then attempted to rent out the front rooms to spectators. He had expected to make over £10,000 from the venture but to his dismay less ambitious touts began selling viewing spaces for a mere ten shillings and sixpence apiece and his project became a financial disaster.

At half past ten exactly the King struggled down from his carriage and gathered his wits and robes together as the signal was given and a solemn procession led by the King's herb-woman scattering aromatic herbs and scented flowers in its path set off along the blue-carpeted walkway towards the Abbey. The King's heavy velvet train, so admired by the Polish dwarf, was supported by eight pages under the direction of the Master of the Robes – Elizabeth's son Lord Francis Conyngham. In spite of his age the King, without his side-whiskers, looked surprisingly youthful that morning as he passed into the Abbey followed by the officers of state carrying the crown, the orb, the sceptre and the sword of state. Behind the leading nobles came the dignitaries of the City of London – among them Alderman Wood, the Queen's main champion throughout the divorce crisis, whose presence provoked the only boos and jeers of the day. A vivid description of the scene in the Abbey was given, appropriately, by the painter Benjamin Robert Haydon who wrote:

> The room rises with a sort of feathered, silken thunder. Plumes wave, eyes sparkle, glasses are out, mouths smile and one man becomes the prime object of attraction to thousands . . . as he looked towards the peeresses and foreign ambassadors, he showed like some gorgeous bird of the east.[45]

As he proceeded up the aisle the King passed an unconscious peeress heading in the opposite direction. The unfortunate woman had fainted and was being carried out by her companions. That July day was one of the hottest for many years and the unfortunate peers and peeresses were so crowded together that few managed to avoid the hot wax that dripped down from the hundreds of candles, ruining their splendid robes. The biographer Robert Huish thought the congregation appeared more like the 'wretched tenants of a slave ship' than the aristocracy of England.[46] Yet they had far greater hardships to endure for the ceremony would proceed relentlessly for another five hours. To everyone's surprise George appeared never to falter at any time that day, even when listening to the Archbishop of York's interminable sermon. The subject for this homily, 'human depravity', was particularly ill-chosen given the reputation of the main participant. Yet the Archbishop droned on remorselessly, exhorting his monarch to bring a new era of morality and the Christian faith throughout his realm and to preserve his people from the 'contagion of vice'. Understandably, the King was seen to fortify himself with a large sniff of the stimulant sal volatile at this point.

When the ceremony finally ended at five in the afternoon the exhausted King withdrew to an anteroom for a few minutes where he flopped on to a chair and mopped his brow. Seizing the opportunity of his absence those who could rushed like lemmings out of the Abbey so that when the King returned he was faced with rows of empty benches and a floor covered with dirt and litter. Eventually the whole congregation was shepherded back into some sort of order and the procession set off back down the walkway on the return journey to Westminster Hall. By now the King's fatigue was evident to all and George looked perilously unsteady on his feet.

Even Lady Cowper felt an unaccustomed sympathy for the unfortunate man who looked 'more like the victim than the hero of the fete. I really pitied him from my heart', she wrote.[47] Many of the 300 guests were in little better condition themselves, not having eaten since six that morning, and were desperate to lay into the coronation banquet. But first, as was the custom, the King had to eat his own banquet.

His first course duly arrived, led in with great pomp if little logic by mounted horsemen. Among them was the Deputy Earl Marshal, Lord Howard, who shocked the lady guests with foul oaths as he struggled to control his spirited horse. As the famished audience watched enviously a trio of elderly peers laboriously served the second and then the third courses. One of them, Lord Anglesea, the one-legged hero of Waterloo, had put on the wrong artificial leg that morning. This, he informed the King, was his riding not his walking leg. But with characteristic fortitude Anglesea dismounted and, supported by pages, managed to clumsily lift the great metal covers from the royal dishes. Remounting, he then backed away from the royal table 'as if from the presence of an eastern potentate' the whole length of the Hall.[48] His colleague, the Earl of Denbigh, who had single-handedly served his sovereign with turtle soup, quail and capon found that he now needed the help of Lord Chichester to carve a royal portion from a giant pineapple weighing over eleven pounds. But the King's attention was not taken solely by the food. Mrs Arbuthnot, who had earlier spotted him kissing his diamond to Lady Conyngham in the Abbey, reported to the Duke of Wellington that he continued to nod and wink at the same lady throughout the banquet.[49] All this would have been clearly visible to Henry Conyngham who, at his wife's insistence, had been given a seat close to the King.

Still none of the famished guests had eaten a morsel themselves and they had now to wait yet again for the King's Champion. On horseback and dressed in full medieval armour, he appeared to have sprung from the pages of a Sir Walter Scott novel. His hereditary duty was to challenge anyone who doubted the King's lawful right to wear the Crown to combat, but as the current champion was an elderly and frail Lincolnshire clergyman, the Reverend John Dymoke, his son had gamely deputised for him. As a form of insurance he had sensibly hired a white performing horse from Astley's Circus, an animal that was used to large crowds, deafening noise and confined spaces. With the challenge completed and the Champion gone the royal dinner was finally judged to be completed and it was the turn of the guests, many now almost delirious with hunger. Like starving beggars they launched themselves into 160 tureens of soup, 160 dishes of fish, 160 hot joints and 160 dishes of steaming vegetables. This was followed by 80 dishes of braised ham, 80 dishes of capons, 80 pieces of braised beef accompanied by 1,190 side dishes, 160 dishes of shellfish, 160 dishes of cold roast fowl and 320 dishes of pastry. In response to the pathetic cries from the starving peeresses and their children who were trapped in the upper galleries, the diners passed up as much food as they could spare. One nobleman was seen to tie up a roast chicken in his handkerchief and hurl it up to his son.[50] By now the King, his spirits much restored by the food and wine, had begun toasting his guests in the greatest good humour. At the end of the day Sir Walter Scott thought the expense fully justified by the success of the occasion and he recalled the day in a description worthy of one of his own historical novels:

> The aisles crowded with waving plumage, and coronets, and caps of honour, and the sun, which brightened and saddened as if on purpose, and now darting a solitary ray, which catched, as it passed, the glittering folds of a banner, or the edge of a group of battle-axes or partizans, and then rested on some fair form, 'the cynosure of neighbouring eyes', whose circlet of diamonds glistened under its influence.[51]

Yet Benjamin Haydon, who had been so enthusiastic at the start of the day, was finally disillusioned on noting that many of the doorkeepers had been drunk and offensive as they manhandled the guests, and that the Duke of Wellington had totally failed to conceal his contempt for his old rival Lord Anglesea. But not even Haydon could fail to join the chorus of approval for the star of the day: the beautiful Miss Fellows, who had performed her role as the King's herb-woman admirably. She and her herb girls in their Renaissance dresses of ivory gauze had delighted everyone. Years afterwards,

Haydon could still nostalgically recall every detail about them: 'the grace of their action, their slow movement, their white dresses'. He remembered the scene as 'indescribably touching; their light milky colour contrasted with the dark shadow of the archway, which, though dark, was full of rich crimson dresses that gave the shadow a tone as of deep blood'.[52]

Exhausted but exhilarated by the success of the day King George IV finally hauled himself up into his carriage and set off back to Carlton House. But they had only travelled a mile when the coachman discovered the way ahead blocked by two overturned carriages, forcing the royal party to make a detour. This diversion took the cavalcade through some of the darkest slums of Westminster, the scene of the worst rioting during the Queen's trial. Fearful of another encounter with the mob George yelled out of the window for the military escort to ride closer to the royal carriage. At one point, completely lost, they passed over a disused and decrepit wooden bridge spanning a dank canal. The following day it was found to have been condemned long before and never used. Those who inspected it agreed that it was a divine miracle that it had not collapsed under the weight of the royal party.[53]

For the ordinary people of London the day ended with a parade through Hyde Park led by two elephants pulling a golden carriage followed by an adventurous balloon ascent fuelled, for the first time in England, by coal gas instead of hydrogen. The aviator, a Mr Green, enjoyed a perfect flight and reached the open country to land at dusk in a field at South Mimms in Hertfordshire – so missing the magnificent fireworks that completed the day. Through this display of lavish entertainment and his own consistent good humour the King appeared to have been restored to the affections of his people. It was hard to believe that only a year had passed since he had been so reviled and hated and the Queen cheered in the streets of London.

But for Queen Caroline the coronation was the scene of her final public humiliation. Determined to be present at any cost she had set off at 5.30 a.m. in an open carriage with her friends Lord and Lady Hood. With her usual fecklessness she had not bothered to apply for a ticket from any of her political supporters and, arriving late, she was refused entry at one door after another. As William Cobbett, who witnessed the scene, wrote indignantly, 'when she got to the door and made an attempt to enter, she was actually thrusted back by the hands of a common prize-fighter'.[54] Worse was to come, for when the mob outside the Abbey recognised her they crowded round and began shouting 'shame'. But the Queen gave as good as she got, cursing them fluently in foul English as they began chanting, 'Go! Go! Go to Como!'[55] It was her last and most humiliating experience of the fickle London mob. Three weeks later she was dead and the crowd changed its mind yet again, deciding they loved her after all. As her funeral cortège passed through London on its way to Harwich en route to Brandenburg the mob forced it to divert through the city centre. But by then the King and Elizabeth Conyngham were on their way to Ireland. The last popular ballad written about the unfortunate Queen ended appropriately with the following verse:

'Ere the daughter of Brunswick is cold in her grave,
And her ashes still float to her home o'er the tide,
Lo! George the triumphant speeds over the wave,
To the long-cherished isle – which he loved like his bride.

# FIVE

## *A Trip to Ireland*

With the trauma of the royal divorce and the stress of the coronation behind him, the King was in unusually good spirits when he set off on 31 July 1821 to commence his state visit to Ireland. When Elizabeth's friend Countess Granville had first heard of the proposed trip in February that year she told another member of the court, Lady Morpeth, in confidence that the whole idea had originated with Lady Conyngham. It was, claimed Lady Granville, Elizabeth's big opportunity to demonstrate to society her power over the King, for a royal visit to Slane Castle meant recognition for the whole Conyngham family. The King, she thought, would be delighted to escape with his beloved as 'he is more in love with your friend [Lady Conyngham] than ever and . . . sits kissing her hand with the look of the most devoted submission'.[1] George had indeed talked of little else that year and had told everyone how eager he was to see Dublin and to visit the home of the Conynghams. To head off the gossip that would inevitably occur if they travelled together it was decided that Elizabeth should go on alone and cross from Holyhead in one of the royal yachts. Although George appeared to have made his peace with the British public, the unrest at the time of the royal divorce hearing had left its scars. Having experienced the fury of the London mob he approached the trip to Ireland with some trepidation, not knowing how the notoriously unruly Irish would receive him. It was little more than twenty years since the bloody Rising of 1798 and the Irish were famous for long memories.

To avoid the discomfort of the long coach journey to Holyhead in North Wales the King, accompanied by members of his household, the Marquess of Buckingham and the Tory politician W.H. Freemantle, took the sea route. They boarded the yacht the *Royal*

76

*George* at Portsmouth, and cruised slowly around the English coast to arrive at Holyhead on 9 August. But the King was no sooner ashore than a messenger arrived carrying a despatch from London warning that Queen Caroline was dangerously ill. In consultation with the ministers accompanying him he decided to wait a day before proceeding to Ireland. The obvious venue for an overnight stay was nearby Plas Newydd, the home of George's friend the Marquess of Anglesea. He had barely sat down to dinner with Lord Anglesea that evening when a second messenger galloped up with news that the Queen's condition had worsened.[2] After further discussion the King decided to remain at Plas Newydd rather than risk alienating public opinion by continuing immediately with what could be seen as pleasure trip to Ireland. He did, however, send word on to Dublin that because of the Queen's illness his welcome there must be quiet and dignified. The next morning as the *Royal George* waited at Holyhead for a favourable wind another messenger arrived – this time with the information that Queen Caroline was dead.[3]

It was barely three weeks since Caroline had been refused entry to the coronation at Westminster Abbey and the humiliation of that day appears to have destroyed both her spirit and her health. This 'Bedlam Bitch of a Queen', as Sir Walter Scott called her, had suddenly developed a serious stomach condition that made her appear haggard and depressed. Ignoring doctors' advice she dosed herself heavily with laudanum and went off to the Drury Lane theatre to watch a dramatic re-enactment of the coronation with the famous actor Robert Ellison playing the part of the King. A few days later she returned, under some strange compulsion, to Drury Lane but during the performance became seriously affected by diarrhoea. As the curtain came down she dragged herself to her feet and curtsied to the audience with such a haggard face that even Lady Anne Barnard, who claimed to detest her, 'burst into tears to see royalty and pride so broken down and humbled'.[4] Caroline was taken home suffering stomach pains of such intensity that even doses of opium and castor oil, large enough to 'turn the stomach of a horse', as Henry Brougham said, had little effect on her suffering. After nine days of torment she died in agony on 8 August at Brandenburg House, having whispered to her friend, the faithful

Lord Hood, 'je ne mourrai sans doleur mais je mourrai sans regret'.[5] An autopsy revealed that she had died of an obstruction of the bowel, probably the result of cancer. Her will left everything to her adopted son Billy Austin who she insisted had been fathered by Prince Louis Ferdinand of Prussia, rather than being the natural son of a London docker as she had earlier claimed. But the unfortunate Billy was to get nothing as the profligate Caroline's debts far exceeded her assets. As a last gesture of defiance she asked that a silver plate bearing the words 'Caroline of Brunswick: the injured Queen of England' be attached to her coffin. The plate was duly produced from under the coat of her dogged supporter Alderman Wood when the cortège rested at Chelmsford. Wood stepped forward and screwed it to the coffin only for the King's representative, Sir George Taylor, who had been ordered to keep an eye open for anything contentious, to order its removal before the funeral party could be allowed to proceed to Harwich.[6]

For George, the Queen's death was a release from the anger and embarrassment that she had long caused him and to have shown sorrow at the news would have been a gross act of hypocrisy. He did, however, manage to disguise his obvious relief and behaved at first, or so his companions claimed, with commendable dignity and compassion – ordering the flags of the royal squadron to be lowered to half-mast as an act of mourning. 'He reacted', said Lord Castlereagh, 'as we could have wished.'[7] Yet it is not difficult to imagine his true feelings now that the threat of Caroline's unpredictable behaviour was removed from him. Although he could not, while the Marquess was alive, marry Elizabeth Conyngham, they could look forward to a period of tranquillity together. But in London his ministers had a different agenda and Lord Liverpool began immediately to discuss with his cabinet a proposal to marry the King off to a suitable European royal. W.H. Freemantle was convinced that the government already had a likely European candidate in mind and he told his friend the Marquess of Buckingham that they were preparing 'to cook up a match for the King with a Princess of Tour and Taxis' (*sic*) at the behest of the Austrian Minister, Count Metternich. What, he wondered, would Lady Conyngham do about that, particularly as he had heard rumours that she had her own daughter in mind for the new vacancy of royal bride![8]

# A Trip to Ireland

After ordering a period of court mourning of six days the King decided to press on at all speed to Ireland. Rather than make the crossing under sail in the *Royal George* he embarked on the new steam packet *The Lightning* instead. It set off at full speed on the morning of 12 August, the King's fifty-ninth birthday, and even without the company of his beloved mistress his friends noticed that he was 'uncommonly well during his passage and gayer than it might be proper to tell'. Throughout the six and a half hour crossing the King never once appeared on deck, remaining below with his companions. Hardly had the ship left port when, led by the King, the entire royal party began downing liberal measures of brandy and water followed by large quantities of wine and whisky punch. The drink and sea air must have sharpened George's appetite for, according to the Duke of Buckingham, the whole party were encouraged to join him in eating goose pie and drinking whisky, 'of which his Majesty partook most abundantly, singing many joyous songs, and being in a state, on his arrival, to double in sight even the numbers of his gracious subjects assembled on the pier to receive him'.[9]

When *The Lightning* docked at Howth Harbour a few miles from Dublin late on the afternoon of 12 August 1821 the King was obviously the worse for drink. As a gesture of mourning he had ordered a black crepe band to be sewn on the left sleeve of his plain blue coat while on his head he had placed, at a jaunty angle, a yachting cap with a gold band and stood waiting to disembark, his face bronzed by the sunshine. As the crowd spotted his portly figure waving from the deck it roared with enthusiasm. The King stepped ashore to be shown a symbolic outline of his first footsteps on Irish soil that had been carved on the quayside in anticipation of his visit. As the King passed under a rickety triumphal arch described by Creevey as being only fit for Jack-in-the Green on a May Day, a burly local fisherman, Pat Farrell, came forward to shake his hand vigorously. The King, mellowed by drink, was delighted by his warm reception and catching sight of his friend the Earl of Kingston in the crowd called out 'Kingston, you black whiskered good natured fellow! I am happy to see you in this friendly country!'[10] Then spotting another old friend from London, Denis Bowers Daly, George stepped unsteadily forward and pumped his hand too. Unfortunately, at that very moment a quick-fingered thief took the opportunity of relieving Daly of both a sixty-guinea watch and his wallet. Jostling through the crowd the King noticed a large rural-looking man waving at him. 'Are you a farmer?' he enquired unnecessarily. 'Troth I am, your Majesty's honour,' the man replied, whipping off his hat and bowing deeply. Eager to demonstrate his knowledge of rural affairs the King asked him if he had a cow. 'Troth sir, I haven't,' the rustic replied. 'Then,' declared the King, 'you shall have one. I think every poor Irishman should have at least a cow, a pig and some fowl.' These words of wisdom were greeted with rapturous applause by the crowd. An aide must have made a note of this encounter for a few days later the farmer was quietly presented by the King's secretary, Sir Benjamin Bloomfield, with a milch cow and two pigs – 'with his Majesty's compliments'.[11]

There could hardly have been a more auspicious start to the royal visit and the King set off for Dublin already convinced that the Irish were the finest people in Europe. Elizabeth's old friend, the Countess of Glengall, who was in Dublin at the time, had lived there long enough there to be suspicious of all this boisterous enthusiasm. She claimed to be appalled and embarrassed by the crowd's wild behaviour as the royal cortège entered the city of Dublin. Thomas Creevey too was shocked to see not a single token of mourning for the late Queen, although his own sable dress provoked one Irishman later that day to enquire who exactly he was commemorating. Creevey's first sight of Dublin city was not auspicious either:

> Rags hung from every window which are called flags . . . no one in mourning. They clawed and pawed him all over, and called him his Ethereal Majesty . . . They absolutely kiss his knees and feet, and he is enchanted with it all. Alas! poor degraded country! I cannot but blush for you.[12]

But it was already clear, not least to the King, that the Irish looked upon him in a far more favourable light than did his English subjects. For their part, they considered his visit a favourable omen for the improvement of their own miserable lot. As Mr Gregory, a typical Irish country gentleman, recalled in his memoirs twenty years later, 'what hopes were raised by his Majesty's visit! The Catholic Bishops, the Catholic nobility and gentry came from the provinces to hear the message of peace and goodwill. The peasants of Galway and Mayo laid by their pikes and blunderbusses and listened for it.'[13] The government back in London were quick to capitalise on the unexpectedly warm reception for the monarch and the official published record of the royal visit eulogised his arrival in glowing terms: 'what a scene . . . the greatest Monarch in the world sails in a common steam packet, lands among his subjects, unaffected, unattended, unguarded'.[14] Astonishingly, given that the Rising had occurred little more than twenty years earlier, not a single soldier lined the route as the cavalcade passed along the North Circular Road – the Rotten Row of Dublin whose streets Lord Norbury observed 'were ill paved but well flagged'. As they approached Phoenix Park the cortège had grown to over 500 carriages accompanied by a reputed 3,000 gentlemen on horseback. Everyone in the King's party was cheered by the dense crowds lining the streets and even the Foreign Secretary, Lord Castlereagh, the most hated man in Ireland, was given a desultory cheer. Lady Glengall thought, however, that they must have mistaken Castlereagh for someone else. The Foreign Secretary's warm reception by the crowd also puzzled Thomas Creevey, who wrote:

> Think of their having applauded Castlereagh! It is exactly as if a murderer were brought to view the body of his victim, and that he was to be applauded for his crime; for Dublin is but the mangled corpse of what it was; and he – the man whom they huzza – the cut throat who brought it to its present condition.[15]

Entering the gates of Phoenix Park, where the King was to stay at the Viceregal Lodge, the procession stretched back through the city for over a mile. George had by now pinned a huge bunch of shamrock to his hat, which he repeatedly pointed to with one hand whilst placing the other sentimentally over his heart. The crowd loved the whole performance and, in a way that seemed peculiar to the English visitors, shouted enthusiastically rather than cheering or hooraying. Perhaps the Irish did not know how to cheer, observed John Wilson Croker caustically, 'for they have not had much practice in the expression of public joy'. The English visitors were further amused to see two drunks stopping a third from cavorting on the pavement. 'He is a scandal to our country,' they shouted in explanation, 'what would strangers think if they saw him!' News of the King's arrival had by now spread to the countryside around Dublin and two peasants on their way to market, hearing the commotion, abandoned their cart in a ditch and mounted the horses. They galloped excitedly to catch up with the cavalcade, even managing to trot alongside the royal carriage, much to the King's amusement. One brave Dublin urchin leapt on to the royal carriage step and crouched there throughout the journey, braving a constant whipping from the coachman to earn a hearty handshake from the King when they reached Phoenix Park.[16] At the Viceregal Lodge the King's servants leapt down and attempted to close the gates on the following crowd but the King waved them angrily aside and beckoned the cheering mob to follow him all the way up to the house. Stepping from his carriage on to the lawn he made a short but jolly speech concluding, 'I assure you my dear friends, I have an Irish heart and will this night give proof of my affection towards you in bumpers of whiskey punch!'[17] The near-delirious crowd urged him not to stint himself on the measures.

That evening the King, in clear violation of mourning dress for his late wife, appeared at dinner dressed in a bright blue coat with yellow buttons. Clearly in the best of form he ate heartily then began discussing the day's events with his companions. All admitted that they were astonished and overwhelmed by the unexpected friendliness of the Irish people. One of the party, Lord Sidmouth, later claimed that throughout the entire visit he had not heard an unpleasant word spoken nor seen a sullen look from anyone. What amazed them most, as Englishmen, was that it was 'the lowest classes' who seemed the most delighted with the King. After dinner as Lords Sidmouth and Londonderry strolled together in the park they were accosted by a Dublin whore, who told them excitedly that 'this night is the King to have all the fat women in Ireland'. In view of the King's current predilection for plump mistresses both Lords thought her comments highly appropriate.[18]

The next day even the Irish papers, usually highly critical of the English, were wildly enthusiastic about the royal visit and full of vehement declarations of loyalty to the King. Curiously George's popularity appeared non-sectarian, being shared by Orangeman and

Catholic alike. Many remembered that as Prince of Wales he had shown his sympathy for Ireland and that his Carlton House faction in Parliament had often voted in support of the twelve Irish members. More importantly, he had openly opposed the military coercion of the Irish people in 1797 when, as the country had stood on the brink of rebellion, he had written a prophetic warning to the then Prime Minister, William Pitt:

A strong military force may secure temporary advantages but no force can long coerce a nation of four million people united in sentiments and interests. I must once more most earnestly recommend conciliatory measures and I abjure you to pause on the awful brink of civil war and to avert its fateful consequences.[19]

Knowledge of this intervention may well have led one rebel survivor of the 1798 Rising to tell the King on the second day of his visit that although he had fought against his father George III he was now prepared to die for his son. It was a sentiment endorsed by Lord Cloncurry, an Irish peer who had been imprisoned in the Tower of London for supporting the United Irishmen. Cloncurry approached the King and suggested 'a waiver of all bygones', warmly inviting him to visit his house.[20] Yet whatever their appreciation of the King's political sympathies the Irish also warmed to his easy-going character and were understandably delighted to discover an Englishman who like themselves was no stranger to the temptations of strong drink and emotional excess.

When the doors of the Viceregal Lodge eventually closed that first afternoon the King was reunited with Elizabeth Conyngham, who had come down from Slane where she had been preparing the castle for his visit. For the next few days the lovers remained out of sight in the grounds of the Lodge while the rest of the royal party went through the motions of observing a period of mourning for the late Queen Caroline. Charles Arbuthnot, who was present, told his wife that although the King attended the official engagements he spent most of his time alone with Lady Conyngham and 'never asked a creature into the house, never spoke to any of his attendants and seemed completely engrossed by his love'.[21] Those days in Dublin and Slane were to be the most enjoyable in their long relationship –

almost a honeymoon. Freed of the restrictions of Court life in London the King could relax and simply walk and talk with Elizabeth. It would be the only genuine holiday that they would ever enjoy together as much-discussed plans to visit France and Italy would never come to fruition. Yet, as in much love as he undoubtedly was, George could still be entranced with, as the *Dublin Advertiser* reported, 'the fresh beauty of the Irish ladies with their graceful and symmetrical forms and their soft and silvery voices'. At the Installation Ball a few days later he was said to have been in excellent form as he was introduced to 1,000 young Irish ladies. They were all, he declared, as well dressed as any he had seen at St James's. When told that 100 more had arrived too late to meet him the King good-naturedly put his coat back on and returned from his dressing room to give them each a smacking kiss.[22] Perhaps it was this flirtatious gesture that prompted Elizabeth to refuse to sit next to him at dinner that evening. Her unexpected froideur infuriated the King and he stormed off in righteous anger only to be followed a few minutes later by an alarmed Elizabeth, who persuaded him to return to the drawing room. The next morning the lovers were seen to have made up their quarrel and to be on the best of terms again.

It had been agreed that Elizabeth should set off alone on 18 August and travel the twenty-odd miles to Slane to be ready to formally greet her royal guest. George attended a splendid review in Phoenix Park that day and two days later received the leading Irish clergy of both faiths. More dinners and receptions followed but by now he had been separated from Elizabeth for six days and could bear the deprivation no longer. On the very day that his late wife was to be buried in her family tomb in Brunswick, he brusquely cut short a public breakfast in his honour at the Royal Dublin Society and set off for Slane. His obvious impatience and desire to be gone annoyed the rest of the royal party, who thought that he should have given the assembled guests more than just a few minutes of his time. Yet the lure of Elizabeth was too potent and with barely a goodbye to the assembled crowd he climbed aboard his carriage and, accompanied by a small troop of cavalry, set off at full speed for Slane. His journey that day later gave rise to a romantic but erroneous belief in County Meath that the long, straight road from Dublin to Slane had been specifically constructed at royal command to speed him to his beloved mistress. Travelling at the brisk rate of ten Irish miles an hour the cavalcade was soon clear of the city and cantering out into the countryside. Bystanders cheered them all the way to Finglas, where they halted and the King, realising that there was no danger, sent half his mounted escort back to Dublin.[23] Maintaining full speed they changed horses at the village of Ashbourne, halfway to Slane, and then just an hour after leaving Dublin, the royal carriage rushed through the lodge gates at Slane and arrived at the main door of the castle.

News of the King's impending arrival must have gone ahead of him for Elizabeth was waiting on the Castle steps 'dressed out as for a drawing room'. George climbed down eagerly from the carriage and took his hostess, to the astonishment of the servants, in a prolonged and passionate embrace. Then after a brief but cheery greeting to the Marquess and the rest of the Conyngham family, who had already arrived from England, they hurried off together for a more intimate reunion in Elizabeth's private drawing room. There they remained alone for the rest of the afternoon until reappearing for dinner. George was relaxed and in the very best of spirits as he joined the rest of the Conyngham family for dinner beneath chandeliers blazing with candlelight. Lord Conyngham had ordered the outside of the castle to be illuminated that night and the whole village of Slane had joined in the celebrations by putting lighted candles in their windows. For miles around bonfires blazed on hilltops along the Boyne Valley to welcome the King.[24] When it was time for bed Henry Conyngham went to his room on the first floor while above him on the second the King and Elizabeth retired to rooms conveniently situated next to each other. It was a memorable start to what George would later describe as the happiest days of his life.

Always an admirer of innovative architecture, George was able the next morning to explore the castle and its ground in detail. He was, according to Mr Gregory, a neighbour of the Conynghams and a frequent guest during the King's visit, entranced by the whole romantic aspect of Slane Castle. Standing high on the north bank of the River Boyne it overlooks a sweep in the river bordered by fine woods. The castle itself had been rebuilt in the gothic revival style a decade before Elizabeth had married Henry Conyngham. The design was by the architects James Wyatt and Francis Johnston, and clearly pleased the King. 'The house he is justly delighted with,' wrote Mr

Gregory, 'especially one round room, and he praised the good taste of a drawing room in the Country having no window curtains but white muslin'.[25] One of the King's aides, the Duke of Montrose, who had been sent ahead to check that everything was fully prepared for the royal visitor, had also been enchanted by Slane Castle and by the ballroom's beautiful fan-vaulted ceiling in particular. He described it, oddly given its location, as 'the finest place I ever saw in England or Scotland'.[26] A less appreciative account had been given a decade earlier by an English traveller, George Hardinge, who described it as 'neither old enough to be picturesque nor quite new enough to look elegant'.[27] But all were agreed on one thing; its splendid setting on the River Boyne was incomparable.

That second day Elizabeth was determined that the King should meet some real Irish people, in this case the local County Meath gentry. At mid-morning they all set off in carriages and drove the short distance to Townley Hall, the home of a celebrated local character, Blaney Balfour esquire. After some merry banter with the jovial Balfour the King and Elizabeth got back in their carriage and 'without a guard of any kind' set off along the riverbank.[28] At Oldbridge they paused for Elizabeth to point out the obelisk that marked the site of the Battle of the Boyne then continued on, taking in the small grey villages and low rugged hills until they arrived at the mouth of the Boyne and enjoyed a fine view of the Irish sea. That night, back at Slane, the King enjoyed another good dinner and was seen to be still in the very best of form. As the next day was Sunday the King decided that he would accompany the Conynghams to morning service at Slane Church. But so many of the local peasantry had gathered in the village to see their sovereign pass that the cheering crowd had to be held back by his small escort of soldiers. Alarmed by what he considered over-zealous pushing and shoving by the military, the King angrily intervened and ordered them to stand back. 'Don't mind them,' he called out, 'the people mean no harm.' As the party returned to the castle a young woman from the village pushed her small daughter forward and urged her to kneel and kiss the King's hand. But with characteristic bonhomie George gently refused the gesture. 'No,' he said, 'but I will kiss her.' He then stooped down and to the delight of both the crowd and his hostess kissed the child's cheek.[29]

At yet another enjoyable dinner in the candlelit ballroom that evening the King remained in splendid form and was clearly delighted to be a guest of his old friends the Conynghams. Mr Gregory noticed that George sat close to Elizabeth and was constantly kissing her hand. 'The King', he wrote, 'never drank wine without touching her glass with his, holding her hand under the table all the time he was drinking.' Such was his enthusiasm for Ireland, George told the assembled company, that he had devised a novel plan to enjoy it more. Turning to the Irish Attorney General he asked him, quite seriously, if it would be possible to send the current Lord Lieutenant of Ireland, Lord Talbot, back to London and for him, the King, to take over the job himself![30] Everyone roared with laughter at this except Princess Esterhazy, who had accompanied her husband the Austrian ambassador on the trip. She was more concerned with watching the more cautious reaction of the Irish gentry towards the King. She later told Prince Metternich that the Irish ladies seemed more reserved towards Lady Conyngham and appeared shocked that Lord Conyngham seemed totally unperturbed by his wife's behaviour as he wandered about repeating delightedly 'the King is father to us all'.[31]

The next day Elizabeth took her royal guest to meet another member of the local gentry. This time the honour fell, appropriately, to a Mr Smith, who enjoyed local fame by having fathered fourteen living children. When told, a few weeks earlier, that he would be entertaining the King of England to lunch Mr Smith panicked and decided that his residence Annesbrook in the nearby village of Duleek looked far too modest for such a distinguished guest. Smith took immediate steps to improve it in record time and the result was an architectural folly worthy of the creator of the Royal Pavilion himself. An enormous portico stretching from ground to roof was quickly built on to the front of the existing house, together with a large gothic banqueting hall. Sadly the latter was never to be seen for when the royal party arrived the King confessed that he was suffering from an annoying bout of diarrhoea. As it was one of the hottest days of the year George decided to picnic under a shady tree on the lawn outside. Although clearly disappointed, Mr Smith declared himself entirely delighted with the royal visit. Sadly, having been completely ruined by his costly home improvements, he was forced to declare himself bankrupt within the year.[32] According to the Countess of Glengall there were many Mr Smiths in Ireland at that time, too ready to spend beyond their means in putting on a grand display for the King, and she lamented that 'far from doing good to this wretched country, his visit is making people spend money which they don't possess'.[33]

The ubiquitous Mr Gregory was again a guest at dinner on the final evening at Slane when the Conynghams entertained not only their Irish friends but also the Russian and Austrian ambassadors from London and their wives. What most delighted Gregory, a man more used to the provincial ways of Dublin, was the King's relaxed affability to all his fellow guests and above all the impeccable manners that Gregory thought fully justified George's reputation as the First Gentleman of Europe:

> In two minutes after the king came into the room, he thawed the ice and put everyone at ease . . . a wonderful memory, the opportunities he has had of hearing, witnessing and collecting all the good anecdotes of every kind, and a talent for mimicry quite surprising. He talks a vast deal, but I think not from natural garrulity, but because his rank makes it necessary for him to originate every subject, and perform a kind of solo to which what others say is little more than an accompaniment. He listens with great good breeding, however, assents in an encouraging manner when he agrees with you, and his contradictions, tho' politely given, are frank and peremptory.[34]

Mr Gregory was delighted to see that, as a compliment to his hosts, the King tried every dish on the table and predictably sampled every drink 'very heartily, but nothing like excess'. Gregory also noted how he graciously complimented Lord Conyngham on the high standard of the cooking at Slane that so contrasted with the poor fare served up by his brother, the Duke of Gloucester, who, he claimed, had a talent for giving bad dinners. With everyone laughing and joking the King became concerned lest the European diplomats present might feel excluded from the merriment. Gregory again noted approvingly that 'after he had amused us, his subjects, with English and Irish stories he turned to the Foreigners, and for a time giving them French ones, which he does admirably, and with the accent of a Parisian, and perfect power over the language'. Less impressed was Lord Burghersh, who later complained to Mrs Arbuthnot that the King had virtually ignored him the whole evening and seemed again more concerned with clinking glasses with Lady Conyngham. As the meal progressed George moved on from wine to the powerful local brew, hot Potteen Punch, which he found much to his taste. By the end of the evening it had given him such a thirst that he had returned to downing bottles of claret. The atmosphere was so convivial that the entire company remained in the drawing room until half past one in the morning. When a supper tray was brought in at midnight everyone was still so replete from the lavish dinner that it was removed again untouched. Even the quiet living Mr Gregory had by now succumbed to the heady atmosphere of the evening, if not the abundant alcohol. The next day he had to apologise to his female friends for not remembering exactly what Lady Conyngham, her daughters and the European ambassadors' wives had worn the previous evening.[35]

After the relaxed atmosphere of Slane Castle George found it difficult to drag himself away to Dublin. But on 27 August he returned reluctantly to the city without Elizabeth to perform official duties for the next few days. One such duty was a dinner at Trinity College, where the wines were again reported to be good and the music excellent. The King remained in excellent spirits and when one of his party, the elderly Lord Norbury, slipped and fell George leapt nimbly forward and dragged him to his feet. At this Norbury, known as an incorrigible jester, thanked him and said, referring to his peerage, and to general amusement 'this is not the first lift your Majesty has given me'.[36] As he left the college that night the King was cheered loyally by the students but for the first time since they arrived in Ireland some members of the royal party, notably Lord Castlereagh, were booed by the crowd. At a public dinner the next day a local alderman provoked what could have been an even more embarrassing scene by proposing in the King's presence the well-known Orange toast 'to the glorious memory of King William'. Royal embarrassment was averted by the quick-thinking Lord Fingal, who leapt to his feet to intervene with an alternative pledge, so saving George from being seen to publicly endorse a naked sectarian ploy. As Croker wrote perceptively, 'if the toast had been put every man, Protestant and Catholic, would have believed that the Alderman acted under the influence of Dublin Castle'.[37] Significantly, the King's own attitude to the Irish problem was revealed when at that same dinner he urged his audience to work for 'peace, no ascendancy . . . kindliness, conciliation'.

The next day, 3 September 1821, as the King prepared to leave Ireland he was informed that the Irish people had been so moved by his visit that there was a move in Dublin to build him a palace there. When Thomas Creevey was told of the scheme he thought it a melancholy farce and commented cynically, 'palaces in the air and drunkards under the table are the order of the day. Ireland I am ashamed of you.'[38] Unaware of the slightest criticism George kissed Elizabeth goodbye at the Viceregal Lodge then set off for Dun Laoghaire harbour, which had just been renamed Kingstown in his honour. As he stood on the quayside he graciously accepted farewell gifts from the people of Dublin. One, a marble chimney-piece hewn from the quarries of Connemara, still adorns the Carlton Club in London but the most significant present was a crown of laurel leaves from Daniel O'Connell, the undisputed leader of Catholic, Nationalist Ireland, which the Liberator presented to the English king on his knees. It was a symbolic gesture of peaceful reconciliation that would unfortunately come to nothing. Moved by this tribute the King replied:

> I never felt sensations of more delight than since I came to Ireland – I cannot expect to feel any superior nor many equal till I have the happiness of seeing you again. Whenever an opportunity offers wherein I can serve Ireland, I shall seize on it with eagerness. I am a man of few words. Short adieux are best. God bless you, my friends. God bless you all.[39]

As the ship sailed away George could take satisfaction from the fact that he had enjoyed in Ireland a popularity that had always been denied him in England. To the Irish he had proved that he was a man of charm whose graciousness, kind heart and good manners had appealed to their own instinctive good nature. But he was still a novelty and they had not seen enough of him to become disillusioned, as his English subjects had, by his increasing bad temper and reclusiveness.

All thoughts of Ireland disappeared when the ship ran into a violent storm and, in the King's own words, 'many of our crew and company were deadly sick but the very worst was my poor self . . . the oldest and most experienced sailors were petrified and para-lysed'.[40] Some of the royal party became so terrified at the towering seas that they ran up on deck and clung to the rails in the throes of uncontrollable seasickness. In complete contrast to the general panic George was reported to have shown great coolness and courage. His escape from a watery grave was, he later claimed, due entirely to the mercy of the Almighty and the love of Lady Conyngham. Yet the voyage had taken its toll and the King was completely exhausted when the royal party landed at Holyhead. He had intended to spend the night at the home of Sir Watkin Williams Wynn near Oswestry on the way back, but the baronet had left a note for him at Holyhead asking him not to call as his wife did not know the ladies of the King's party. This was a clear but guarded slight to Elizabeth who Williams Wynn wrongly suspected might be travelling with the King. By now the strong wind had abated and the King decided to re-embark and sail on round the Welsh coast to the port of Milford Haven. Still weak from the stress of the stormy crossing he described himself to a companion as 'completely shattered and torn to pieces by the effects and sickness of an eight and forty hour tempest'.[41]

His spirits were restored, however, when he saw Elizabeth, who had gone on ahead in another of the royal yachts, waiting for him on the quayside at Milford Haven. She was, thought Thomas Creevey, never in a better humour nor more beautiful as she stood with the King discussing whether or not they should proceed to London by road. But the arduous 270-mile journey along the unpaved roads of West Wales and the lack of anywhere comfortable to stay before Gloucester held little appeal. To the relief of the whole party the King decided that they all should re-embark once again and sail round Land's End to Portsmouth as originally intended. It proved to be a near-disastrous mistake for when they put to sea the light breeze soon strengthened into yet another gale. As the ship ploughed on huge waves broke over her deck and at one point the tiller was lost and the ship lay on her beam-ends. If it had not been for the fortitude and experience of Captain Paget, the King said later, they would all have been lost as even the most experienced sailors were terrified. But reassured by the presence of Elizabeth, the King seemed to maintain his cool demeanour throughout the voyage though one of his companions claimed to have seen him discreetly invoking the help of the Almighty from time to time.

Eventually the wind died and the ship sailed safely on to Portsmouth, where the royal carriage was waiting. Some way out of the town the King recognised a carriage on the road ahead as that of Lord and Lady Harcourt. When they overtook he insisted on stopping and joining the Harcourts for a leisurely chat. George gave them a dramatic account of his adventures in Ireland and of his deliverance from a watery grave. Again he attributed the salvation of the entire party to the almost divine presence of Lady Conyngham.[42] Then with a cheery wave he rejoined his own carriage and they set off again for London arriving back at Carlton House on 6 September, a fortnight after leaving Holyhead.

Most English politicians agreed that the King's visit to Ireland had been a great personal success. The Tory John Wilson Croker thought it had not only 'assuaged the violence but also removed the rancour of party in Ireland'! At the other end of the political spectrum the Irish poet Tom Moore spoke for many of his fellow countrymen when he declared that from now he was a confirmed monarchist. Many of the ordinary Irish shared Moore's unexpected admiration for the King and one Dublin politician even suggested that King George IV of England should be re-christened 'King Paddy the First of Ireland'. The radical press in England, however, took a far more jaundiced view of the triumphal progress, believing that the warm and friendly welcome George had received was totally undeserved. As Lord Dudley commented sourly, 'the King seems to have behaved not like a sovereign coming in state and pomp to visit a part of his dominions but like a popular candidate come down upon an electioneering trip'.[43] But the euphoria of George's visit was short-lived and by Christmas it was the violent business of sedition and revolt as usual in Ireland. The *Dublin Annual Register* spoke for many ordinary Irish people when it said 'the events of October, November, and December destroyed all the splendid anticipations to which His Majesty's visit had given rise . . . the gaudy and hollow bubble of conciliation soon burst, and a system of outrage, robbery, murder, and assassination commenced'.

# SIX

## *Trading Places*

Reinvigorated by the success of his Irish visit and with the memory of the Slane idyll still fresh in his mind the King found it difficult to resume his official duties in London. Although his ministers bombarded him with requests for meetings to deal with urgent state business he brushed them aside and after three disconsolate days at Carlton House made good his escape to Brighton. There Elizabeth was waiting and the lovers resumed their intimacy, with George continuing to ignore the official despatches from London. His stubborn refusal to attend to state business infuriated the Prime Minister, Lord Liverpool, who considered that much of the blame for the King's increasing fecklessness could be laid at the door of Lady Conyngham. The monarch was being seduced, in every sense, he told the Duke of Wellington, from his responsibilities by a woman who was known to be a secret Whig sympathiser.[1] The Duke shared his Prime Minister's almost paranoid belief in Elizabeth's duplicity and confessed that he too was convinced that she was deliberately poisoning the King's mind against all his ministers. At a dinner party a week after their return from Ireland Lord Liverpool repeated to Princess Lieven his grave suspicion that Lady Conyngham was a closet Whig and was actually passing the King's private opinions concerning important political matters on to her brother, the Whig MP William Denison. Furthermore, claimed Liverpool, over the past year the Opposition leader Lord Grey had been seen attending the same dinner parties as Lady Conyngham, where he had often appeared to be whispering to her in private. The Princess sensibly pointed out to him, however, that as she had everything to lose by a change of government it was unlikely that Elizabeth would flirt with the opposition. Furthermore, the Princess added, would the Whigs, who were constantly preaching high moral standards in public life, want to risk their reputation by coming to power as the result of their intrigues with a royal mistress? The true reason for Lady Conyngham's hostility to the Tories, the Princess suggested, was not political but personal. When Lady Conyngham had first appeared at Court the wives of Lord Liverpool's own Tory ministers had deliberately and quite rudely snubbed her. Now she was simply repaying that score by encouraging the King to make life difficult for their husbands. The most sensible course of action, she suggested, was to hand the problem over to the Duke of Wellington and let him deal with it.[2] Whatever the past disagreements between them the King maintained an unwavering respect for the great hero and even Lady Conyngham could never risk coming between them.

Had she known how strongly Wellington shared his Prime Minister's antipathy towards Elizabeth, the Princess would probably not have given such advice. Although he had been forced to make some concessions in his public attitude towards Elizabeth, Wellington continued to voice his hostility in private. As the victor of Waterloo the Duke felt that had earned his many honours by his own efforts and he resented the easy path to similar rewards now being offered to the Conynghams. What he found particularly distasteful was Elizabeth's middle-class origins, her fascination with what he considered the mundane, and her constant attempts to seek advancement for her family and friends. Once he complained to Harriet Arbuthnot that on a recent journey with Lady Conyngham downriver to Hampton Court 'she did nothing but talk of who had the appointments and what they made by them and how much their coals and candles were worth. There never was such an avaricious, vulgar woman.'[3]

Tory resentment of Lady Conyngham had already manifested itself the previous year in what at first appeared to be a petty dispute over royal appointments but soon developed into a serious conflict that threatened to bring down the government. It concerned the traditional right of the party in power to make appointments in the royal household. These had traditionally been arranged by mutual agreement but in April 1821 when the Canonry of Windsor became vacant the King, to please Lady Conyngham, filled the position without consulting a single minister. His choice for the post was the

Reverend Charles Sumner, the curate of a small country parish at Highclere in Hampshire, whose sole claim to distinction was that he had once been tutor to all three of Lady Conyngham's sons. Sumner had been promoted over the heads of several long-standing and better-qualified candidates. When the government was informed of the proposal it was outraged. A dangerous precedent would be set if the monarch rather than his government was allowed to make such appointments and Lord Liverpool warned the King that 'serious inconveniences' would result if Sumner's appointment went ahead.[4] The King's friends were equally hostile and none more so than Princess Lieven, who warned Prince Metternich that the British government would not accept this blatant challenge to its power. The Princess shared Tory suspicions that Lady Conyngham was indeed the instigator of the dispute and was using it as a trial of strength with the government.[5] Although she had maintained a cordial, if guarded, friendship with Elizabeth – essential if she were to retain access to the King – the Princess held her in no more esteem than did the Duke of Wellington and once described her in these most unflattering terms:

> Not an idea in her head, not a word to say for herself; nothing but a hand to accept pearls and diamonds with, and an enormous balcony to wear them on . . . she is a fool and just the kind of malicious fool who might do a great deal of harm. All sensible people regret Lady Hertford . . . Can one imagine anything more absurd than an amorous and inconstant Sexagenarian who at the beginning of his reign, gives up all his time to a love affair? It is pitiable.[6]

Outside the political world of Westminster there was little public concern over what appeared to be a petty dispute about a clerical appointment – not even a bishopric. Nor did news of the conflict between the King and his ministers reach the ears of the cartoonists, always eager to capitalise on any royal discomfiture. Realising that a swift resolution of the problem was essential, Lord Liverpool urged the King to reconsider his actions, at the same time reassuring the cabinet that he was determined to oppose the Sumner appointment whatever the cost. His colleague Lord Sidmouth left the meeting feeling that it was the worst political crisis he had experienced since joining the government a year earlier. Another minister, the Foreign Secretary Lord Castlereagh, was so concerned that he took it upon himself to write to the royal secretary, Sir Benjamin Bloomfield, urging him to persuade the King that Sumner's appointment would be 'prejudicial' to the fundamental relationship between Crown and State.[7]

Why Elizabeth had chosen to risk controversy by championing the career of a man so little known in the church is hard to fathom. But in spite of her self-serving reputation she had always shown her gratitude to those who served her well and it was through her introduction that Charles Sumner met the King, who found him both intelligent and personable. George fully endorsed Elizabeth's firm conviction that Charles Sumner would make an excellent Canon of Windsor. As the storm between the King and his ministers intensified Elizabeth urged him to stand firmly by his decision and not to give in to their threats. She reassured George that it was his sole prerogative to choose candidates for positions in the royal household and at her insistence a terse note was sent to Lord Liverpool reiterating that 'the nomination of the Rev. Mr Sumner to the vacant Canonry of Windsor would be very acceptable to the King's wishes as Mr Sumner's strict piety, exemplary conduct and great learning peculiarly recommend him for this mark of royal favour'.[8]

It was obvious that neither side was prepared to give way and as the crisis deepened it was left to the king's secretary Sir Benjamin Bloomfield to attempt some form of mediation. Five times in three days he rode fruitlessly back and forth to London in the hope of brokering a compromise. But his efforts appeared to have failed, for a few days later Lord Liverpool assembled his cabinet and told them that as the King remained intransigent he was now prepared to offer his resignation. The Duke of Wellington nodded his assent, convinced that the Prime Minister had no alternative. 'It was', said the Duke, 'an extraordinary state of affairs – the constant hostility between master and servant.'[9] Having decided to deliver the ultimatum personally Lord Liverpool drove down to Brighton and informed George of the cabinet's unanimous decision. Faced with the political chaos that would follow and by the certain prospect of an even more hostile Whig party coming to power, George hesitated for a few minutes before totally capitulating. It seemed that in the final instance he preferred to risk the wrath of his mistress to the certain loss of his government.

When told of the King's humiliating climbdown Elizabeth accepted the defeat with surprising good grace, knowing that he would now be obliged to make it up to her in other ways. Perhaps another fine necklace would soon appear. She even produced a face-saving formula herself by asking Charles Sumner to write a letter to Bloomfield saying that after much thought he had decided to withdraw his candidacy as he did not wish to cause the King 'the uneasiness of a single instant'.[10] It was an acceptable resolution for all involved and the government readily approved the King's suggestion of an alternative position for the Revd Sumner. In a game of ecclesiastical musical chairs the Royal Librarian and Chaplain at Carlton House, Dr James Stanier Clark, was appointed the new Canon of Windsor and Charles Sumner promoted to Clark's old post with an increased salary of £300 a year and 'a capital house opposite the Park gates'. Sumner had lost little by his ready compliance and had earned the government's gratitude for he was later made Canon of Worcester, then Bishop of Llandaff and finally elevated, with more discreet assistance from Elizabeth Conyngham, to the prestigious See of Winchester.

The Sumner affair had been a significant if little publicised event in British history; for the first time in living memory a royal mistress had almost succeeded in overriding the government's wishes by placing her own candidate in an official office. The political fall-out did little for Elizabeth's already tarnished reputation. It was, thought Robert Huish, 'a miserable business for the very laws of the constitution had been infringed and all to gratify the ambition of a female'.[11] At the time, May 1821, it seemed likely that the loser in the Sumner affair would certainly be Lady Conyngham herself, for henceforth any decision by the King would be closely scrutinised by ministers intent on finding any evidence of Lady Conyngham's malign interference. But her nominal defeat should be seen, in reality, as a clear-cut victory, for she had demonstrated to the world that she enjoyed the King's confidence. Whatever society thought of her, it could no longer ignore the fact that Lady Conyngham now had the greatest possible influence on the King's decisions. One of the first to realise this fact was Harriet Arbuthnot, who claimed to be shocked by what she saw as Lady Conyngham's growing arrogance. 'Lady Conyngham has no sense of shame about her connection with the King,' Harriet wrote. 'She continually boasts of her influence over him and of her knowledge of public affairs, which she has not the discretion enough to keep to herself.'[12] Charles Greville, too, saw startling evidence of Elizabeth's new power and growing confidence one evening at the Brighton Pavilion. As they all sat down to dinner a footman entered carrying a note for the King announcing the death of the Marquess of Cornwallis who had been, among many things, Master of the Royal Buckhounds. Later, as they got up from the table Elizabeth turned to Greville and asked him casually if he would care to nominate someone for the vacant post:

> I thought she was joking. 'Not at all,' she said, 'today we can give it to whom we like. I have nobody in view in whom I am interested; if you name someone it will be done this evening; for tomorrow Lord Liverpool will have a candidate to propose to the King, and it will be too late.'[13]

It was certainly no idle boast, for Elizabeth had recently ensured that one of her oldest friends, Thomas Assheton-Smith, had been appointed Lord Lieutenant of Caernarvonshire rather than the more obvious candidate, Lord Gwydyr, who was enraged at the snub. It was also known that she had intervened successfully in another ecclesiastical appointment by persuading the King to veto Lord Liverpool's nomination of a Mr Colbourne for the vacant Deanery of York. Her reason, she told the King, was that Colbourne was a brother-in-law of the Tory Robert Peel, who was in turn a relative of the despised Hertford family. When she was told of these successful machinations Princess Lieven began to see Elizabeth Conyngham in a new light. Whatever Elizabeth's apparent vulgarity she was a clever woman with undoubted power over the King and would make a useful ally in the Princess's pursuit of her own secret political strategy, to get the King more closely involved with his fellow European monarchs against his ministers' wishes.[14] From the time of the Sumner affair the Princess set about cultivating Elizabeth far more assiduously than before and encouraging her to persuade the King to pay less attention to ministerial advice on foreign policy and more to developing closer ties with his friends on the Continent.

But the Duke of Wellington continued to keep his distance from Elizabeth, confessing himself shocked by her increasingly successful manipulation of the King. He confided to Harriet Arbuthnot that he suspected her next move would be to try and secure an English peerage for her husband.[15] In this he was proved correct when just before the coronation in July 1821 the Marquess of Conyngham was created Baron Minster of Minster Abbey in Kent. As an English peer Lord Conyngham would now have a seat in the English Parliament and the political credibility that went with it. Many were as mystified as Wellington that the King had chosen to elevate the amiable but unremarkable Henry in this manner. There could be no other explanation than that it had been done as a generous reward for his wife. From Elizabeth's perspective it was well-merited recognition of her important position in the royal household and a message to society that Lady Conyngham had lost nothing by her involvement in the Sumner affair and still maintained her influence at court.

Then just before the coronation the second major political crisis of that year occurred, again clearly fomented by Lady Conyngham, and concerning another appointment disputed between the Crown and Parliament. The prestigious office of Chamberlain of the Royal Household was currently held by the Marquess of Hertford. Although George had abandoned Isabella Hertford as his mistress in 1819 he had decided to retain her husband, Francis, as his Chamberlain. For the next two years Hertford's almost daily presence was a constant irritation to Elizabeth, symbolic as it was of the old domestic order at Brighton. She told the King that she was convinced that Lord Hertford was reporting any rows or disagreements between them back to his wife. Even if this accusation was true it appears unlikely that Isabella would have gossiped to her friends about them, for she was known as a woman of the firmest principles and the utmost propriety. Once when asked if she had been aware of the King's growing admiration for Lady Conyngham and if he had ever talked to her about it, she replied imperiously that, intimately as she had known the King and as openly as he had always talked to her upon every subject, he had, quite properly, never once ventured to speak to her about his mistresses.[16]

Adept at making life impossible for those she had once decided were her enemies Elizabeth, from the moment that she openly became the royal mistress in 1819, began lobbying the King to have Francis Hertford replaced. After two years of Elizabeth's implacable hostility the wretched Francis Hertford finally decided that he could endure the humiliation no longer and in July 1821 suddenly resigned.[17] Elizabeth had already decided that the next Chamberlain should be none other than her own husband. When told the news that the plan had the King's full approval the government was utterly astonished. The sheer effrontery of the proposal again united them in implacable opposition to this blatant attempt at nepotism. Unmoved by their hostility, Elizabeth claimed that the appointment made good sense and urged Lord Liverpool to consider it dispassionately. For with Henry as Chamberlain the Conynghams would gain official status in the royal household and much of the public gossip and innuendo concerning her relationship with the King would cease. George repeated that he saw the good sense of Lady Conyngham's argument and informed the Prime Minister that he proposed to confirm the appointment forthwith.[18] Predictably Lord Liverpool again threatened to resign, as he had done over the Sumner affair. But why, demanded the King, should he not have the right to choose his own Chamberlain – a position that was neither political nor ecclesiastical? However, having come close to personal humiliation over the Windsor Canonry affair, George was unwilling to risk it again and in consultation with Elizabeth, who soon realised that Lord Liverpool would never agree, he presented the Prime Minister with a compromise plan. He was now prepared to withdraw the proposal but as he had already promised Lord Conyngham the position it would be only fair to compensate the disappointed peer with the less controversial post of, say, Master of the Horse.[19]

Convinced that the Prime Minister would readily agree to his suggestion the King was dumbfounded when Lord Liverpool again refused, arguing that the granting of this office too was the sole prerogative of the government. Moreover, although he did not say this to the King's face, as Master of the Horse Lord Conyngham would have the honour and privilege of being able to use the royal livery on his own carriages. This Lord Liverpool thought would cause a great scandal in society, for who could explain why the obscure Marquess of Conyngham was being so honoured if not for condoning his wife's association with the King? Liverpool was adamant – if the King persisted in this matter then he and his entire cabinet would renew their offer to resign.

For the next few weeks the bitter dispute dragged on with neither side prepared to give way. This time the King was even more furious with his ministers' intransigence than he had been over the Sumner affair. Not only had they dismissed his face-saving compromise out of hand but they also appeared to be intent on ignoring his wishes in other matters too. The most wounding example of this had been their behaviour over the late Queen's funeral arrangements. George had given explicit instructions that the cortège should proceed by boat down the Thames rather than going by road to the port of Harwich en route to Germany.[20] Ignoring his sensible request the government had allowed Caroline's coffin to pass through the very centre of London, thus providing the mob with a last opportunity to demonstrate their fickle loyalty to the Queen's cause. Predictably a yelling, cheering crowd assembled as the coffin passed to give the unfortunate Queen a rousing send-off. The whole business, according to the King, had been so incompetently handled that it amounted to little more than a deliberate and personal insult to himself. So angry did he become with the government that his normally perfect manners were temporarily abandoned and he behaved with uncharacteristic rudeness to both Lord Liverpool and the Duke of Wellington.

When Wellington next invited him to dinner at Apsley House in London George curtly refused. Instead, accompanied by Elizabeth, he went to Devonshire House where they dined with the young Duke of Devonshire, one of the most eligible young men in the country and already marked out by Elizabeth as an ideal match for her eldest daughter, Lady Elizabeth. As the national hero Wellington was ill-accustomed to such brusque treatment and felt the slight keenly, taking it as both a political and personal insult. When next they met on official business he asked the King with characteristic bluntness, 'if you do not like us, why do you not turn us out?' The

King, realising the danger of provoking a serious political crisis, refused to reply – at which Duke merely bowed coldly and walked silently away.[21]

As a sound military strategist Wellington realised that he must recover the situation by attacking on a different front and, to her great surprise, he called unexpectedly on Elizabeth the following day to discuss the problem face to face. Disarmingly he began by telling her that in spite of all the rumours she may have heard, personally he had no objection to Lord Conyngham having an official position in the royal household, providing it was the right one. In fact, he positively welcomed the idea now that the details of the forthcoming royal visit to Hanover had been agreed and the King was keen that both Conynghams go with him. Although the trip to Hanover was principally to enable George to be crowned King of his other realm, it had a secret diplomatic purpose too. Lord Castlereagh, the Foreign Secretary, was concerned lest the growing antagonism between Russia and Turkey involve Britain in a wider European conflict. His plan was to build a closer understanding between Britain and Austria to guard against such an event. This is where the King's assistance would be invaluable for it was known that the Austrian Minister, Prince Metternich, both liked and admired King George. Castlereagh had arranged that they meet privately together in Hanover and discuss a closer friendship between Britain and Austria.[22]

As the King's close companions on this important mission, Wellington told Elizabeth, the Conynghams could provide him with invaluable personal support. But if they all travelled together merely as friends then the whole of Europe would gossip about Lady Conyngham's relationship with the sovereign. The questions asked would be, 'who the Devil is Lady Conyngham? What post does she hold? What business has she with the King?'[23] But if Lord Conyngham had an official role to play in the royal household rather than just being there as the husband of the royal favourite, their presence would more credible. Lord Conyngham should be given an impressive but non-controversial position in the royal household. Then they could all go off to Hanover together, leaving the government to get on with the real business of running the country. But, added Wellington, for this plan to succeed it must be proposed not by him, for the King was still too angry with him, but by Lady Conyngham herself. Elizabeth considered the proposition and, ever the realist, agreed. To her great amusement, she now found herself in an unexpected and unlikely alliance with the Duke of Wellington.

The stratagem worked perfectly. When the suggestion was put to the King he instantly agreed, recognising the value of this face-saving arrangement in a dispute that was threatening to destroy any remaining goodwill between himself and his ministers. So Wellington was invited down to Brighton and asked exactly what office he and Lord Liverpool had in mind for Lord Conyngham. The Duke suggested that it be Lord Steward of the Household and, as a bonus, Constable of Windsor. As a further reward for his compliance Henry would also be appointed a member of the Privy Council. When told that he must resign in favour of Lady Conyngham's husband the serving Lord Steward, Lord Cholmondeley, protested so vehemently that he had to be placated with the Order of the Garter and a peerage for his son in his own right.[24]

Although this latest controversy had ended satisfactorily for all parties Wellington still privately resented having to make deals with people like the Conynghams. When Elizabeth thanked him profusely for his help in the matter he replied coldly that he had not acted personally but only in the best interests of the King's ministers and her gratitude should be reserved for them. Their sole concern in this matter, he told her pointedly, had been to uphold his majesty's dignity and honour. Elizabeth, never slow to respond to a slight, replied sharply that on the contrary it was the ministers who should be grateful to her for they only remained in office because she had, on numerous occasions, persuaded the King not to sack the whole lot of them. They should also know that she and Lord Conyngham had decided, to avoid further friction, not to accompany the King on the forthcoming visit to Hanover after all. It had taken hours of pleading on her part, she said, before he finally agreed to let her remain in London. Lord Liverpool and his ministers should reflect on that and cease continually blaming her for their own inability to deal with the King.[25] Wellington admitted himself taken aback by her vehemence but as a plain-speaking soldier himself he respected her directness. From that moment he decided that he would never again prevaricate with Lady Conyngham but would deal with her openly. Their relationship now became one of grudging mutual respect and the Duke in future did not hesitate to consult Elizabeth before putting any difficult or controversial issue before the King. She dealt with him in like terms but confessed herself intrigued that all three of them, the Duke, the King and herself, remained unpopular and were the butt of the cartoonists' humour. Once when she asked him why this was Wellington replied bluntly, 'it is the King that is unpopular and we share it with him'.[26]

Elizabeth's decision not to go with the King to Hanover must have been difficult for from the very start of their relationship they had shared a romantic dream that one day they would travel to Europe together, preferably to Italy. Having completed his official duties in Germany the King would then have been free to continue on to Venice for a private holiday; it would have been his reward for enduring the unmitigated boredom of Hanover for a month. But in spite of all Wellington's efforts the government was privately delighted that Lady Conyngham would not, after all, be going with the King. They remembered that when he returned from Ireland an embarrassing series of mocking cartoons had appeared in the print-makers' windows depicting the happy pair cavorting at Slane Castle and tramping the Irish countryside as if on some wild, abandoned honeymoon. Another such romantic escapade, particularly on a state visit to Europe, would, thought Lord Liverpool, bring the King and the monarchy into even greater disrepute.

For George the loss of his intimate companion on this pleasurable odyssey was galling. He even complained to his friends that he would miss the company of Lord Conyngham, for in spite of his unprepossessing appearance and pedestrian character there was, according to the King, no more agreeable companion. But duty demanded that he go alone and that he must prepare himself thoroughly for what would be an important diplomatic mission at a time of political unrest in eastern Europe. So Elizabeth went down to Brighton and George remained disconsolately in London so that Foreign Secretary Castlereagh could brief him for his forthcoming meetings with Metternich.

When she heard that the King would be meeting her lover Metternich, Princess Lieven, who had not seen him since his return from Ireland, hurried round to Carlton House to find him sprawled out on a sofa and dressed in a lilac silk dressing gown with an incongruous velvet nightcap. He apologised immediately for receiving a lady in bare feet but claimed that he was too exhausted to find his slippers. Yet he was not too tired, she noted, to recount the events of his Irish adventure in great detail for over two hours. By the time she was ready to leave, now exhausted herself, George seemed restored to his usual good spirits and rewarded her patience with 'two smacking kisses' as a parting gift.[27]

Later that week, on a blustery late September day that must have reminded him ominously of his recent perils in the Irish Sea, the King set off to take ship at Ramsgate. He had decided to board the royal yacht there rather than at Dover, where a year earlier the inhabitants had disgracefully insulted him by cheering the arrival of the late Queen Caroline. His last night in England was to be spent at the Kentish house of his old friend the genial cockney, Sir William Curtis, yet another entrepreneur to have risen from humble origins to great wealth in Georgian England. Curtis had invented a more efficient process for making the sea biscuits that were then the essential fodder of the Royal Navy. That evening, relaxing in the vulgar comfort of Cliff House, the King's nerves were calmed with many draughts of his favourite cherry brandy until, overcome by apprehension and alcohol, he and his host eventually fell fast asleep at the table.[28]

Next morning he was up at dawn and arrived at the quayside at nine o'clock sharp, still suffering from a memorable hangover. There he was joined by the rest of his party including Lord Castlereagh. After a thankfully uneventful crossing in calm seas the ship arrived at Calais where among the crowd lining the dock stood the forlorn figure of his once bosom friend George, Beau Brummel. Now a bankrupt, Brummel had, like so many of his countrymen, fled to France to escape his creditors. Although Brummel stepped forward and attempted to speak, George brushed past him with barely an acknowledgement.[29] Climbing briskly aboard their carriages the royal party set off at full speed for Brussels where that evening George dined quietly with the Prince of Orange, one-time suitor of his late daughter Princess Charlotte. Rejected by the headstrong

Charlotte, the Prince had married a Russian Grand Duchess instead, who appeared at dinner wearing a vast array of fine diamonds that clearly impressed the King. George bowed to her and said, 'Madame, vous etes tres brillante'. Then as if reminded of Elizabeth he bent over and whispered in her ear that her gems were worthy of the famous Lady Conyngham herself![30]

The following day George fulfilled a long-held ambition to visit the field of Waterloo. Having listened dozens of times to the Duke of Wellington's own account of the conflict he was familiar with every minute detail. Now accompanied by the great man himself George drove slowly around the battle site before alighting from his carriage and wandering about on foot in the pouring rain. As the Duke, walking beside him, yet again recounted the events of that great day the King appeared to poke about in the mud with his walking stick in distraction. The cause of his wandering attention was soon revealed when he abandoned the Duke altogether and went off in search of the Marquess of Anglesea's leg. This had famously been struck off by a cannon ball at the height of the battle as Lord Anglesea sat on his horse beside the Duke. When George at last found the stone that marked the final resting place of the lost limb he waved his stick triumphantly in the air before, ever the sentimentalist, bursting into tears.[31]

Sightseeing completed, the party rejoined their carriages and proceeded on to Hanover where, on 7 October, the King was given an enthusiastic welcome in spite of his known antipathy to the city. The following day, in Hanover cathedral, George IV was crowned for the second time that year in a simpler and far less costly ceremony than the extravaganza at Westminster Abbey. As in Ireland he found the ordinary people of Hanover far more sympathetic to him than the London mob had ever been. Everywhere he went he was followed and cheered by a large, good-natured crowd, even though his enjoyment of their applause was spoilt by the nagging pain of the gout that had returned to plague him. This small German kingdom had long been seen by the Hanoverian rulers of Britain as a place to avoid – other than as a final bolthole in the unlikely event of a revolution in Britain. Those members of the family who had plucked up the courage to visit returned to London with cautionary tales of the boredom of Hanover. The current disgruntled ruler was one of the King's younger brothers, the irascible Ernest, Duke of Cumberland, who had been sent there as a punishment by his father for disreputable behaviour in London.[32]

As the weather in Germany had turned unseasonably cold the King decided to complete his engagements in Hanover but not to travel on to Carlsbad or Vienna as Lord Liverpool had originally suggested. For the next month George endured the tedium of life at the Hanoverian court with its monotonous routine of formal assemblies without either wit or colour. His sole consolation was the series of meetings he held in conjunction with Lord Castlereagh and Prince Metternich, who had joined him there from Vienna. George had long admired the Austrian minister who, when visiting London in 1814, had conferred on him the spectacularly ornate Order of the Golden Fleece. George was delighted with it for he collected such honours as schoolboys would later collect postage stamps. As they met for the first time in over seven years the King took Metternich's arms warmly and planted a firm kiss on both his cheeks before launching into a bombastic oration likening the Austrian statesman to Julius Caesar, Cato, Gustavus Adolphus, Marlborough, Pitt and other great figures in history.[33] When they finally got down to business both men found themselves in surprising agreement on many of the issues discussed. What concerned Metternich most was the question of Turkey and the Russian threat to its crumbling empire. To his surprise he found George more sympathetic to the Russian position than he had been led to believe and far more amenable to a resolution of the dispute than his Tory ministers back in London. As the meetings progressed each found the other a most agreeable companion and recognising that, like himself, Metternich was suffering a distressing separation from his most intimate confidante, George suggested that they must both lament the absence of the witty and amusing Princess Lieven.

Now in considerable pain from gout, George was unable to disguise his suffering and was clearly missing the support and sympathy of Lady Conyngham. The sunny mood that had characterised his arrival in Hanover changed to one of sullen irritability as when he refused point-blank to receive a deputation of English émigrés living in Hanover. His discomfort was further compounded by injury when he slipped on the wet cobblestones one morning and twisted his ankle. For the rest of his stay he was forced to rely on a sturdy walking stick for mobility. What had begun as pleasant duty now became a tiresome ordeal.

Several days before the end of his official visit the King could endure the pain no longer and, cancelling all remaining engagements, set off back to England. It was an uncomfortable journey for a man with gout and an injured ankle as his carriage rumbled along the pot-holed roads of northern Europe. Arriving at Calais he was further depressed to encounter a brisk wind that threatened another rough sea passage, this time to Dover. But the wind dropped and the crossing and subsequent journey up to London proved more bearable than he had expected. Still hobbling on his stick, on 8 November George finally reached Carlton House, where Elizabeth was waiting to restore his spirits. That evening at dinner, perhaps in celebration of their reunion, he began his odd habit of taking snuff from her bare clavicle, a custom among Continental lovers that he may well have witnessed in Hanover.[34]

Even curtailed as it had been, the royal trip to Hanover was considered by the government to have been a great success and earned the King the unaccustomed gratitude of his ministers. The British public, who knew nothing of his talks with Metternich, remained unimpressed by their monarch's European jaunts and the satirists claimed to be perplexed by all this gallivanting about to Ireland, Belgium and Hanover. Was the King about to give up his throne, they speculated, and retire to Slane Castle or was he planning to run off to the Continent with the portly Lady Conyngham? One cartoon encapsulated what was thought to be the King's own confusion. It shows him wearing a French coat and German cap and smoking a meerschaum pipe as he tosses coins to his British subjects. One bystander declares, 'he is a Hanoverian at heart', a second replies, 'no, he is an Irishman', while a third insists, 'he said he and his brother were the only ones in the family who were not Germans'.[35]

# SEVEN

## Battle of the Drawing Rooms

Having done his duty by the government the King could be denied a holiday no longer and he rushed post-haste down to the Brighton Pavilion with the Conynghams. There he stayed for a whole week holding only one official dinner party, which included his erstwhile travelling companion, Lord Castlereagh. Another guest was Princess Lieven, eager to learn news of her lover Prince Metternich. As she arrived she was treated to another series of smacking kisses by the King, who later told her at dinner of a strange rumour concerning Metternich that he had heard in Hanover. It was said that her beloved Prince was having an affair with the King's own sister-in-law the Duchess of Cambridge. Laughing at her obvious embarrassment he advised the Princess to respond in like manner and make Metternich jealous by starting a romance of her own in London. Why not a pick a member of my own cabinet, he teased, and surely the best candidate must be his handsome and highly intelligent Foreign Secretary, Lord Castlereagh sitting right opposite.[1]

There could hardly have been a more incongruous candidate for passionate lover than Robert Stewart, Viscount Castlereagh, a man universally detested by the mob and second only to the Duke of Wellington in the demonology of extreme Toryism. Although an immensely capable minister, Castlereagh was cold and patrician in manner, displaying both the virtues and vices of the Anglo-Irish ascendancy. Never a populist, his close association with the King in the matter of the royal divorce had so enraged the London mob that it besieged his London house for days – forcing him to take refuge in the Foreign Office. In Ireland he was, if anything, even more un-popular, having been actively involved in the suppression of the United Irishmen at the time of the Rising and later as a keen

109

supporter of the Act of Union of 1801. The fact that he was also in favour of Catholic Emancipation was completely ignored by his enemies. At Westminster, Lord Castlereagh was disliked by the Whigs and loathed by the Radicals. Yet the King, although wary of Castlereagh's high-minded principles, nevertheless admired his undoubted political talents and thought him the obvious choice for prime minister if Lord Liverpool ever resigned, as he constantly threatened to do. While the King grudgingly respected Castlereagh, Elizabeth simply abhorred him. It had not always been so, for when the Conynghams first arrived from Ireland Robert Castlereagh had, of course, helped introduce them to London society. But as Isabella Hertford's nephew and motivated by family loyalty his attitude abruptly changed when his aunt was abandoned by the King in favour of Lady Conyngham. It was, he thought, a matter of such personal honour that the issue could not easily be glossed over. While most of his fellow ministers grudgingly accepted the presence of the Conynghams as a fait accompli and grumbled about them discreetly, Castlereagh remained openly critical of them and of the King's decadent behaviour in openly flaunting his new mistress.

The first sign of an impending crisis between George and his highly principled Foreign Secretary occurred in February 1821 when the King proposed clipping Queen Caroline's wings by reducing her state allowance from £50,000 to £30,000 a year. The measure was clearly important to George but Lord Castlereagh, perhaps unwisely, chose to speak out openly against it.[2] Then when Elizabeth's son, Lord Francis Conyngham, declared to his Tory colleagues that he intended to support the motion in Parliament, Castlereagh went up to him and warned Lord Francis that it would be imprudent for him to do so 'in his position' – a clear reference to his mother's compromising relationship with the King. Lord Francis resented the implication and angrily demanded to know what exactly was meant by 'his position'. He warned that if Lord Castlereagh intended to insult his mother then he must give satisfaction in a duel.[3] It was a confrontation that Lord Francis must have expected to face one day, knowing that his mother's behaviour had provoked such universal disapproval. The challenge was wisely ignored and situation defused by Castlereagh, who explained that his only concern was that as Lord Francis was a member of the King's intimate circle it would look to the country as if the King himself was supporting the motion to impoverish his wife.

This confrontation marked Lord Castlereagh's increasingly open hostility towards the Conynghams in which he was enthusiastically encouraged by his equally patrician wife Emily, the daughter of the Earl of Buckingham, a longstanding friend of the Hertford family and 'a great crony' of Isabella's. In October 1821 Emily Castlereagh began what became a prolonged and famous 'battle of the drawing rooms' by refusing to invite Elizabeth to one of her coffee parties. Her excuse was that Lady Conyngham had failed to observe the polite conventions of London society by leaving her calling card at the door. Moreover, she complained to her friends that just because the King chose to have her as his favourite 'all the Ministers' wives and adherents were expected to pay her court'. She, Lady Castlereagh, had no such intention. Her husband agreed completely, adding that his wife 'was much too high minded to pay court to any one, much less to a woman whose only notoriety arose from so shameful a cause'.[4] Emily Castlereagh made a particularly powerful enemy for Elizabeth because she was one of the seven lady patronesses of Almacks, the club that dominated London social life. Soon the war between the Foreign Secretary's wife and the king's mistress escalated, with each lady seeking to outscore the other with invitations and exclusions. But Elizabeth Conyngham was not just another lightweight actress who could be pushed easily aside, for she had inherited the determination and strength of character of her father and was in unassailable control of the King's social life. Rather than the Conynghams becoming pariahs it was the Castlereaghs who found themselves increasingly excluded from the best drawing rooms in London. Lord Castlereagh, who still considered himself on good terms with the King, was deeply wounded by this social rejection and complained that George was now ignoring his wife and had 'ceased to treat her with the familiar kindness . . . and now never enquired after her'.[5]

As the weeks passed what had begun as a petty dispute between two women began to affect the important political relationship between the King and his ministers. Princess Lieven, an intimate of both parties, returning from a visit to the Royal Pavilion warned the Duke of Wellington that the King was in a foul mood and was now considering a change in his government and 'all caused by Lady Conyngham . . . I am persuaded that all this disgust to his ministers is caused by their wives not having crouched to Lady C which has made her furious'. She told the Duke of a conversation they had at dinner the previous evening when Elizabeth asked the King disingenuously, 'when your majesty changes your government, do you change the Foreign Minister also?' The King smiled enigmatically and replied 'that will be according as I like'.[6] Then his mood changed and he launched into a heated attack on Lady Castlereagh for her unseemly rudeness towards Lady Conyngham, complaining that his own ministers treated him equally badly. In fact, he protested to his guests, anyone who was a friend of himself and Lady Conyngham had been 'marked out for all sorts of contempt and insult'.

The next round in the battle came the following summer when the King was making preparations for a second trip to Europe – this time to attend the Congress of Nations at Verona. Again he seemed determined to take Elizabeth with him and finally to visit Italy and all the other romantic places they had long discussed. At Verona he would, for once, be in a European setting and free to talk to his fellow monarchs, much as Metternich had suggested in Hanover the previous year. But Lord Liverpool, now alarmed by the growing friendship between George and Metternich, had become increasingly apprehensive about the trip. The prospect of the King of England let free to discuss foreign policy with the leaders of the most despotic regimes in Europe was too much to bear. Castlereagh, having witnessed the King and Metternich together in Hanover, agreed, and reminded the rest of the cabinet, if they needed reminding, that Britain's foreign relations must remain the business of the government not of the monarch. After much dithering it was decided that the royal visit should go ahead as long as the Foreign Secretary went along to keep an eye on the King and advise him on what to say. Given that Lord Castlereagh was Foreign Secretary the whole project now ground to a halt as the King stated firmly that he would not travel without Lady Conyngham, and she adamantly refused to travel with Lord Castlereagh. There was now an added complication for Lord Londonderry, as Castlereagh had now become, could not be expected to go on such an important mission without his wife. As Emily Londonderry and Elizabeth Conyngham refused to speak to each other or appear in public together there was a total impasse. This petty dispute threatened to make the British government the laughing stock of Europe. An appeal to the King produced only disdain and he repeated that he had promised Elizabeth that she could go with him to the conference, Lord Londonderry or not, and he intended to keep his word.

Princess Lieven, although amused by this petty squabble, decided that some kind of rapprochement must be attempted for it was in Austria's interests that the King should meet Metternich again in Verona. The only solution, she decided, would be to attempt some kind of accommodation between Lady Conyngham and the Londonderrys. The prospects of doing so were not good, for as she complained, 'I see no means of bringing about reconciliation with Lady Londonderry. There is the bitterest prejudice against her . . . the King grows more arrogant and despotic every day, the favourite has complained to me; and her son is leaving, because he cannot stand it any longer.'[7]

Then something quite unexpected happened. A few days later, while driving in her carriage in a quiet area of Hyde Park, the Princess was astonished to see the solitary figure of Lord Londonderry riding towards her. It appeared that this casual encounter had been carefully planned for he quickly dismounted, walked over and began discussing the royal trip to Europe. He assured her of his firm belief that the King's presence in Verona was essential for the continuing good relations between both their countries. Nor did he object, in spite of the rumours circulating at Westminster, to the King meeting Prince Metternich again in private. His sole condition was that he, as Foreign Secretary, must be on hand to advise and counsel him. They both agreed that the best way to put this reasonable position to the King would be at an informal social occasion rather than at a formal audience.[8] At Castlereagh's behest the Princess now wrote to the King, using all her charm to suggest that he invite Lord Liverpool and Lord Londonderry to dinner at the Pavilion in order to resolve the matter.

When he entered the royal dining room a week later Lord Londonderry was shocked to find that he had been deliberately placed beside his bitter enemy, Lady Conyngham. At first the atmosphere was so tense and Lord Liverpool so tongue-tied with embarrassment that the other guests found it hard to conceal their amusement. The stratagem appeared to have worked, however, for the atmosphere quickly relaxed and when Prince Metternich was mentioned the King took Elizabeth's hand affectionately, saying that he would give anything in the world for her to meet the great statesman. 'And so she shall,' murmured Princess Lieven encouragingly. But the King seemed less convinced and merely sighed mournfully at her words.[9] Although the evening was judged a success nothing had been resolved and the next morning the protagonists went their separate ways as neither party was prepared to advance the reconciliation further.

The strain of fulfilling his duties as Foreign Secretary while involved in this petty social conflict with the King and his mistress was clearly beginning to take its toll on Lord Londonderry. He had always been a cool and distant figure at cabinet meetings but his colleagues noticed that he was now in constant ill-humour and quickly roused to anger, frequently complaining that the King no longer appeared to confide in him. Even the Duke of Wellington was dragged into the dispute when summoned to Windsor and told that it was not just the Foreign Secretary who was intransigent but the entire Tory cabinet. George repeated his accusation that both he and Lady Conyngham were sick of being treated with contempt by the ministers and their wives.

Princess Lieven doggedly continued her efforts to bring about a lasting reconciliation. Her next attempt was to persuade Elizabeth to accompany her on a visit to Lady Londonderry's house – that lady having agreed to receive them politely. 'I had promised to bring her, and there was great joy at the thought that this wretched quarrel was over,' she told Metternich, 'but she gave me the slip and I am furious.'[10] But Elizabeth too was feeling the strain of the interminable dispute and decided to leave London for a short holiday. The Princess, frustrated by the whole business, suggested waspishly in a letter to Metternich that Elizabeth might have suddenly developed a conscience about her scandalous relationship with the King and that her sudden departure was occasioned more more by 'an unaccustomed attack of prudishness'.

When she returned in May 1822 Elizabeth found the King facing yet another dilemma involving the Londonderrys. While she was away he had been asked by the government to give a formal dinner for the visiting Crown Prince of Denmark and his wife. As it was a state occasion he felt he had no option but to invite his Foreign Secretary and his wife. He hoped that Elizabeth would understand and agree to attend. Predictably she refused, and in desperation George implored her at least to discuss the matter with their mutual friend and honest broker, Princess Lieven. Delighted at another opportunity for mediation, the Princess reminded Elizabeth that as this was indeed a state occasion it was the government and not the King who were the real hosts and she could not possibly lose face by attending herself. Furthermore, if she attended but insisted that the Londonderrys be excluded, it would cause an international scandal. The whole of Europe would surmise that the King of England was deliberately snubbing his own Foreign Secretary at the behest of his mistress. For her part, the Princess assured Elizabeth, Lady Londonderry had confessed that she bitterly regretted her original slight to Elizabeth and had spent the past year quietly searching for a way to atone.[11] That evening Elizabeth informed the King, to his great surprise, that she would attend the dinner after all, and that he was free to invite the Londonderrys.

Scarcely had this skirmish been resolved when, the following month, the rivalry broke out again. This time it was brought about by Elizabeth's old rival Lady Hertford. Even with the passage of time Elizabeth could still be provoked by the slightest reference to Isabella Hertford and the role she had once played in the King's life. Ireland was again in the grip of famine and to raise money for its relief the ladies of Almacks, including Lady Londonderry, suggested an 'Hibernian Ball' be held. The 'patroness' chosen for the occasion was the Duchess of Richmond, who promptly co-opted her old friend Isabella Hertford on to the organising committee. Elizabeth, who could have expected an invitation to join the party, was deliberately excluded. This was a calculated and deliberate slight that she could not afford to ignore. Her revenge was not slow in coming for within a few days she had persuaded the King to endorse a rival ball under his royal patronage. This was organised 'under the auspices of a new set of ladies', meaning the old set but with the notable exclusion of the Duchess of Richmond and Lady Hertford.[12] This new committee was, of course, presided over by Lady

Conyngham. The battle of the rival balls caused great excitement in London producing, as Lady Holland put it, 'much malice and charity strongly blended'. The King, of course, went only to Elizabeth's ball and the whole evening turned out to be a spectacular success with the Drury Lane theatre beautifully decorated for the occasion with exotic tents, a special box for the King and one equally grand for the Lady Patronesses. The girls from the opera danced quadrilles, each wearing a costume paid for by one of the young male guests. Even the sceptical Mrs Arbuthnot was impressed by the evening and wrote to her husband that 'the whole coup d'oeil was such as no country but our own could provide for the magnificence of the dress and the beauty of the women'.[13] She did not mention, however, that Lady Londonderry had arrived and attempted to annoy Elizabeth by sitting down uninvited in a seat beside the King. Elizabeth was furious and, according to Lady Holland, looked 'cross and askance'. The situation was saved by a handsome Parisian actress who was visiting London, a Mlle Le Vert, who placed herself directly in front of George and began flirting outrageously with him, successfully distracting the King from Lady Londonderry's embarrassing attentions.[14] Finally, the night was Elizabeth's and Lady Hertford was described the following morning as being 'incensed at this practical retort from her successful rival'.

By now Princess Lieven was exhausted by her self-imposed but thankless task of peacemaker between the Conynghams and Londonderrys. She confessed to Metternich that 'there can be no more difficult job than getting round a woman's vanity, when one can appeal neither to her reason nor to her decent feelings'.[15] In spite of all that had happened Lord Londonderry remained as hostile as ever. When the Princess unwisely boasted to him that it was she who had persuaded Lady Conyngham to allow his wife to attend the dinner for the Danish Prince, Londonderry flew into a rage, threatening to resign and crying 'you have shown me my position . . . our position clearly. Things cannot go on like this. We cannot put up with a Lady Conyngham who is powerful enough to offer us such affronts.' So violent was his reaction that the Princess became alarmed, pleading with him not to throw away a distinguished political career because of a petty quarrel with an empty-headed woman. But Londonderry was not listening. No longer, he ranted, would he be the King's humble servant – nor was he prepared to continue sacrificing both his honour and his pride:

> As for the journey, I wash my hands of it. The King has Liverpool; let him arrange with him. I shall accept his words, and if I continue to serve him, I shall decide according to whether my wife is or is not included in the expedition, what course I have to take.[16]

After a year of constant stress and overwork something had finally snapped in Lord Londonderry's mind and he was never to regain his mental composure again. Paranoid delusions began to overwhelm him. Later that same day his half-brother Lord Stewart called on him and was so shocked by his condition that he called immediately for his carriage and raced round to Princess Lieven's house. When he arrived he appeared almost as distressed as his brother. It was all the fault of this endless and stressful battle with Lady Conyngham, he told her. His brother had become obsessed with the meeting in Verona and was struggling to do his duty in the face of wilful obstruction by other parties. Now, he added ominously 'the cup has overflowed' and the unfortunate Londonderry was convinced that enemies in Parliament close to the King were plotting against him. At this the overwrought Lord Stewart burst into tears himself and begged the Princess to get Lady Conyngham to do something, even if it were only an open declaration of hostility, as Lord Londonderry could no longer stand the pressure.[17]

Unknown to Lord Stewart, Elizabeth had earlier that day decided to end the dispute herself by informing the King that she would accompany him to Verona after all, even if the Foreign Secretary and his wife were in the party. The only reward she required for this largesse, she told him, was that Florence must now be included in their itinerary. The King was delighted and summoned Princess Lieven down to Brighton the next day. After swearing her to secrecy he told her the good news. Characteristically she again took full credit for Elizabeth's sudden change of heart. 'I think I have brought it off,' she wrote to Metternich, 'I had a long talk with Lady C, I made her quite excited about the prestige that she would acquire for the King in Europe by deciding to go with him on the journey.'[18]

But on her return to London the next day, the Princess again found Lord Stewart on her doorstep, this time in even greater distress at his brother's deterioration. Stewart appeared so anguished that the Princess decided to break her promise to the King and tell him the good news immediately. The war of the drawing rooms was over, she declared, and everyone will be delighted when the Conynghams and the Londonderrys celebrate their reconciliation by going off to Verona together. But Stewart seemed barely to be listening to her as he repeatedly shook his head before launching into another tirade. His brother had now become so paranoid that he was convinced that the Duke of Wellington had been behind the dispute all the time. It was he who had persistently poisoned Lady Conyngham's mind against him so that he could go to the Verona conference himself. Now the Duke, according to Londonderry, was secretly trying to involve Lady Conyngham in other even more dastardly plots intended to bring about Lord Londonderry's total disgrace and downfall.[19] These wild accusations from Lord Stewart, who clearly believed much of it to be true, alarmed the Princess, who did her best to calm him. She assured him that it was all nonsense and that it was ludicrous to think that Lady Conyngham was in league with the Duke of Wellington, of all people. In fact, she had not seen him for weeks and he had certainly not been present at any time the royal visit to Verona was being discussed. Her calm good sense eventually prevailed and seemed to calm Stewart, who agreed to return to his brother and persuade him that his worries were mere delusions. That evening the Princess wrote how shocked she had been by the distressing scene and by these 'illusory terrors that have been conjured up', and how fearful she was of their consequences.

A few days later Lord Londonderry called on the Princess in person. She was appalled at the change in his appearance. Ghostly pale and trembling with emotion, he appeared to have aged five years in as many days. He looked, she thought, a broken man. His terrifying paranoia was now clearly spiralling out of control, for he suddenly accused her too of being part of the conspiracy against him. He made no mention of the good news that the problem of Verona had been amicably resolved but repeated his threat that, if Wellington took his place in Verona, he would resign instantly from the government. After all she had done to resolve the situation the Princess was shocked and disappointed by these wild accusations yet as they parted she reminded Londonderry of a longstanding engagement to dine with her a few days later.[20]

When he arrived on the evening in question the Princess was astonished to see that Lord Londonderry appeared to have undergone another bizarre transformation and was now apparently his old self again. He told her that he had gone down to Brighton to see the King and that all the problems concerning Verona had been amicably resolved. He was clearly in the best of spirits: witty, lively and perceptive enough to reject her politically compromising offer, given the British government's wariness of Austria, to send a private greeting on his behalf to Prince Metternich. All he would say was, 'tell him that I am hoping to see him soon'. As the party retired to the drawing room a delighted Lord Stewart came up and took her arm. 'You have made the King obey you on every point,' he warmly congratulated her, 'my brother found him as prepared as if he were under orders.'[21]

But it had all been for nothing for, without consulting his ministers, Lord Liverpool had decided that the royal visit to Verona must be postponed until the following year. Having witnessed the chaos that even the prospect of such a trip had produced, the Prime Minister was now more wary. He had also become convinced that the prospect of the King blundering about Europe with Lady Conyngham in tow and discussing British foreign policy at a time of international tension was too appalling to contemplate. He informed George privately of his decision and asked him instead to fulfil a long-standing promise that the government had made that the sovereign should visit Scotland as soon as possible after the coronation. When she heard the news Princess Lieven was furious, considering it a poor reward for all her hard work. She was not the only one to be disappointed by the Prime Minister's abrupt decision. When she called on Elizabeth Conyngham three days after the cancellation she found her slumped on a sofa with eyes red from weeping. Elizabeth thrust a letter from the King into her hands. 'All is over,' she announced dramatically, 'he writes to me this morning to tell me that his plans are changed, that he is going not to the Continent but to Scotland and he has sent for his Ministers to tell them.'[22] It was final confirmation that all the Princess's protracted scheming with Metternich to get the King to Verona had come to nothing. In a last desperate attempt to save the situation she persuaded Elizabeth to write to the King urging him not to agree to Lord Liverpool's proposal until she, Elizabeth, had discussed it with him. But as she was about to leave the drawing room with the letter in hand, Lord Francis suddenly entered. He told them that he had come straight from Carlton House where the King was already in conference with his ministers discussing the final details of his trip to Scotland. Like the realist she was, the Princess finally realised that further discussion was useless. Accepting defeat she wrote wearily to Metternich that evening:

> Lord Liverpool has pulled so many strings, and frightened the King so much by means of newspaper articles . . . the King is in tears, the favourite is in tears; they are all in despair. I give as much autocratic advice as I can; but I have to deal with two women – the King and his mistress . . . what a weathercock he is; the last person to speak to him carries the day.[23]

She consoled herself with the thought that at least the King would meet Metternich again the following year. But two days later even this arrangement seemed under threat when she arrived for dinner at Lady Cowper's house and found to her surprise – for the Cowpers were leading Whigs – that Lady Conyngham was there too. The guest of honour that evening was the Whig leader Lord Grey, who had apparently been invited so that he could meet Lady Conyngham. It was an obvious attempt by the opposition to ingratiate themselves with the King through his influential mistress. Knowing that the Whigs were totally opposed to the royal visit to Europe and closer ties with Austria, the Princess decided that she must sabotage the evening. First she insisted on being placed next to Lord Grey at table and then worked hard on holding his attention throughout the meal. When the party retired to the drawing room she continued to monopolise Lord Grey, so that Elizabeth was unable to talk with him for the entire evening. 'I prevented all secret talks between him and the Marchioness,' the Princess boasted triumphantly to Metternich. Yet Elizabeth must have been aware of her machina-

'ROYAL HOBBY's or the Hertfordshire Cock-horse!', anonymous but probably by George Cruikshank, 1819. Lady Hertford rides George IV like an early bicycle.

'A Sketch from Brighton', by William Heath, 1822. The Conynghams promenading with their daughter Elizabeth.

George IV, by Sir Thomas Lawrence, 1822. *(Reproduced by permission of the Trustees of the Wallace Collection, London)*

Elizabeth, Marchioness of Conyngham, after the portrait by Sir Thomas Lawrence.
*(Birmingham Museum and Art Gallery)*

Engraving of Dorothea
Benckendorff, Princess Lieven.
*(Copyright of the Duke of
Wellington)*

Viscount and Viscountess
Castlereagh, afterwards 2nd
Marquess and Marchioness of
Londonderry, by Sir Thomas
Lawrence. *(By permission of
National Portrait Gallery and
Blicking Hall)*

The Duke of Wellington and
Mrs Arbuthnot, by T. McLean.
*(Copyright of the Duke of
Wellington)*

'Baise-Mon-Q', possibly by William
Heath, 1820.

'The Deepot', by William Heath, showing a defiant Lady Conyngham surveying her booty, 1830.

'Brobdignag Cottage', anonymous, 1824. This depicts the Royal Lodge at Windsor that became the love-nest of the King and Elizabeth Conyngham.

Harriette Wilson, engraving by Cooper from an original drawing by Birch. *(Reproduced courtesy of the Hulton Getty Picture Collection)*

The Royal Lodge at Windsor, engraving by W.R. Wright, 1827.

'A Kingfisher', by
C. Williams, 1826.

Sir William Knighton,
after the painting by
Sir Thomas Lawrence.
*(Reproduced by
permission of the
Royal College of
Surgeons)*

tions for at dinner she had turned to a fellow guest, Lord Clan-william, and asked him in loud and clear voice whether he had heard that Lord Londonderry was going to the Congress in Verona. At once Lord Grey exclaimed in surprise 'What? Londonderry? What Congress? Is there to be a Congress?' At this Elizabeth smiled and said calmly 'but of course there is to be one'. Grey, thoroughly alarmed, said 'if there is a Congress there is mischief . . . break it up immediately and send the Holy Alliance to the devil'.[24] A few days later in Parliament the Whigs began bombarding the government with questions about a secret European congress of which they had been told nothing.

But for Lord Londonderry events were moving towards a terrible resolution as his personal and political problems drove him into the final stages of mental collapse. Politically his plans for an alliance between Britain and Austria to keep the Russians out of the Mediterranean had been frustrated by the Turks massacring the Greeks on the island of Skios and the British government in consequence having to give way to Russian demands for action against them. At home he had seen his plans for the King to attend the Congress destroyed; moreover the long and damaging dispute between his wife and the King's favourite had prevented him from having any further influence at Court. As if this were not enough there was another, darker, problem, linked to his own sublimated homosexuality.

A month earlier the Bishop of Clogher, the son of the Irish peer the Earl of Roden, had been arrested for having sex with a soldier in a common alehouse in Westminster. The news of this bizarre event seemed to galvanise Londonderry into a morbid fear that a similar fate awaited him. This was not mere paranoia, as he had told friends that he was being blackmailed for a similar crime. A few months earlier he had visited a brothel and had, so he claimed, found that the woman provided was in fact a man in woman's clothing, so he ran panic-stricken from the house. The perpetrators of this strange charade had recognised him and were now attempting to obtain money by threatening to reveal the details to his wife. The stress, he told his secretary Lord George Seymour, was enormous. Clapping his hand to his forehead he turned to Lord George and said 'my mind is, as it were – gone'.[25]

Seymour told Lady Londonderry of this strange conversation but failed to inform any of the minister's political colleagues. After all that had passed Emily Londonderry was determined to say nothing that might embarrass the government and kept silent herself about her husband's true mental state, attributing his agitation merely to overwork.

As none of his colleagues knew that the Foreign Secretary was suffering a severe mental breakdown he was allowed to continue with his political duties unchallenged. When he had completed the now redundant itinerary for the royal visit to the Congress of Nations, he had taken it personally to Carlton House for approval by the King. At first George seemed not to notice his Foreign Secretary's agitated condition when he entered and began reading the document aloud. Then realising that Londonderry was not listening the King looked up to see him staring fixedly at the ceiling as if in a trance, eyes rolling from side to side. Alarmed, the King demanded to know what the matter was. 'Listen,' whispered Londonderry, 'that is my footman at the door and he will not go away.'[26] Realising that something was seriously wrong the King ordered him to return home immediately and get a doctor to come and bleed him – the King's own favourite remedy for any condition. But Londonderry seemed unable to comprehend his words and, grasping the King's arm in panic, he sank to his knees and moaned:

Have you not heard the news, the terrible news? I am a fugitive from justice. I am accused of the same crime as the Bishop of Clogher. I have ordered my saddle horses; I am going to fly to Portsmouth and from there to the ends of the earth. I must leave by the little gate in your garden.

George was shocked by this bizarre self-accusation but, kindly as ever, took his hands and urged the distraught man to calm himself. But Londonderry pulled abruptly away and began laughing sarcastically, accusing the King of being an enemy just like everyone else. All of London hated him, he said, people were even crossing the street to avoid him. Continuing this paranoid tirade he then began accusing himself of every imaginable crime. Once again the King tried to calm him and repeated his sensible advice that he should go home and be bled. At this Londonderry dramatically produced a document from his pocket and waved it in front of his sovereign. This he claimed was sure proof that he was being blackmailed. Then suddenly he froze and collapsed again at the King's feet in tears. In a moment of terrible clarity he looked up and cried out, 'I am mad. I know I am mad. I have known it for some time.' Then before rushing from the room he took the King's hand and begged him to keep his secret.[27] As soon as he was gone the King, deeply upset, summoned the Duke of Wellington, who by chance had been waiting in an anteroom to see him. George urged him to contact Londonderry's doctor at once and tell him of their concern for his patient. Then, in a typically kind-hearted gesture, he wrote an affectionate letter to his Foreign Secretary, again urging him to seek medical help. A second letter warning Lord Liverpool of the Foreign Secretary's collapse was despatched to Downing Street. Wellington – who had set off at a gallop from Carlton House – managed to overhaul and stop Lord Londonderry's carriage. The Duke implored him to follow the King's advice and go straight to his doctor but he merely smiled sadly and, turning from the Duke, ordered his coachman to drive on.[28]

Exhausted and exasperated by all this turmoil George was grateful to get away to Scotland even though he had once again failed to persuade Elizabeth to go with him. Henry Conyngham had, however, agreed to accompany him as far as Edinburgh before travelling on alone to his estates in Ireland. In George's absence Elizabeth announced that she would take a short holiday with her daughter Lady Elizabeth, who had recently been unwell. Everyone thought it likely that Elizabeth would soon be summoned to Scotland, however. As William Freemantle put it, 'I should not be surprised if accident brings her to Edinburgh about the same time!'[29] George had thrown himself into the Scottish preparations with the same enthusiasm that he had shown in planning his coronation. Tailors and jewellers were summoned to Carlton House and the firm of George Hunter of Edinburgh was chosen to provide his formal ensemble of sixty yards of satin plaid tartan set off by a Highland bonnet decorated with gold and jewelled ornaments, an elegant claymore of polished steel and a large pair of Highland pistols. To keep him cool in this weighty outfit a travelling case of eau de cologne was added at a cost of £32.[30] Not even in his younger days when he was a recognised arbiter of fashion and an avid collector of uniforms – he owned eight full-dress field-marshal outfits – had George spent so extravagantly on his appearance. Where he intended to wear his new opera pelisses, astrakhan Polish caps, white beaver morning gowns and rich, gold 'marmalouk' sword belts is hard to ascertain. One blue silk coat alone had so many alterations that it kept a tailor and his two assistants in constant employment for three weeks at a cost of £600.

It was a sign of the rapid technological change that had occurred in recent years, even since his voyage to Ireland, that when the King set off for Scotland on 10 August 1822 the royal yacht was towed down the Thames by one of the new steam packets, the *Comet*. Significantly the King's new friend and future secretary, William Knighton, travelled with him and was given the cabin next to his own. The current incumbent of the post, Sir Benjamin Bloomfield – now increasingly out of favour – was relegated to a more distant one.

George never seemed to have much luck when travelling by sea and sure enough four days later the party sailed into the port of Leith in a torrential rainstorm. The Scots more than made up for the appalling weather, however, by welcoming their sovereign almost as enthusiastically as the Irish had done. The melodramatic reception ceremony had been planned in every detail by the King's great friend and admirer, Sir Walter Scott. The famous novelist, resplendent in the Campbell tartan, stood on the quay ready to greet the monarch as he was rowed slowly towards the cheering crowds on the harbour wall. As the King set foot on Scottish soil for the first and only time in his reign, Sir Walter stepped forward, bowed deeply and presented him with a splendid silver St Andrews cross 'on behalf of the ladies of Edinburgh'. Others came forward offering him other gifts and words of welcome, among them the Earl of Kellie, who discreetly handed George a small wooden casket with the instruction that he was not to open it in public. That evening when alone the King lifted the lid to find that it contained a merkin, a small wig made of pubic hair collected, as was the custom then, from several of the King's earlier mistresses. He had sent it to Edinburgh in 1783 as an amusing gift for a local aristocratic sex and drinking club.

The gifts presented, Sir Walter commenced a 'traditional' Scottish welcoming ceremony of his own devising that included handing his sovereign a libation of his favourite tipple, cherry brandy. To the hurrahs of the excited crowd he downed it in one before climbing clumsily aboard a waiting carriage for the short drive to Edinburgh. On his hat were pinned a St Andrew's Cross and a bold sprig of heather, in the manner of the shamrock that he had worn in Ireland. That evening Sir Walter returned home to Abbotsford with the precious glass the King had drunk from still in his coat pocket only, to sit on it accidentally at dinner.[31] But the day had been a triumph for Scott who, more than any man, became responsible for the creation of the nineteenth-century myth of Highland Scotland that was launched by this royal visit of 1822.

Without his 'intimate companion' the King spent a lonely first night in Scotland at the bleak granite fortress of Dalkeith Castle. His host was its youthful custodian, the sixteen-year-old Duke of Buccleuch. To the embarrassment of the other guests George drank heavily all evening but refused to let his young host keep pace with him. As a servant went to fill the young Duke's glass with cherry brandy the King waved him angrily aside, crying out 'no, no it is too strong for his Grace to drink'. Next morning at HolyroodHouse the King appeared, to general but suppressed amusement, decked out in full Highland rig – the dramatic effect being somewhat spoilt by the flesh-coloured tights he insisted on wearing beneath his kilt. It was the birth of an image that would later appear on the lid of many a shortbread biscuit tin. More incongruous even than his own appearance was that of his old friend, Sir William Curtis, the sea biscuit tycoon. Despite not having a single drop of Scottish blood in his veins, Curtis stood proudly beside his sovereign decked out in an even more flamboyant approximation of Highland dress complete with a kilt of the Stuart tartan. One jaundiced Scottish observer, John Lockhart, complained that Curtis 'cast an air of ridicule and caricature over the whole of Sir Walter's Celtified pageantry'.[32] The ridiculous appearance of the two pseudo-Highlanders was, of course, a gift to the London satirists who for the rest of the year teased the 'Celtic' King in numerous cartoons and rhymes. But to the weavers of tartan and to the authors of sentimentalised clan histories the royal visit launched a profitable new tourist industry.

The commercial exploitation of George's visit to Scotland had begun even before he had set foot on that country's soil, for one man with a keen eye for a business opportunity had placed mahogany planks on the landing stage before the King's arrival. A week later they were taken up and made into souvenir snuffboxes that sold by the hundred.

For the next few days the King fulfilled his official duties in a relaxed and informal atmosphere, quite convinced that the Scots loved him just as much as did the Irish. Then as his visit drew towards a close, a messenger arrived from London with the shocking news that Lord Londonderry was dead. It appeared that soon after the King had left for Scotland it became public knowledge that the Foreign Secretary had suffered a mental collapse. Two days after Elizabeth Conyngham returned to London following her short holiday, Princess Lieven called on her and as the two women sat talking in the drawing room Lord Francis Conyngham suddenly burst in, as pale as death.

'Londonderry is dead!' he gasped. Elizabeth immediately sprang up and clutched her hands to her head, crying out 'good God, then he has destroyed himself'. Lord Francis seized his mother's arms, saying 'no mother, he had an apoplectic fit'. But Elizabeth shook her head in disbelief. 'No,' she repeated, 'he has killed himself, he was mad.'[33] As Charles Greville noted in his journal, Lady Conyngham was one of the few people at court who knew the seriousness of Lord Londonderry's condition because the King had told her of the harrowing interview at Carlton House. Visibly distressed by the encounter, George had told her that he was so upset that he doubted if he would sleep a wink that night.

As news of the Foreign Secretary's death spread through London Princess Lieven, an intimate witness of his tragic decline, wrote to Metternich telling him that she was sure Lady Conyngham blamed herself for not informing Londonderry's wife of the events at Carlton House, even though the King had sworn her to secrecy. Oddly the Princess refused to accept that Londonderry's suicide had been caused by a mental collapse, although 'terrible remorse was playing on his conscience. But he was not mad when he killed himself. Nobody can quote a word he said that he was not sane. There is no evidence except his conversation with the King.'[34]

The facts of Lord Londonderry's death are well documented. Returning from Carlton House after his emotional meeting with the King he called briefly at his town house before setting off for his country seat at North Cray in Kent. There his wife, forewarned from London, summoned the local physician Dr Bankhead, who saw at once that Londonderry was in a suicidal mood and ordered her to lock up her husband's pistols and all sharp instruments such as knives and razors. Then, two days after the King had left for Scotland, the tragedy occurred. Londonderry had seemed to pass a tranquil night but something about his demeanour the next morning so alarmed his wife that she summoned Dr Bankhead again. Leaving her husband to dress she called the servants together and gave them their orders for the day. Meanwhile Bankhead had arrived and was shown straight to the bedroom but found it empty. It appeared that when left alone Londonderry had gone through to his dressing room and retrieved a small penknife he had hidden in a drawer of his desk. At the very moment that the doctor entered the room Lord Londonderry, standing by the window, slashed the carotid artery in his neck. Turning to Dr Bankhead he murmured quietly 'it is of no use', then with blood spurting from his throat he fell forward, dead, on the carpet.[35]

The news shocked London society and produced predictable criticisms of his fellow ministers for not helping the troubled man. The mob was at best indifferent to his fate and few tears were shed as Londonderry was buried at Westminster Abbey. One of his old enemies present, an ageing United Irishman, reported that 'great personages walked in procession, holding the pall; but the people shouted at the porch'. The Whig politician Thomas Creevey, a life-long opponent of the late Foreign Secretary, gloomily pondered the implications of his sudden death and wondered if it presaged a similar end for the dissolute monarch himself:

This time last year he was revelling with his Sovereign in the country he had betrayed and sold, over the corpse of the Queen whom he had so inhumanly exposed and murdered. Ah Prinney, Prinney! your time will come; and then your fame and reputation will have fair play too, my boy.[36]

Lord Byron, who had once likened Castlereagh to the Devil, thought his violent end well merited. It might, he thought, 'serve as some consolation to the nations, that their oppressors are not happy, and in some instances judge so justly of their own actions, as to anticipate the sentence of mankind'. Byron had put his low opinion of Lord Londonderry even more succinctly in an earlier verse that uncannily echoes the thoughts of Lady Glengall at the time of the royal visit to Ireland: 'So he has cut his throat at last! He! Who? The man who cut his country's long ago'.[37]

Not since the murder of the Prime Minister, Spencer Perceval, in 1812 had there been such a sensational political event as the suicide of Lord Londonderry. Although the King had sided with Elizabeth in her long dispute with the Londonderrys, he had always admired his Foreign Secretary as a skilled mediator between himself and the cabinet. In view of this, he told Robert Peel that it was 'the greatest loss he had ever sustained'.[38] For Elizabeth Conyngham there remained a legacy of guilt. She had used the King as weapon against Londonderry, producing confusion and dilemmas that added to the stress on a conscientious and deeply neurotic man. She had also manoeuvred the King into choosing between his affection for her and his duty to the most able minister in his government. Although blameless of his suicide she was certainly responsible for much of the stress that eventually destroyed him. Did the King harbour any resentment towards her for her part in the death of his most able minister? Certainly after 1822 numerous witnesses report a cooling in their relationship and frequent disagreements. His old easygoing amiability appears to have left him as deteriorating health and incessant gout came to dominate his life. Not surprisingly he became ever more morbid and one subject came to dominate his conversation – the imminent prospect of his own death.

# EIGHT

## *Spending It*

As far as the great majority of the British public was concerned Lord Londonderry was no great loss. Nor for that matter were the conflicts and intrigues of Tory politicians of any real interest. What dominated the lives of ordinary people was the grim struggle to survive, for times were hard. With the end of the Napoleonic Wars had come a near-collapse of world trade and the introduction of the Corn Laws, which had sent the price of bread soaring not only in the new industrial cities of north but also in rural areas where farm workers already lived on the edge of starvation. Yet the incomes of great landowners like the Conynghams and the Hertfords continued to grow, with average rents from land increasing fivefold between 1790 and 1830. As the ruling classes spent money as never before, the desperate poor were increasingly attracted to violent expressions of discontent resulting in the Peterloo Massacre of 1817 and the Cato Street Conspiracy of 1820. These events had a profound effect on the King, increasing his fear of the mob and encouraging his compulsion to lock himself away at Windsor with Lady Conyngham. Shelley's bitter sonnet 'England in 1819' captured the radical mood of those years and the growing contempt of the labouring poor for the aristocracy and the crown:

> Princes, the dregs of their dull race, who flow
> Through public scorn – mud from a muddy spring,
> Rulers, who neither see, nor feel, nor know,
> But leech-like to their fainting country cling . . .

After the tragedy of Peterloo George had been hissed in the street by a huge mob, an experience he never forgot, and on her way to visit him Isabella Hertford was almost 'tipped out of her carriage' by the

129

crowd and had to be rescued by the Bow Street Runners.[1] The King must have been aware that the poor had plenty to complain about but their plight continued to be irrelevant to him. Consequently he made no attempt to curtail or even disguise the prodigal lifestyle so widely mocked by the satirists. As Charles Greville, a frequent guest at Carlton House, so succinctly put it, 'poverty, and vice, and misery must always be found in a community like ours, but such frightful contrast between the excess of luxury and splendour and these scenes of starvation and brutality ought not to be possible'.[2] Yet the King went blithely on with his sybaritic lifestyle, ignoring public opinion and indulging his mistress in a manner unprecedented in a British king. His punishment was a vicious and sustained mocking by his critics, who considered him a gullible fool incapable of sound judgement and increasingly controlled by a cunning and avaricious mistress. A typical cartoon of the period, 'The Depot' by William Heath, shows Elizabeth Conyngham standing with hands on hips in front of a vast cupboard stacked with moneybags labelled '£100,000'. She stares defiantly back over her shoulder at the viewer and asks 'do you think I care for the opinion of any of you?' Another caricature, this time by Paul Pry, ambiguously titled 'Sketch of a Lady – Playing with a Sovereign', bears the caption 'When Kissing and Cooing and toying are done, Tis Gold must enliven the lover'.

Although Lady Conyngham was blamed for much of the King's extravagance in the 1820s she was just the latest excuse for him to spend prodigally. Since breaking free of his father's strict financial control at the age of eighteen, he had indulged in a wild and costly lifestyle. By 1789 his extravagance had run up a colossal personal debt of over £300,000 – much of it owed to London tradesmen. When, in desperation, one of his London jewellers, Grays, threatened to sue for their money George's then treasurer, Colonel Hotham, complained to him that 'it is with grief and vexation that I now see your Royal Highness . . . totally in the hands, and at the mercy of your builder, your upholsterer, your jeweller and your tailor'.[3] George's financial predicament proved all the more embarrassing because the public appeared to know every intimate detail of his expenditure. George and his equally spendthrift brother the Duke of York were constantly mocked in such cartoons as 'The

Insolvent Brothers'. When the government decided not to risk bailing him out George turned in desperation to his ex-cook, Louis Weltje. Now a Brighton tavern owner Weltje, a man with a thousand useful contacts, suggested to George that they enlist the help of the shadowy Irish financier, Nathianiel Parker Forth – agent for the fabulously wealthy Philippe, Duke of Orléans, cousin of the King of France.

The anglophile Duke was well known in Britain as a hard-drinking sportsman and a leading patron of British bloodstock. Given the huge sum needed to stave off his creditors Weltje suggested that George ask Orléans for a loan of £200,000, which the Prince promptly upped to £300,000, arguing that his brother needed money too. The security for the loan would be the revenues from the Duchy of Cornwall to be redeemed once George succeeded to the throne.[4] Once again the Prince had committed an act of treason comparable to his earlier morganatic marriage to the Catholic Maria Fitzherbert by signing such an agreement without his father's knowledge or consent. Luckily for George and his brother the unfortunate Philippe Égalité, after throwing in his lot with the Jacobins and signing his cousin King Louis XVI's death warrant, was himself arrested and guillotined by Robespierre in 1794 and the debt became void.

With this new capital the Prince wiped out his old debts but, true to form, immediately incurred many new ones. But his personal expenditure on gifts and luxuries was dwarfed by the prodigious sums he lavished on grandiose building projects. This passion for architecture had begun years earlier when he radically altered his London home, Carlton House. No expense was spared; five leading British architects participated, the finest craftsmen were employed and hand-picked fittings were imported from the Continent. Even the great marble fireplaces seemed constantly on the move as they were carted from one room to another for the Prince to give his opinion in situ.[5]

As the Prince and the architect James Wyatt experimented with exotic combinations of Chinese, gothic and classical, Carlton House became the prototype for the later extravaganza at the Brighton Pavilion. Carlton House was the design sensation of the day and here, as at Brighton, George indulged his talent for entertaining in style. A series of sumptuous breakfasts, balls and fêtes were held, culminating on 19 June 1811 in a celebration of his Regency. Two thousand representatives of the nobility and gentry of Britain and Europe sat down to dinner at a supper table over 200 feet in length bisected by a stream of real water flowing down the middle. The following day the Prince unwisely opened the house to the public and thousands arrived to gape in awe at this architectural spectacle but in the mêlée many spectators were injured and hundreds of shoes lost. The correspondent of the *Morning Chronicle* witnessed the chaos:

> The number of stray shoes . . . was so great that they filled a large tub, from which the shoeless ladies were invited to select their property. About a dozen females were so completely disrobed in the squeeze, they were obliged to send home for clothes . . . and one lady was so completely disencumbered of all dress, a female domestic, in kind compassion, wrapped her up in an apron.[6]

Grand as it was, Carlton House soon proved too small for entertaining on the scale that the Prince demanded and even rejigged and renovated it was no more than an inflated mansion rather than the splendid palace he desired. Without more ado he promptly demolished it and turned his attentions to the Brighton Pavilion.

While his greatest expenditure was on architecture, gifts to his friends and mistresses consumed a significant part of his income. For years he had bought expensive presents from all the leading London jewellers. Among his favourite shops were Hamlets, whose proprietor was facetiously known as 'The Prince of Denmark', Thomas Grays and Phillips in Bond Street. In these three establishments alone he had, by the time he took up with Elizabeth Conyngham, already spent over £54,000 on jewellery for Maria Fitzherbert. But the main beneficiary of his custom was the official royal jeweller, Messrs Rundell, Bridge & Co. of Ludgate Hill. Their account books reveal that in 1819 he bought Lady Conyngham an eye-catching necklace consisting of 'thirty-seven remarkably large oriental pearls', which cost him, or rather the nation, a staggering £3,150. That same year, as was his custom with all new mistresses, he commissioned a miniature portrait of himself framed in diamonds, which he presented to the new incumbent. Two years later his continuing obsession with Elizabeth had led him in a two-month period to spend a further £400 on a pair of diamond earrings for her, £437 on a pair of pearl bracelets, £530 on an emerald necklace and £740 on a lesser pearl necklace. In the decade that they were together George IV spent an astonishing £105,618 with Rundell, Bridge & Co. alone on presents for Elizabeth Conyngham.[7] Not surprisingly the King was described by the miserly proprietor of the firm as 'our greatest Patron and Best Friend'. So well did Rundell do out of his royal patron that he was once reputed to have offered his own bankers a loan. When he died at the age of eighty Rundell left over £1,400,000 – the equivalent to £70,000,000 today, in the largest will ever registered in Britain.

Purchased secretly by the King's secretary, these gifts were then flaunted without discretion by Elizabeth in the flamboyant manner of the newly wealthy middle class. This vulgar display produced much criticism from the older members of the aristocracy who formed the royal circle. On seeing Elizabeth in her new finery at a ball at Carlton House the waspish Lady Cowper told her brother, William Lamb, 'the family pearls she talked about last year have increased greatly, the string is twice as long as it was, and such a diamond belt, three inches wide, with such a sapphire in the centre'.[8] It was the presence of this famous sapphire on the King's mistress that most shocked observers for it was virtually a Crown jewel. The sapphire had been left to George, perhaps as a gift of reconciliation, by the last of the Stuart dynasty, the Cardinal Duke of York. He had then given it as a wedding gift to his daughter Princess Charlotte in 1816. When, to the despair of the nation, she had died in childbirth the following year the King asked her husband for its return on the pretext that he needed it for the coronation. In reality he wanted it back to give to Elizabeth Conyngham, who then decided to wear it as the centrepiece on a jewelled belt that she had made. George wholeheartedly approved of her action, sharing with her a love of ornate jewellery, orders and decorations. Such was his enthusiasm for these things that he designed the new Order of St Patrick and owned personally no fewer than fifty-five versions of the Order of the Garter. Elizabeth's magpie fascination with regalia matched his own, so that she even persuaded the King to inaugurate a new private decoration, a precursor to the Victorian Order, to be given solely to his friends. Princess Lieven was chosen to be the guinea pig to launch it in public. In April 1821 she complained:

> He has given his portrait to wear on a blue ribbon . . . Lady Conyngham wants to wear it; but it must be started by someone else; and the public must amuse itself at the expense of that someone; then Lady Conyngham will wear it when the joke is stale. I am the person considered most suitable.[9]

Expenditure on such luxuries only encouraged the mounting criticisms of the king and his greedy mistress. But any new attempt to curb the royal profligacy seemed doomed to failure because George was simply incapable of living in other than an extravagant manner. Yet there was a paradox in his character. Spendthrift that he undoubtedly was, no other British monarch in modern times had such a kind and generous heart. Quietly and consistently he subscribed large sums to numerous charities and was capable of acts of personal generosity to his friends, his servants and to even the humblest individual. When told that one of the local Brighton tradesman had attempted suicide through financial distress, the King immediately took out his pocketbook and removed the contents, over £700 in bank notes, telling his servant to send it at once to the unfortunate man. 'Bid him make use of these,' the King said, 'I may perhaps owe him something, and under such circumstances the routine of payment must appear odious.' Again, when his friend the equally extravagant Georgiana, Duchess of Devonshire, 'whose needs were perennial, and her means of raising money practically exhausted', was in trouble he provided her with a substantial personal loan.[10]

The King's wanton indulgence of Lady Conyngham drove his Keeper of the Privy Purse, Sir Benjamin Bloomfield, to distraction for he had to account personally to the government for the King's expenditure. The King, Bloomfield told his confidants, had completely lost his wits over the woman and the Privy Purse was already exhausted by paying for diamonds for Lady Conyngham. One of those who witnessed Bloomfield's constant lamentations was Charles Arbuthnot, who agreed with him that it was quite shameful the way Lady Conyngham covered herself in jewels.[11] Condemnation of Elizabeth's persistent avarice became widespread in spite of an ingenious scheme she devised to head off the criticism. Henry Hobhouse, the Under Secretary at the Home Office, claimed that she told the King in 1822 that in future 'she could not receive any [gifts] unless a similar one was made to her daughter!'[12]

The flamboyant and self-indulgent lifestyle of the lovers continued to irritate the public, fascinate the satirists and make life difficult for Benjamin Bloomfield. Contemporary prints portrayed them as the fat sybarite and his plump, greedy woman, Elizabeth being shown so fat that her eyes are almost oriental slits in her moonlike face. In most cartoons she appears with a half-moon decoration on her head in the form of a 'C', intended as a vulgar double meaning on the first part of the word Conyngham. In one year alone, 1820, over 800 scurrilous cartoons featuring either the King or Lady Conyngham appeared. The King was as much distressed by their extent as he was by their content. In a vain attempt to curtail the flow he ordered Bloomfield to use the secret service fund to suppress them. Using a go-between, one Josh Calkin, Bloomfield went furtively about London attempting to stem the flow of ridicule. Between 1819 and 1822 he handed over more than £2,600 of the taxpayers' money to bribe cartoonists not to publish their work. The best-known publisher, J.L. Marks, received £35 for withdrawing one particularly vitriolic cartoon, followed by another £500 for destroying dozens more. Marks admitted that these secret payments not only provided him with a lucrative second income but also saved him the cost of printing ink and paper. The most acerbic cartoonist of all, the great George Cruikshank, received a further £100 from Bloomfield for promising 'not to caricature His Majesty in any immoral situation'. Cruikshank then, ingeniously, devised a more subtle way of making his point by showing the King as a penitent sinner dressed in a white sheet.[13]

Such nefarious activities took their toll on Bloomfield too, as he became increasingly critical of his royal master. It was now apparent that the current royal secretary had proved no more successful than his predecessors in curbing his master's extravagance; on the contrary, it had increased significantly with the advent of Lady Conyngham in 1819. In 1821 embarrassing questions about the

King's lifestyle were being asked in Parliament and the Prime Minister Lord Liverpool had came under increasing pressure from his ministers to intervene in the King's financial affairs. Summoned to a private meeting by Lord Liverpool, Bloomfield gave him a solemn assurance that he would do all in his power to curb the King's wild spending. A new financial regime was introduced into the royal household based upon the novel concept of accountability. From that point on every area of expenditure was closely scrutinised and rigid economies ordered by Bloomfield, who was desperate to honour his promise to the government.

The chief victim of these new economy measures was, not surprisingly, Lady Conygham, who reacted with indignation to what she considered the meddling interference of a petty official in the way, as Lady Stewardess, she ran the king's household. George was instructed to tell Bloomfield to mind his own business, a message he hesitated to pass on. But the stress of reconciling a penny-pinching secretary and demanding mistress began to take its toll on the King. He frequently lost his temper with Bloomfield and was seen grabbing him by the collar and giving him 'a good hearty shake'.[14] Such treatment further alienated the secretary, who in March 1822 complained bitterly to Charles Arbuthnot that the King no longer shook hands or even spoke when he entered the room. He also claimed that, to his great embarrassment, he had been shockingly abused by the King in front of one of the royal cooks. Nevertheless Bloomfield was so persistent in his task of curtailing the household expenditure that Elizabeth finally decided that, like Lord Hertford before him, Bloomfield must be driven from the royal household forthwith. As with every conflict at Brighton or Windsor it soon became public knowledge that the Marchioness of Conyngham was determined to get rid of him at any cost. There was even a rumour that she wanted the post of Secretary herself to add to her current title of Lady Stewardess. But those closer to events at court dismissed such gossip out of hand, considering that Lady Conygham and Sir Benjamin had too much in common ever to really fall out. This same idea had now occurred to the satirists, who depicted them as a pair of thieving servants conspiring to fleece their master in his own house:

Ben Bloomfield and the fat old cook
Herself a perfect larder
A simple jig together took
The tune was Shave the Barber

But there were reasons other than financial for Elizabeth Conyng-ham to want to see the back of Benjamin Bloomfield. Not only had he originally been recommended for his post by the despised Isabella Hertford, he had also, against Elizabeth's clearly stated wishes, insisted on maintaining a warm friendship with the Hertford family. Elizabeth was concerned that, like Francis Hertford before him, Bloomfield might be carrying tales back to the enemy. While remaining 'very civil' to his face and refusing to criticise him too harshly in front of the King she now took every opportunity to subtly undermine him behind his back. One effective stratagem was to encourage her son Lord Francis to offer to help the King with some of the secretarial tasks that Bloomfield currently performed. As the resentful secretary told Charles Greville that December, 'Francis goes to the King every morning, usually breakfasts with him, and receives all his orders'.[15] Bloomfield had no doubt that in spite of her continuing smiles Lady Conyngham was responsible for this. She was, he told Greville, secretly scheming his ultimate downfall and disgrace. As proof Bloomfield offered the startling claim that he had been told as much by a certain Frenchman whose ex-mistress was now the lover of Lord Francis Conyngham. This woman had heard Lord Francis openly boasting of his mother's power over the King, of all the jewels that he had given her and of how she intended to get rid of the main witness, Sir Benjamin Bloomfield.[16] This story soon became so well known in society that even a foreign visitor to England, Captain Gronow, refers to it in his diaries, adding the twist that Elizabeth's jewels really belonged to the Crown and that as Bloomfield was the only one to know the truth he had to be removed.

As part of her strategy to replace Bloomfield with a more amenable Keeper of the Royal Purse, Elizabeth had begun grooming a suitable replacement – the egregious society physician and gynaecologist, Sir William Knighton. One of Knighton's first and most clandestine duties had been to conduct Elizabeth in a hired carriage to Carlton House without the knowledge of Sir Benjamin. Now under her subtle and insidious pressure Bloomfield's self-confidence began to wilt. He began to lose his grip on affairs and, in turn, the confidence of the King. When his salary was abruptly stopped by royal command Bloomfield knew his departure was imminent. In desperation he began lobbying his political cronies at Westminster and openly blaming the Machiavellian scheming of Lady Conyngham for his threatened downfall. His natural audience should have been the Whig opposition but they were unimpressed by his complaints of royal betrayal for Elizabeth's brother and a member of their own party, the irreproachably respectable William Denison, had told them a different story. His sister, he revealed, had told him in confidence that the real reason for wanting Bloomfield removed was a strange event that had occurred in Dublin a few weeks before the royal visit. Bloomfield had gone ahead to supervise the final arrangements and had decided one evening to visit a local theatre. In an attempt to impress what he believed was an important representative of the King himself the manager of the theatre ordered the national anthem be played as Bloomfield entered his box. The audience, believing that a member of the royal family had joined them, stood up and joined in a rousing chorus of 'God Save the King'. Unwisely tempted by this unexpected adulation Bloomfield had stepped forward, smiled and bowed royally to the audience.[17] When told of this hilarious event the King's usual sense of humour failed him and he told friends that he took Bloomfield's behaviour as a 'personal affront to himself'. As a result Bloomfield was immediately excluded from the glass-walled sitting room at the Brighton Pavilion known as the 'Magic Lantern' where the King met his intimates every day.

Yet another, and more credible, explanation for Bloomfield's demise was given by the courtier Sir William Freemantle who in a letter to the Duke of Buckingham claims that an unannounced audit of the previous year's coronation expenses revealed in the spring of 1822 that a large sum of money was unaccounted for. When Bloomfield was questioned he admitted that the deficit resulted from a large purchase of diamonds that he had made, as he put it, 'by order of the King'.[18] It appeared that George had blithely added some personal gifts to the coronation expenses much as a salesman might add a purchase from the hotel shop to his bill. In spite of his predicament the King was adamant that Bloomfield should have held his tongue. This awkward revelation served to confirm George's growing conviction that Bloomfield was losing his touch, for in the past he could always be relied on to bury such compromising evidence beyond fear of detection. What particularly appalled the King was that Bloomfield had implicated him in the affair, although it is difficult to see what else the wretched man could have done other than to confess to stealing the money himself. The destination of the diamonds was no mystery to William Freemantle, however, who was certain that they had ended up adorning the neck of Lady Conyngham. Indeed they may well have been the jewels that she kissed so publicly during the coronation ceremony. It was a sorry business resulting, thought Freemantle, 'from an intrigue in the party now governing at the Pavilion'.[19] Again in the mysterious passage of scandal from court to cartoonist a print by J.L. Marks appeared putting the blame for the whole sordid affair entirely on the King and his crafty mistress.

GEORGE IV (fondling Lady Conyngham): Turn him out! . . . Have I not a right to give my precious stones to whom I like?
LADY C.: let me have the care of your purse.
GEORGE: You shall, my Cunning-one, and my precious stones too.

Obligingly Marks sent a proof copy of this across to Carlton House before running it off in volume. The King was horrified and immediately sent Bloomfield down to Fleet Street for the last time to deal with Marks. This was to be the last such secret payment, for when the sanctimonious Sir William Knighton became royal secretary he ordered that the practice cease. Bloomfield handed over £45 to stop the publication and Marks, having surreptitiously printed off a few copies for reference, destroyed the plate in front of him. No evidence existed that the money was ever drawn nor was any receipt given by the publisher. Given Bloomfield's shady past dealings it would not be surprising if some of these bribes, as rumoured, did find their way into his own pocket. Indeed in the year before his dismissal Bloomfield, realising that his lucrative position would soon be gone, was rumoured to have spent over £100,000 on buying property in Ireland.[20]

Benjamin Bloomfield was a man who knew many secrets. Whatever peculation he may have been involved was less important to the King and his mistress than his potential for exposing their own secrets. The King was, therefore, greatly relieved when his ministers agreed, at his insistence, that Bloomfield must be induced to go, and go quietly. In return for his acquiescence he would be rewarded with a generous settlement. With Sir William Knighton's assistance the King wrote to the Prime Minister, Lord Liverpool, asking him to abolish the post of Private Secretary. This he thought would make Bloomfield's departure appear as a political rather than a royal decision, so providing the face-saving stratagem that Bloomfield desired. Lord Liverpool then informed Bloomfield of the cabinet's decision, taking great pains to exonerate both the King and Lady Conyngham from any blame in the matter. He assured him that it was not from 'any preference to any other individual, nor from want of any personal confidence' that his office was to be abolished. As compensation he was offered the Governorship of Ceylon or, if he preferred, his current salary for life and, at the King's suggestion, the Order of the Bath.[21] Bloomfield thought he merited far more than this and insisted that he should, at least, be given an English peerage. When the King was told of this demand he flew into a rage and threatened to do to Bloomfield what he done with the late Queen – ostracise him and drive him out of society.

Eventually Bloomfield, ever the pragmatist, came to an agreement with his master. Although he refused the offer of Ceylon he agreed to accept the Bath, a sinecure worth £650 a year and the Governorship of Fort Charles in Jamaica, which he would later exchange for the post of Minister at Stockholm. But he excused himself from receiving the Bath from the King's own hand; for that he would have to go down to Brighton where he would have to again face his hated nemesis, Lady Conyngham.[22] Bloomfield accepted his fate with equanimity and, having been a libertine all his life, unexpectedly embraced Christianity as an apparently devout convert to Methodism. Soon passers-by were amused to see on the door of his London house in Portman Square a large white placard bearing the words 'At Prayer'.

This royal largesse appalled those like Thomas Creevey who had always despised Bloomfield, considering him little better than a common footman, 'having made himself a fortune by palpable cheating and robbery in every department'.[23] Although constantly suspected of sharp practice Bloomfield had, nonetheless, been a popular character and his demise was attributed by the press entirely to the baleful influence of Lady Conyngham. Yet another wave of criticism of this seemingly all-powerful and wilful woman now swept through London and the cartoons and satires mocking her became even more bitter. This incessant abuse from the media had a marked effect on public opinion. When the Conyngham family next arrived at the Windsor races the crowd applauded the King but hissed and hooted Lady Conyngham. This public animosity must have had its effect on the Conynghams, invulnerable as they appeared, for at the end of the year John Wilson Croker, a shrewd observer of the royal scene, thought the whole family was behaving far more meekly. Only the most ill-natured of people, he thought, could now find them in any way objectionable for as he told a friend:

> You have heard of their intrigues for station and office – all false. I know and can assure you that they asked for nothing – and the King's kindness towards Lord Conyngham, natural as it was, was not only spontaneous upon His Majesty's part, but, I might almost say, imposed upon him.[24]

Croker's kind words would have had little effect, however, on the King's sisters, who had got on very well with Bloomfield. They continued to ignore Elizabeth much as they had done from the start of their brother's affair with her, arguing that since their brother had forbidden them to speak to the late Queen Caroline on the grounds of her immorality he could not now expect them to converse with his mistress.

Yet in spite of the private and public hostility she provoked there were many in Britain who entertained a sneaking regard for Elizabeth and an admiration for the way she had taken control of the King's domestic regime at Brighton. Another diarist of the period, Charles Wynn, told his friend the Duke of Buckingham that even the congregation of the fashionable Caledonian Chapel in Hatton Garden knew what was meant when the Presbyterian preacher, Mr Irving, whenever Lady Conyngham was in the congregation, spoke not of the heavenly mansion but of the heavenly Pavilion.[25]

# NINE

## *Playing Politics*

While the domestic drama of Bloomfield's reluctant departure dominated events at Brighton the political life of the country began to focus on the problem of George Canning. With Lord Londonderry gone, this highly capable and intelligent political maverick was the natural choice for the important office of Foreign Secretary. The problem for the Prime Minister, Lord Liverpool, was that both the King and his increasingly influential mistress heartily disliked Canning and were opposed to his presence in the cabinet. At this time British governments thought the sovereign's consent essential before making any senior ministerial appointment. As far as George and Elizabeth were concerned Canning had already demonstrated his unsuitability for high office by giving his sovereign deep personal offence. It was common knowledge that in 1820 Canning had become involved in a brief but highly embarrassing sexual episode with the late Queen Caroline. On the pretext of discussing her impending divorce she had invited him to dinner one evening, got him drunk then made love to him vigorously on her drawing room sofa.[1] Canning had been literally seduced into taking her side against the King. For a man of his political astuteness he appeared, on this occasion, to have been incredibly naive, but for Caroline this was a proven way of recruiting a man for her cause and she had dealt with the equally unfortunate Henry Brougham in a similar manner. Caroline made sure that Canning's fate became known to his colleagues and the newest and most promising member of Lord Liverpool's ministry was so compromised that he had no alternative but to resign as President of the Board of Trade.

The death of Lord Londonderry appeared to many in the Tory party to be the ideal opportunity to bring about Canning's return to high office and they implored Lord Liverpool to ignore the King's objections. It was fortunate for them that Canning was even in London for after months of pleading Lord Liverpool had eventually persuaded the King to agree his appointment as Governor-General of India. However Canning's departure had been unexpectedly delayed by bureaucratic wrangling and he was still in London when Londonderry's death was announced. At once many of Canning's Tory colleagues began clamouring for his appointment. Fearing a serious split in the party Lord Liverpool was forced reluctantly to carry his cabinet's demand to the King. George cleverly avoided an outright confrontation by passing the dilemma and the responsibility for a solution back to his Prime Minister by asking 'if I could get over that which is so intimately connected with my private honour, all might be well, but how, my friend is that to be effected?'[2]

Although dismissed at the start of their relationship as an empty-headed woman, Elizabeth had by 1822 become a significant influence on the King's political thought and opinions. Anyone seeking to persuade the King on a particular issue, as the Duke of Wellington had found, now thought it wise to lobby Lady Conyngham first. Princess Lieven, her nose deep as ever in the political intrigues of the time, told Metternich on 5 September that Lady Conyngham was currently closely involved with the King in delicate negotiations with Lord Liverpool over the appointment of George Canning. 'She knows what the King wishes, and his Ministers don't. . . . On this point she is very discreet . . . the King has his mind made up. Which way it is made up I have no idea.'[3]

What is surprising is that George had begun to involve Elizabeth in his political responsibilities in a way that he had done with no previous mistress. Without the knowledge of his ministers he asked Elizabeth to use Princess Lieven as an emissary to sound out European reaction to Canning's proposed appointment as Foreign Secretary. At Elizabeth's request the Princess contacted both the Tsar of Russia and the Austrian Minister, Prince Metternich. A few weeks later she reported back to Elizabeth that given Canning's reputation as a decided liberal in foreign affairs, it pleased neither. Once again Elizabeth urged the King to stand firm against the appointment but George again came under pressure to bend to his Prime Minister's wishes. In the meantime Canning had found influential but discreet support within the royal household from the King's new secretary,

Sir William Knighton, who like him was a maverick and outsider. After all the previous skirmishes with ministers the King no longer had the stomach for a prolonged fight and he decided to end the dispute on the best terms he could get. A few days later when Elizabeth entered his dressing room George told her that he proposed, reluctantly, to agree to Canning's appointment. At this she threw up her hands and gave 'a cry of alarm', at which the King said to her bluntly, 'very well, if you like I will not appoint him; I will change the Government and put in the Whigs'.[4] Elizabeth reportedly gave another cry of alarm at that prospect for in spite of her supposed friendship with the opposition leaders she knew full well the consequences if the government fell. The blame would undoubtedly be laid at her door. But the King insisted that that was the only realistic alternative to the present impasse since Lord Liverpool had assured him that the government could not stand without Canning. The best he could do was to try and gain future concessions from Lord Liverpool in return for agreeing to Canning's appointment. 'I have', he said, 'sacrificed my private feelings . . . for the good of the public service . . . I therefore look with confidence to a similar return.'[5]

On 8 September the King formally announced his defeat in the matter and said to his ministers, 'very well gentlemen. Since you are determined to have him, take him in God's name but remember I tell you he will throw you all overboard.'[6] Privately he told Lord Liverpool that in ignoring his private feelings he was making the greatest sacrifice in his life and to make sure that Canning knew it. He should also remind the new Foreign Secretary that 'the brightest ornament of his crown was the power of giving grace and favour to a subject who may have incurred his displeasure'.[7] But Canning showed little initial gratitude for this supposed royal largesse, for he had bitterly resented the King's constant hostility towards him. In a fit of pique he refused at first to accept the appointment, saying that it was like being giving a ticket to Almacks, the most exclusive society club in London, on which someone had written 'admit the rogue'.[8] But the Duke of Wellington, although on the opposite wing of the Tory party, advised Canning not to be a fool and urged him to accept the office. The Duke was delighted with the outcome, particularly as he was recovering from a serious illness and Lady

Conyngham had written to tell him how great had been their relief when Knighton brought word that he was better and that the King had agreed to take Canning. She hoped that 'now the King had yielded his inclination to the wishes and advice of his Ministers, that they would behave to him better than they had done'.[9]

With his new and supposedly dangerous liberal Foreign Secretary in place the King went into another emotional decline, perhaps apprehensive of how his fellow European monarchs would react towards him. As always when he became fearful of public opinion, he stopped going out, spending most of the day in Elizabeth's company when not attending to state business. These seemingly incessant confrontations with his ministers were clearly taking their toll on his health and when Princess Lieven saw him soon after Canning's appointment she thought him much changed, commenting that he had 'aged a great deal in the last three months'.[10] To his perennial gout was now added, according to Emily Cowper, who had spoken to one of his doctors, 'irregularity of the pulse, occasional pain about the praecordia, sensation in the left arm and sudden breathlessness'.[11]

Since his return from Ireland the King had shown an increasing tendency to avoid his responsibilities in London, preferring to remain at Brighton with Elizabeth and his close circle of friends. This not only infuriated his ministers – who were forced to travel constantly down from London to negotiate state business – but also, more ominously, withdrew him from the public view. By the spring of 1823 George IV had been absent from the public scene for so long that the newspapers speculated gloomily that he must have gone the way of his poor father and become a mad recluse. Wellington, who had weekly audiences with him, thought the King in sad decline and began to feel that he would be dead within the year. News of George's supposed decline soon reached the ears of his brother the Duke of York, the heir to the throne. The Duke was now seen to be paying unaccustomed attention to public affairs. Fears of an impending royal demise must have touched Elizabeth too, for Princess Lieven thought she appeared to be 'taking precautions against the future'. When the Princess attended a reception at the Conynghams' London house Elizabeth said to her sadly 'what a pity now if all this were to end; for you must admit that it is charming'.

As she said these words, the Princess noted, she gazed around her drawing room, which was like an over-decorated 'fairy's boudoir'. What she would regret most if the King died, the Princess suggested acidly to Metternich, would be the loss of his diamonds, pearls, handsome furniture and good dinners and his ability to promote the interests of her family. But the King, she thought, was only too aware of all this for, 'here is a lover with his eyes wide open . . . any one but myself might take it into her head to become her rival'. For the King had whispered to the Princess after dinner that very evening, 'you see how she takes advantage of her position to push her family. Oh, she knows very well when she is well off.'[12]

As an insurance against the future Elizabeth began to build bridges with the now highly influential Mr Canning. He in turn saw the good sense in accommodating, if not the King himself, then his influential mistress. At first nothing could be done to improve the relationship as George remained firm in the opinion, which he claimed to share with the Duke of Wellington, that Canning was an incompetent. He was no more capable of conducting foreign affairs, George pointedly told Princess Lieven, than her own baby. In particular he resented Canning's suggestion that he should invite the King and Queen of the Sandwich Islands, who were visiting London, to dinner – protesting that he was not prepared to sit at a table with such a 'pair of damned cannibals!' He did not have a much higher opinion of Lord Liverpool, who had got him into all this trouble, for even if the Prime Minister lived to Doomsday, he told Wellington, he would 'never be made fit for the high office, to which I raised him'.[13]

Consequently from the moment of his appointment George had seized every opportunity to embarrass and annoy his new Foreign Minister. He even sent Sir William Knighton to the Continent on secretive missions without informing the Foreign Office, as he should have done. Then in a direct violation of diplomatic procedure he sent a personal letter to Prince Metternich inviting him to come to England and stay at the Royal Lodge so they could discuss the international situation in private. On the one occasion that Canning was himself invited to Windsor he was goaded by the King into an outburst in which he declared his conviction that Metternich cared nothing for democracy and was hell-bent on wiping out all constitutional government in Europe. The King, delighted by the reaction he had caused, replied jauntily that he saw no harm in that at all 'as long as our constitution is among them'.[14]

As if in response to this royal provocation Canning, in the spring of 1824, accepted an invitation to a banquet at the Mansion House given by the Lord Mayor Robert Waithman, a keen supporter of the late Queen. Canning went along knowing full well that a large portrait of Caroline would be displayed ostentatiously in full view of the diners. George was furious when he heard and raised his bid in this poker game of insults by, at the instigation of Princess Lieven, inviting a number of European ambassadors down to Windsor for a whole week where he and Elizabeth entertained them in private. The party, consisting of the Austrian Lievens, the Russian Esterhazys, their aide Baron Neumann and the French ambassador, Prince Polignac, was immediately dubbed 'the Cottage clique' by the newspapers. At first delighted at her part in getting the King to disobey his ministers, the Princess was soon complaining that these regular get-togethers were proving to be so dreary and boring that she felt close to tears. Each monotonous day brought the same routine for the guests: an afternoon drive or boat trip on the river followed by gargantuan dinner with conversation so stupid that she began to doubt her own sanity. Once, she claimed, when the boredom had caused her to fall asleep at the table she awoke to find the company silent and the King gazing at Lady Conyngham with an expression in which 'sleep battled with love'. Elizabeth, in turn, sat staring at an enormous emerald on her arm while her daughter, beside her, toyed with a large ruby at her neck.[15] Frequently the tedium and formality of these occasions produced a tension among the guests that only laughter could relieve. On such an evening, the Princess told Metternich, during an unusually long silence after grace she was seized with an uncontrollable fit of laughter that soon infected Lady Elizabeth Conyngham and then Admiral Nagle, who knocked over a bottle of wine in his merriment. This gave everyone the excuse to join in. The King made it even more hilarious by assuming that they were all laughing at him.[16]

By June the following year the monotony of life at Windsor had begun to take its toll as George's increasingly short temper and Elizabeth's unconcealed boredom led to the first serious quarrel between them. Elizabeth complained bitterly that she felt under a 'terrible restraint and confinement' and was determined to leave Windsor and go abroad. So serious did the situation become, according to Thomas Creevey, that the King's old friend Lord Lauderdale was called in as mediator to dissuade Elizabeth from actually leaving. Lauderdale reminded her that she had become involved with the King of her own free will and that it was now 'her bounded duty' to submit and go through with it.[17] After much consideration that must have included a realisation that it would mean giving up the royal patrimony forever, Elizabeth relented and withdrew her threat.

A year had passed but the hostility between the King and his Foreign Minister continued unresolved. Then in August Canning decided to break the impasse and drove unexpectedly down to Brighton and offered Elizabeth's son, Lord Francis Conyngham, a post in the government as his Under-Secretary of State at the Foreign Office. Lord Francis was delighted at the offer for he had recently married Lady Jane Paget, the daughter of the Marquess of Anglesea. The relationship between the King and his ministers was now so bad that they objected to the marriage taking place at the state-owned Carlton House. The King suggested that the couple use the Royal Lodge at Windsor instead and, generous as ever, purchased for them as a wedding present Hollygrove, a large house in Windsor Great Park. Canning's offer of a government position to Lord Francis was seen by all parties as a clever move, even though it was later revealed that he had already offered it to four other Tories who had all declined.[18] This apparently spontaneous gesture was immediately reciprocated and both the King and Lady Conyngham implored him to stay on for dinner that evening. Canning's move demonstrated his astuteness in realising that a grateful mistress would produce a more compliant King. For as Princess Lieven shrewdly guessed, the idea of Lord Francis's appointment had not originated with Canning at all but with Elizabeth herself. It was she who had first suggested it to the King and he had taken it up with alacrity, knowing that the time was ripe for Canning to make a gesture of reconciliation. 'He is a clever man,' the King told her, 'he is trying to win me over . . . I wanted him to give Francis the post and he did it.' But the Princess, who did not think much of Lord Francis, considered it merely cynical opportunism by Elizabeth, for 'the young man is no use in the office and the mistress wants this done because it means a salary of £3,200; and money is always the surest way to her heart'.[19] The real loser in the Canning affair proved to be Princess Lieven, who had been as much opposed to Canning as any of the European governments. The new Foreign Secretary would now frustrate all her attempts to bring about closer contacts between George IV his fellow monarchs. Yet she continued to see Elizabeth Conyngham as an invaluable source of information about the King's political opinions and to encourage his now unlikely trip to Europe. As she told Metternich:

> Have seen the favourite. She welcomed me in a most gushing way; but I did not receive any interesting information . . . she is not particularly well disposed to Mr Canning and laughed with me over his cleverness in the giving the post to her son adding 'I should have been a fool not to take advantage of it' . . . she sighed a score of times over the King not going to Verona. I told her we must manage it better next summer.[20]

The Princess also saw in Canning's appointment the increasingly powerful hand of Sir William Knighton, 'the man-midwife who is really Prime Minister'. She believed that Knighton was now the coming power at Court. He was rumoured to be cultivating Canning to further his own ambition to be appointed a Privy Councillor but 'Mr Canning who regards him as his declared enemy, said curtly that he would never consent. The refusal naturally offended the man-midwife, and he is not a man to be offended with impunity . . . everyone is afraid of him from the King downwards. He controls newspapers, caricatures, public business. He works underground.'[21]

Knighton himself was absent in France at the time, having gone to Bagneres at Elizabeth's request to give his expert opinion on the medical condition of her eldest son, the Earl of Mount Charles. She had told Knighton that although she was keen to visit the sick young man herself she feared leaving the King alone at Windsor. He thought the reason for this was that the King might take up with someone else in her absence and although 'she could do without his love she could not do without his diamonds'.[22] Knighton arrived in

France to find the medical facilities so inadequate that he insisted that Lord Mount Charles be transferred at once to a hospital in the city of Nice, then in Italy, before returning to England himself. As an experienced doctor Knighton was able to make sure that the sick young man received the best treatment available. But his efforts were in vain for a few months later in January 1825 Henry Mount Charles died and his mother, overcome with grief, insisted on leaving Windsor to go into mourning in London.

There is a curious postscript to the story for Lady Charlotte Bury, a lady-in-waiting to the late Queen Caroline and one of the great gossips of the age, later claimed that Lord Mount Charles had secretly married a young woman in Switzerland. She had given birth to a son who was consequently the legal heir to the Conyngham titles and land. Elizabeth was determined that her second son 'dear Frank' should succeed his brother and she instructed her old protégé Charles Sumner, now Bishop of Llandaff, to travel secretly to Switzerland and to offer Mount Charles's widow a large sum of money if she agreed to conceal both her marriage and the existence of the boy. The widow accepted and Sumner was rewarded on his return with the more prestigious Bishopric of Winchester. This demonstrated, wrote Lady Charlotte, not only Lady Conyngham's deviousness but also her power over the King, for 'she can achieve whatever she wishes'.[23]

Bereft of his intimate companion for the first time in months the King grew increasingly morose and bad-tempered with those around him. Although Elizabeth claimed to be too distressed by grief to return to Windsor for some time George, always suspicious of her fidelity, began to suspect that other matters might be keeping her in London. He had long known that his brother Frederick, Duke of York, held a secret passion for Elizabeth and thought he might even now be paying court to her. These jealous suspicions increased dramatically when Elizabeth, uncharacteristically, failed to reply to his letters. When she did finally return to Windsor a month later she shocked him even more by confessing that the Duke of York had indeed been most attentive to her in London and had sent her a touching letter of condolence. This appeared to confirm George's fears and in a furious rage a week later he used his brother's mild criticism of the management of the civil list to subject him to such a haranguing that the wretched man left the Royal Lodge without a word.[24]

With Elizabeth restored to him the King's anger soon subsided and he took new enjoyment from their domestic bliss. The management of the household was now left exclusively to the Marquess of Conyngham as George and Elizabeth spent more time together. Each evening they now dined privately upstairs, Elizabeth claiming that she was still too upset to see anyone. For several weeks no guests were invited to the Lodge until this second honeymoon period had run its course. Inevitably Elizabeth's mood again changed and there were signs of the return of her old dissatisfaction, which Charles Greville noticed she did little to hide:

> She sometimes endeavours to assume popular and gracious manners but she does this languidly and awkwardly . . . she carries ennui to such a pitch that even in the society of most intimate friends she frequently owns that she is bored to death.[25]

Her body language said it all as she slumped down on to a sofa each evening after dinner and lay back with her eyes closed, ignoring fellow guests and not speaking a word. Thomas Creevey, who witnessed several of these petulant episodes, thought it no wonder that the opinion had grown that 'she hates Kingy'. He also thought her 'very restless and impatient under what she calls her terrible restraint and confinement'. Creevey was therefore not surprised when Elizabeth announced to the assembled company at dinner one evening that she was determined to travel abroad in the near future. Princess Lieven also thought these displays of undisguised discontent would eventually compromise her entire relationship with the sovereign. 'How the King will hate her if ever the turn does begin,' the Princess wrote, 'for, considering his extreme kindness to her, she really does make him a most ungrateful return. She detests him, shows it plainly and yet continues to accept all his presents, which are of enormous value.'[26]

But Elizabeth could, at least, enjoy the satisfaction of seeing her favourite son a member of the government. Others saw Lord Francis's appointment as yet another shameful example of Lady Conyngham's blatant nepotism and the wit Lord Alvanley began referring disparagingly to him as 'Canningham'. Some political observers, including Princess Lieven, thought George Canning had fatally compromised himself, for he could never escape the accusation that he had appointed the ill-qualified son of a royal mistress to an important government ministry. The Princess was convinced that from now on Canning would have to cultivate his new friendship with the Conynghams if he wished to retain the support of the King.[27] Duplicitous as always, she took a different line with Lord Francis when he called on her, advising him always to be the King's man and never Canning's. In spite of Canning's known opposition to the project the Princess still hoped, against all the odds, that Elizabeth would eventually persuade the King to override ministerial advice and visit his fellow monarchs in Europe. As part of her new strategy she began to pay more attention to Lord Francis himself, using flattery and encouragement to ingratiate herself with this important new member of the Foreign Ministry.

George Canning meanwhile had begun to enjoy his new popularity with the monarch and his lady and was now to be seen walking in the grounds of the Pavilion with the King's arm draped affectionately around his shoulder. With growing confidence in the relationship he decided to buy a house nearby and even asked George's permission to walk with his wife in the Pavilion grounds. This was readily granted and the refreshing cordiality between King and Foreign Minister proved unexpectedly useful when the King discovered to his horror in August 1825 that Elizabeth's old love John, now Lord Ponsonby, had unexpectedly arrived back from Corfu. A few days after his return Elizabeth had run into him in Lady Jersey's drawing room and had reacted with such emotion, almost fainting away, that when the King was told of it he was thoroughly alarmed.[28] Nothing, it appeared, had changed in fifteen years and Ponsonby's mere presence in London was a clear threat to the King's peace of mind.

In a panic the King summoned his Foreign Minister down to Brighton and implored him to get the wretched man out of the country at any cost. A diplomatic post must be found for him even though 'the handsomest man in England' knew nothing of diplomacy. When Canning promptly suggested that Ponsonby could be made Envoy Extraordinary in far away Buenos Aires the King, according to Princess Lieven, 'nearly swooned with gratitude'.[29] So Ponsonby was sent off to South America and acquitted himself so well there that he was soon made British Ambassador to Turkey. The King was relieved and delighted to see the back of this potential rival and grateful to George Canning too. There were other reasons for him to feel grateful to Canning. As King of Great Britain George was now enjoying the new respect that Canning's tougher and more liberal foreign policy was earning for him among his fellow European monarchs.[30] This he rightly attributed to his government's radical policy of leading the way in recognising the new Latin American states that were breaking away from Spain. George, to his surprise, suddenly found himself elevated from being the fifth member of the old conservative club of European monarchy to the leader of the fashionable new liberalism.

For the next two years the relationship between Canning and the King continued to improve as both he and Elizabeth came to recognise the Foreign Minister's undoubted abilities. She in particular found him open-minded and a welcome relief after the implacable hostility she had endured from the late Lord Londonderry. Then on 17 February 1827 the Prime Minister, Lord Liverpool, suffered a massive stroke that meant he could no longer continue in office. The King, as always in a crisis, went into a decline. As Elizabeth told her brother William Denison, 'he would not permit any one whatsoever to speak to him on the subject of his successor as Prime Minister'. Paralysed by the need to make a decision George remained in seclusion at Brighton, ignoring his ministers' frantic appeals and seeing only servants, tailors and doctors. 'Was there ever such a child or Bedlamite. Or was there ever such a set of lickspittles as his Ministers to endure such conduct,' wrote Creevey. 'What the devil is it come to?'[31]

One of the obvious candidates for Prime Minister was the dull but highly capable Robert Peel but the King disliked his provincial manners, particularly his awkward habit of holding out his hands while talking, and Elizabeth dismissed him out of hand as a kinsman of the still reviled Hertfords. The choice, the King decided, must be between his old favourite, the Duke of Wellington, and his new, George Canning. So both were invited down to the Royal Lodge to be interviewed by the King. By lunchtime Canning had gloomily accepted that his cause was lost and the Duke would get the job. But then the King announced that they should all, including the ubiquitous Princess Lieven, go out for a drive in the pony carriages that were such a feature of life at the Lodge. As they were all about to move off the King suddenly got down from his seat beside Elizabeth and went over to Canning, taking him by the arm and leading him back into the house as he gestured to the rest of the party to drive on.[32] After questioning him in great detail about his attitude to the Roman Catholic issue and receiving an assurance from Canning that he would proceed with caution on the matter, the King without more ado offered him the premiership. On hearing the news later that day half the cabinet, including an outraged Duke of Wellington and Robert Peel, promptly resigned. With little more than the rump of the Tory party as his support, Canning had little option but to ask the Whigs to join him in a coalition. Although their leader Earl Grey personally refused, sufficient Whigs agreed to join him in Canning to make his government viable. To the more extreme Tories George Canning was now anathema. An arriviste son of an actress, albeit an old Etonian, Canning had made little secret of his intention, when Prime Minister, to break the traditional hold of the British aristocracy on public life. In this he had the active and influential support of Sir William Knighton who, ambitious and opportunistic as ever, had already chosen as his reward for pleading Canning's case to the King, the Chancellorship of the Duchy of Lancaster. But neither Canning's political reform nor Knighton's ambitions were to be realised, for three months after taking office Canning fell ill. He died in the first week of August 1827 at the Duke of Devonshire's house at Chiswick. 'This may be hard upon me,' Canning had said on his deathbed, 'but it is harder upon the King.'[33]

# TEN

## *A Nasty Scandal*

Once again the King was faced with the wearisome task of finding a Prime Minister. This time he decided with surprising alacrity to choose George Canning's closest ministerial colleague, the uninspiring Lord Goderich. But when Goderich drove down to Windsor later that same month to kiss hands the King appeared to have forgotten the purpose of his visit. His sole concern appeared to be the pet giraffe that had just arrived as a gift from the Pasha of Egypt. The King was so taken with his new pet that only when Goderich was about to leave, having been introduced to the giraffe, did he remember to officially confirm his appointment as Prime Minister. George also asked him to honour Canning's promise to leave both parliamentary reform and Catholic emancipation well alone for the present. As soon as the new Prime Minister had departed the King returned happily to the far more appealing company of his giraffe.[1]

This exotic animal was the latest addition to the growing royal menagerie at Windsor that so delighted George and Elizabeth. Already it contained leopards and lions and such tropical birds as ostriches, eagles, cranes, macaws and wild swans. The more docile pets, the deer, kangaroos, zebras and giant tortoises, were often led out to be petted by the royal guests. But it was the new giraffe that captured both the King's and the public's imagination that summer. All who saw it were impressed by the animal's grace and beauty. 'Imagine something midway between the eye of the finest Arab horse and the loveliest southern girl,' wrote one entranced visitor, 'with long and coal-black lashes and the most exquisite beaming expression of tenderness and softness united to volcanic fire.' One of the more amiable cartoons of George and Elizabeth together, *The Camelopard or a New Hobby*, shows them mounted together on its

155

back as it is led by a keeper through Windsor Great Park. Elizabeth shared the King's passion for the giraffe and she asked him to have its portrait painted together with its Egyptian attendants. The eminent French artist Jacques-Laurent Agasse was chosen for the task, and the result was much admired. But the giraffe soon became an unexpected liability when it was taken by the cartoonists as a symbol of the King's complete indifference to the plight of his common subjects and his perverse obsession with the bizarre and exotic. Sadly the chill English climate proved unsuitable for the animal and it died suddenly the following year leaving George and Elizabeth heartbroken. But its memory lingered and even when gone the giraffe was still remembered, its skeleton appearing in a cartoon as part of the booty being carried off to Ireland by the Conyngham family after the King's death in 1830.

Unfortunately the offhand manner of Goderich's appointment at Windsor did little for his self-confidence. Notoriously dithering and indecisive, he attempted to fill the role of Prime Minister but soon appeared incapable of uniting a government composed of disparate elements. Lacking Canning's keen intellect and determination Goderich failed to control his ministers and his indecision threatened to reduce the government of the country to chaos. Life became even more difficult for the wretched man when Sir William Knighton began leaking evidence to *The Times* that confirmed Goderich's sheer incompetence.[2] On 8 January 1828 he could take the strain of office no longer and drove down to Windsor where, weeping openly, he tendered his resignation to the King. George, always moved by strong emotion in others, immediately took out his own pocket-handkerchief and implored Goderich to wipe his eyes with it. The sudden departure of a new Prime Minister was so unexpected to those outside Westminster that many, without a shred of evidence, saw it to be the work of the interfering Lady Conyngham. Within a few days of Goderich's departure the Duke of Wellington was summoned to Windsor to be told that he was Prime Minister at last. He found the sovereign still in bed and dressed in a grubby silk jacket and an even dirtier silk turban. As explanation for his unkempt appearance George told Wellington that he had not felt well since Christmas and was constantly racked with gout and rheumatism.[3] With Wellington now firmly in charge of the country political stability soon returned, allowing the King time to deal with another royal scandal that threatened to bring the monarchy into further disrepute.

For some years the infamous courtesan Harriette Wilson had been living beyond reach of her creditors in Paris. To restore her depleted fortunes she had decided to publish her memoirs in London recounting the numerous liaisons she had enjoyed with dozens of the British aristocracy and, so she claimed, a senior member of the royal family. Harriette had seen how successful Mary Ann Clarke, the mistress of another of the King's brothers, Frederick, Duke of York, had been in extracting money from the royal family. Mary Ann considered that the Duke was keeping her short of cash so she had devised an ingenious scheme to counter his meanness. From time to time, usually late at night, she would produce household bills for their love nest in London that needed his signature. Among them she surreptitiously placed authorisations for army commissions which he signed inadvertently and which she then sold on for large sums of money. When news of this scam leaked out it caused a national scandal, not least because of the Duke's own suspected collusion in the sordid business. The scandal even threatened the monarchy until a parliamentary investigation in 1809 found Mary Ann guilty but the Duke innocent. The Opposition, however, seized on the verdict to force the indignant Duke to resign his command of the army. Ever the opportunist, Mary Ann capitalised on the furore by immediately writing her memoirs, of which 20,000 copies were sold in the year of publication alone. She followed this financial coup with another by which she sold the Duke back his own love letters to her for the considerable sum of £10,000. In a final display of opportunism she demanded and was granted a government pension of £400 a year for life.[4] The lessons of the Mary Ann Clarke affair were not lost on Harriette Wilson.

The most successful courtesan of her age, Harriette was the daughter of a prosperous Mayfair clockmaker and had followed the lead of her eldest sister by taking an aristocratic lover at the age of fifteen. Within a few years she had become the most celebrated professional mistress of her time. Relying on a lively personality rather than her mundane looks, she soon became rich enough to have her own box at the theatre. Here she openly entertained friends and lovers in the company of her sisters and other courtesans. Harriette Wilson was in such demand that she was soon able to pick and choose her lovers. She was said to have rejected the overtures of the Austrian ambassador, Prince Esterhazy, because (in the Austrian custom) he kept his hat on in her presence.

Now living under her married name of Mrs Rochfort, Harriette warned London society that her memoirs would shortly be appearing in instalments. They would, she threatened, contain the most intimate details of all her affairs and liaisons with members of the British aristocracy. Those of her old lovers wishing to avoid mention must now pay her a fee or else suffer the consequences. Among the astonished recipients of this novel variation on the traditional blackmail letter were the Duke of Wellington, Lord Brougham and Elizabeth's son, Lord Francis Conyngham. It was Lord Francis, Harriette insouciantly claimed, who had 'persuaded and encouraged' her to put pen to paper in the first place. Harriette and Francis had become lovers when she found herself attracted by his beautiful blue eyes, although she soon discovered that he was 'rather cold but amiable and truly unaffected'. She refused to allow herself to fall completely in love with him, she claimed, 'because he had the tremendous bad taste not to fall in love with me'.[5] She had also been rather put off by his irritating cough and constant ill health. Rather did he inspire in her 'the tenderness of a mamma'. Francis decided that being mothered by Harriette had its erotic attractions and began referring to her in his letters as 'ma chere mama'. These maternal feelings did not stop her attempting to blackmail him into paying a substantial fee not to be mentioned in the publication, although she graciously left it to Lord Francis 'to dedemanger me with whatever sum he thought appropriate'. It was the same formula that Harriette was to apply to her other victims, leaving them to nominate themselves the exact amount they should pay.[6]

So great was her clout in society at this time that Harriette sent these blackmailing letters off to England in the British Embassy diplomatic bag. When the Duke of Wellington received his he told Harriette promptly and famously to 'publish and be damned', but the radical politician and lawyer Henry Brougham proved far less resolute and was even inveigled by Harriette into acting as her

London agent. This was just one of many embarrassing episodes in Brougham's disaster-prone life. Not only had he made the mistake of taking Harriette as a lover but he had also unwisely agreed to defend the late Queen at her divorce trial, doing irreparable damage to his future relationship with the King. Perhaps he had little choice in the matter for, like George Canning, he had accepted Caroline's invitation to a party only to find himself the sole guest. After a tête-à-tête dinner he was promptly and expertly seduced by Caroline on a sofa. A man of great intellectual ability, Brougham nevertheless remained a maverick and a social outsider all his life. It was said of him, 'nothing could check that terrifying energy, power of invention and almost insane inclination to mischief'. Even when Lord Chancellor he continued to conduct himself with a carelessness bordering on the foolhardy. Once, when staying at a country house, he lost the Great Seal of England while playing an after-dinner game of blind man's buff and later, on an official visit to Lancaster, he got drunk and wandered off into a common tavern where he joined a group of working men in a night-long drunken orgy with local prostitutes.[7]

When the first volume of Harriette Wilson's *Memoirs* had appeared in February 1825 it caused a sensation. Cleverly, on the eve of publication she had placed a notice in the London papers announcing that Lords Londonderry, Byron, Melbourne, Burghesh, Avanley, Conygham and dozens more were featured in the work. 'A pretty list indeed,' said Henry Brougham, 'almost every one of my particular friends is among them.'[8] So great was the demand for the book that it was reprinted thirty times in the first year alone. Crowds gathered each morning at the premises of the publisher, John Stockdale, in the Opera Colonnade at Covent Garden, inspiring the enterprising proprietor to set up a bar to provide them with refreshments.

Yet in spite of her well-publicised threat Harriette had failed to mention the Conynghams. Now in 1827 she announced the forthcoming publication of the second volume in which she again promised a detailed account of the private life of, among others, the Marchioness of Conyngham. Among those who had found themselves immortalised by Harriette in the first volume had been Elizabeth's old friend John Ponsonby. Returning to England in

March 1825 he discovered that the whole of London society knew the most intimate details of his affair with Harriette. Ponsonby's friends, among them Sir Robert Lawley, husband of Elizabeth's younger daughter, Maria, commiserated with him. Lawley told a distressed Ponsonby that he was 'as angry at it as you most justly are and on your account, as the effect such a publication must have had upon your first appearance in England was unfortunate'. But Lawley could not resist suggesting to Ponsonby that if he were only twenty years younger Harriette's breathless account of his prowess would ensure him great popularity among eligible young ladies in society![9]

Having seen the notoriety that had descended upon the hapless Ponsonby as result of his appearance in the memoirs, the King and his mistress now awaited the second volume with trepidation. For Brougham had informed them that Harriette intended to include detailed accounts about both of them. A letter from Harriette confirmed the threat that while she did not intend 'to enquire into the causes of the rise of a Jersey, a McMahon, a Knighton or a Conyngham', she would however, relate the touching and intimate story of her own relationship with the young Prince of Wales. At this news George was seen to blanch, for it was common knowledge that something of a sexual nature had occurred between them when Harriette was the mistress of the Marquess of Worcester, an officer in the Prince's own 10th Hussars. Worcester had taken her down with him to summer camp on the Brighton Downs, where she met the Prince. In 1802 she had written him a letter and invited him to write back to her. Never one to miss the chance of a casual amorous encounter, the Prince invited her up to London 'for an interview' but Harriette had apparently changed her mind for she wrote back with an arrogant challenge, 'if you can prove that you are one bit better than any man who may be ready to attend my bidding, I'll even start for London directly'.[10] The Prince claimed never to have replied. But letters between them, in Harriette's possession, appeared to suggest that something had indeed taken place. It was these matters that she now threatened to include in the next instalment of her memoirs.

There was bad news for Elizabeth Conyngham too, for according to the highly embarrassed Lord Brougham, Harriette had other, more damaging, documents in her possession. These were the highly compromising letters written by Elizabeth Conyngham to John Ponsonby soon after her own marriage to Henry Conyngham. The revelation of Elizabeth's infidelity in such circumstances would certainly confirm British public opinion that she was unprincipled as well as greedy. When Brougham told Harriette of the consternation she had caused at Windsor she noted in her journal that 'the Conynghams dread the publication of a Commedy [*sic*] for which I have refused 1000£ desiring to lead a harmless life'.[11] This further vehicle for extortion was to be called *Bought in and Bought Out* and would include not only the secrets of the Conynghams but of the Hertfords too. Harriette followed up this threat by writing again to Lord Ponsonby, confirming that there was a lot more to come including the intimate stories he had told her twenty-five years earlier about his affairs with the society beauty Lady Clare. The only way Ponsonby could stop these revelations was to send her the now-customary £200. But Ponsonby, showing a determination that belied his reputation for easygoing indolence, refused to pay up, declaring that to give in to such insolent blackmail would only 'encourage the woman's desire for plunder and shew her the certain means of gratifying it'.[12] When his principled stand became known near-panic ensued. If the contents of the letters were revealed it would show Elizabeth as a hypocrite and her carefully contrived facade of respectability at Windsor a sham. Sir William Knighton, now the royal fixer in all embarrassing matters, was sent post-haste to try and persuade Lord Ponsonby to withdraw his threat to sue Harriette Wilson for blackmail. Ponsonby defended his right to take action against this 'obscene harpy' but said that out of chivalry he was more concerned for Elizabeth's reputation.

Nothing but my entire respect for Lady Conyngham could force me to abstain from instituting a prosecution against Mrs Wilson for attempting by letters menacing to bring false and foul charges against me . . . I avow myself unable to comprehend why her ladyship should . . . bear the villainies of that woman. What can Lady Conyngham have to apprehend? She has her perfect innocence to support her, and, if the accusations could be substantiated they go only to establish my villainy. I alone could be branded.[13]

Knighton urged him not to proceed even though he had prepared his case and hired lawyers because, 'you cannot relieve the feelings of the distinguished lady mentioned in your letter by dragging her name, and for ought you know, even her presence, into the court of Justice'.[14] Ponsonby took Knighton's advice and ignored all further letters from Harriette.

Now another of Harriette's past conquests took a hand in the murky business. Lord Granville, the British Ambassador in Paris, had from the start of his appointment taken it upon himself to keep a close eye on her activities. Astutely, Granville had not stopped her using the diplomatic bag but ordered that all her letters be opened and copied before being sent on to England. Any delicate information concerning the King or Lady Conyngham was to be sent directly to Sir William Knighton at Windsor. Granville had been prodded into further action by the late Prime Minister George Canning, who had taken the precaution of visiting Paris in person on 30 June 1825 to buy himself out of the dreaded memoirs. Canning had then urged Granville 'not only to lend yourself to any mode of removing uneasiness, but to devise means for that purpose if you can'.[15]

With this new threat from Harriette Wilson, Lord Granville decided to go immediately to the top and requested an urgent meeting with the French king himself. He warned Charles X that Harriette's activities were causing grave embarrassment not only to George IV and Lady Conyngham but also to half the English aristocracy. He reminded the French monarch, perhaps presumptuously, how a scandalous book published earlier in France, *Anecdotes sur Mme la comtesse du Barry* had helped bring down his own monarchy for it had portrayed the then French king, Louis XV, as a drunken lecher controlled by a grasping and interfering mistress. If Harriette's activities were not checked her memoirs might well have the same disastrous effect on the British monarchy.

George had also been making his own discreet attempts to counter the threat of 'Mrs Rochfort', for a year earlier he had sent Sir William Knighton over to Brussels to assess the situation. At the time Knighton thought the danger much overrated and took a less serious view of Harriette's activities than did Lord Granville. Returning to London Knighton advised the King that the best policy was silence and that they all should simply ignore Harriette's threats or reject them in the peremptory manner of the Duke of Wellington.[16] But now Harriette confirmed that she did indeed intend to publish forthwith and that her new volume would certainly contain extracts from the Ponsonby letters. Panic-stricken, Elizabeth implored the King to do all in his power to save her reputation even if it meant an unpleasant compromise with this grasping woman. Harriette, sensing the panic at Windsor, was now convinced that she could command an even higher price for the letters themselves. There were further complications for the Conyngham family too. Although she had allowed Lord Francis to buy himself out of the first volume of the memoirs for a modest sum Harriette had induced him to use his position at the Foreign Office to procure a consulship in Belgium for her husband, William Rochfort. Lord Francis had recommended the appointment but Canning, having paid off Harriette himself, rejected it out-of-hand. Now added to her threat to reveal the contents of the letters she hinted that she would involve Lord Francis after all. She would tell the world what a scoundrel he was, how he had committed adultery with her and treated her 'with all the cold disrespect due to a common prostitute'. This new threat was contained in a letter to Lord Brougham that she ended, typically, by telling him that she was keeping a copy in case he too decided to be unhelpful to her.[17]

Without knowledge of the new threat to Lord Francis the King resolved to act decisively and he ordered Knighton to return to France and make a deal with 'Mrs Rochfort and her hellish gang'. Arriving in Paris Knighton went first to see Lord Granville and relayed to him the King's personal request that the Paris police should put Harriette Rochfort and her close associates under immediate surveillance. From Paris Knighton travelled on to Brussels where Harriette's husband was now in hiding from his creditors. After consultations with Sir Charles Bagot, the British Ambassador, a member of the embassy staff, refusing to give his name, called at William Rochfort's house in Tournai de St Rémy and gave him this firm warning. Rochfort was to tell his wife that she must:

Discontinue immediately and for ever those annoyances which she has long and particularly of late been in the practise of directing against a quarter which she would perfectly understand [failure to comply would lead to] . . . such measures with the Government of this country in respect to her, and to those immediately connected with her, as would infallibly attend with inconveniences to which she had probably never looked.[18]

Brass-necked as ever Harriette, when told of this threat, wrote directly to Bagot demanding compensation for herself and for his failure to give William Rochfort a consulship at Tournai. She helpfully suggested a lump sum of £300 and £100 a year for life. Bagot was careful not to reject her demand outright and referred the matter back to Lord Dudley, the new Foreign Secretary in London. Dudley considered the matter then replied that he saw no option but to agree to some sort of payment. Still Sir William Knighton, who had taken a firm personal stand on the matter, urged the King and the Foreign Secretary not to give in to Harriette's outrageous demands. The strain of it all was now taking its toll on the King in particular. As he told Knighton, 'the Wilson business of yesterday has entirely knock'd me up and destroyed me'.[19]

But Harriette and William Rochfort were under increased pressure from their own creditors, William having narrowly escaped jail when a bankruptcy order was served on him in Tournai. His wife blamed this on the clandestine activities of the British Embassy at The Hague. Desperate for money she decided to settle for the best terms she could get. Sir William Knighton offered her husband a modest but secure minor diplomatic post and an annuity of £100. Harriette would receive a cash sum, quietly diverted from the secret service fund, on the understanding that she cease blackmailing the King and Lady Conyngham once and for all. It was further agreed with Knighton that any further comments on George IV in her memoirs would be both uncontentious and favourable. Harriette accepted and the triumphant negotiator returned to London with the letters – which soon mysteriously disappeared – in his pocket to receive, with his usual smugness, the heartfelt gratitude of the King and his mistress.

# ELEVEN

## *Off to Windsor*

In the early years of his relationship with Elizabeth the King pursued an unvarying daily routine. He would have dressed early, completed his state business soon after lunch then walked from the Brighton Pavilion round to the Conynghams' house in Marlborough Row. On his arrival at four o'clock sharp each afternoon Lord Conyngham would have bowed then discreetly retired to his study leaving the lovers alone together. But as the years passed the King began to lack the energy for this intimate afternoon tryst and preferred to remain at the Pavilion. He would now lie on in bed each morning reading the daily newspapers and only rise in the late afternoon to prepare himself to greet Elizabeth when she arrived for dinner at precisely six o'clock. What remained immutable was the evening ritual, when the lovers would retire to the drawing room and sit together for an hour or two before the King retired to bed at ten o'clock.

Alone in the night George found it increasingly difficult to sleep and spent the long hours tossing and turning. From time to time he would ring a bell for a page to enter and pass him a glass of water that stood on his bedside table a mere foot away. When the insomnia was at its worst he would ring repeatedly to ask the time, even though a perfectly good watch hung beside him on the bed head. His valets became so annoyed and exhausted by these unnecessary demands that they implored Elizabeth to ease their burden by suggesting to the King that he allow them to take turns in waiting upon him on alternate days.[1]

The easygoing atmosphere at the Pavilion that had so impressed George's guests in the early days had also changed as the pain of gout and his increasing breathlessness made him ever more bad tempered. Now he found it difficult to manage even the short walk to the dining table. His once hearty appetite had also declined and it took several fortifying glasses of his favourite cherry brandy before he could summon the energy to take up his knife and fork. As ever he insisted that the central heating system be turned on full, causing the Duke of Wellington, as frequent a guest as ever, to complain that the rooms were 'infernally hot', that the air reeked of scent and that the lights were 'dazzling'. One weekend the Duke considered that even the discomfort of a routine meeting of the Privy Council scheduled for the following day in London would be more appealing. But when he asked the King for permission to return to town George, racked by the pain of gout shouted out 'damn the Council!' and ordered the Duke to stay put at Brighton. The ageing hero of Waterloo was therefore forced to spend the rest of the week lying around awkwardly on cushions with the other guests, playing patience and sipping liqueurs.[2]

A fellow guest, the diarist Charles Greville, was equally disenchanted with life at the Pavilion. The splendour that had once amused now bored him. The food was frequently served up cold and he loathed the 'bowing, smiling sycophants that infested the place'.[3] His royal host often seemed increasingly bored with his own guests too, preferring to sit quietly playing patience with Lady Conyngham before leading the company in to dinner. Gone were the boisterous companions who thronged the Pavilion in earlier days: men such as the playwright Richard Sheridan, 'Old Q', the Duke of Queensbury, 'Cripplegate' Barrymore and Tommy Onslow, the best carriage driver in England. Now a far more sedate class of guest such as the MP Thomas Creevey and his wife sat down to dinner. As close neighbours the Creeveys were on nightly standby to make up the numbers at dinner if more important guests failed to arrive. Their invitation would often not arrive until the evening, giving them little time to dress and scurry round to their punctilious and often drunken host at the Pavilion. Their efforts may not have been justified by the quality of the meal for, according to Lady Holland writing as early as December 1824, Elizabeth had drastically reduced the household budget and 'the good cooks are dismissed; and the dinner is supplied for each guest at so much par tete, which certainly is a miserable way for any decent house'.[4]

Princess Lieven also found the atmosphere at the Pavilion much changed, but she was more shocked by the obvious deterioration in the King's health, which even moved her to express an unaccustomed sympathy for Elizabeth Conyngham and what she now had to put up with:

> He looks ghastly; he is plunged in gloom; he talks about nothing but dying. I have never seen him so wretched; he did everything he could to pull himself together, but in vain. The favourite is in despair, especially over his temper, which is as sour as can be. . . The least thing gets on his nerves – and a crooked candle produces a stream of abuse.[5]

Yet the Princess was amused to see how a pretty face at dinner could still raise his spirits and that at the formal ceremony of the opening of Parliament a year earlier in 1823 she witnessed his sudden transformation from invalid to Lothario when surrounded by attractive women.

> When he came in, he seemed quite crushed. His heavy robes, his crown slipping down on to his nose, his great train making his fat neck look still fatter – everything conspired to heighten the comic effect . . . finally seated on the throne, he looked prostrate. A moment later, he caught sight of me – a smile. Higher still. Lady Morley: he beamed. He began letting his glance wander down the rows; but more often he looked up, with his eyelids going hard at it – and there was his Majesty quite recovered and perfectly well.[6]

The King's ill-health was exacerbated by his increasing weight. He still often ate and drank to excess and misguidedly sought to combat weight gain by constant blood letting. He seemed addicted to the practice and oblivious to its debilitating effects on his once-robust constitution. Realising that any sensible doctor would have forbidden these unnecessary bleedings he resorted to secretly consulting a number of surgeons. Each thought himself the King's sole practitioner on the matter and so agreed to his request whenever asked. Not surprisingly, weakened by bleedings and sustained by large quantities of alcohol, George appeared increasingly unsteady on his feet and incoherent at public functions. Thomas Creevey thought he would certainly lose his mind or even drop dead as a result of the alcohol alone.

Yet in spite of his infirmities the King could still bring himself to make an effort with his guests and continued most evenings after dinner to entertain them in the music room. Proud of his resident German band, he would frequently invite visiting guest musicians to join them and on one memorable occasion the great Italian composer Gioachino Rossini had sung arias to the assembled guests. As late as 1828 the King's voice remained strong and true and he was still ready to join with his orchestra as a soloist or conductor. Even when sitting with his guests as a mere spectator he would keep time with the music by beating heartily on his thigh. One visitor thought it a curious sight to see a monarch so employed. Sometimes George's enthusiasm overcame his judgement and guests complained that his loud singing often spoilt their enjoyment of the music. On rare occasions he would suddenly lose interest in the music and, fuelled by alcohol, would cajole Elizabeth and the other ladies present into trying their skills with an air rifle: on one such evening Lady Downshire reduced the King to uncontrollable laughter when she missed the target and hit an unfortunate violinist in the orchestra instead.[7]

Another regular guest at the Pavilion, John Wilson Croker, gave a more detailed account of that same evening. He thought the King still in excellent form 'but the dinner was, I think, shorter than usual and the cuisine inferior to what it used to be'. His comments seem odd for that same evening George had invited his friends to sample some wild boar that had been sent specially from Hanover. His argument was that German boar tasted far better than English domestic pork in the way that wild pheasant had far more flavour than farmyard chicken. A long debate then ensued as the diners discussed the competing merits of both kinds of flesh. This so bored Elizabeth Conyngham that she abruptly decided to change the subject to the matter of the King's growing reclusiveness. Why, she asked him, had he not honoured his long-standing promise made to her and to the theatre management to take her to see the new play at Drury Lane? George laughingly denied the accusation but Elizabeth insisted that he must explain himself in front of his guests. Surely the British people, she protested, had a right to see their monarch enjoying himself in public. Many would willingly pay up to ten guineas for a box to witness such a spectacle. The King replied that just by promising to attend he had done his duty. All the tickets were sold in expectation of his presence there and he did not even have the bother of having to attend in person. But Elizabeth would not let the matter rest there and appealed to her guests to add their support. As Croker saw it:

> Still the ladies insisted, and at last Lady C, applied to Lord Francis, who said that the man had told him that he did not expect the King but nevertheless his placard gave out that the play was by command, and everyone expected the King. This went on for some time, the King still on the defensive.[8]

What began as a domestic tiff had assumed a symbolic importance for Elizabeth and Croker saw the dispute as a trial of strength between the King and his lover. Did she still have the same power over him as in the past, he wondered, or was George attempting to assert himself and break away? The following week Croker met a fellow guest, Lady Anne Becket, who told him that Lady Conyngham had said the King would go to the theatre and go he did! But Lady Anne agreed with Croker that in spite of this apparent victory, Elizabeth's power over the sovereign had clearly declined.

This episode confirmed the suspicion that the royal lovers were becoming increasingly irritated with each other. A further example of the growing tension came a month later when one evening the conversation turned to the subject of the tragic suicide of Richard Tickell, a celebrated but minor poet who had fallen into debt and then thrown himself out of the window of his apartment at Hampton Court. The fall was apparently so violent that his head made a hole a foot deep in the gravel. The King, characteristically, lamented that if he had known of the poor man's troubles he would have tried to save him from such a miserable end. He then quoted a passage from Tickell's poem 'Anticipation' by heart. When Elizabeth said that she had not read any of Tickell's works the King sarcastically offered to look out a volume out for her. Croker wondered if 'Lady C will find either wit or pleasantry in it. She will read it like an old parliamentary debate.'[9]

Present that evening was Lord Francis Conyngham who, with the death of his elder brother, was now Earl of Mount Charles. Francis was a frequent guest at Brighton whenever his duties at Westminster permitted. For some time he had, with his mother's encouragement, been acting as an unofficial secretary to the King. Forty years younger than his sovereign, Francis provided George with a useful insight into the opinions of the younger generation of London society. In spite of the age gap between them they had much in common – not least a scandalous past involvement with Harriette Wilson. Yet although he had obtained his present post at the Foreign Office largely as a result of his mother's relationship with the King Lord Francis found their domesticity tedious. Irritated by their unchanging daily routine he once asked his mother why she spent every evening playing patience with the King when she had already passed the entire morning with him doing exactly the same thing. Life at the Pavilion, he complained, had become so insufferably boring that he was sorely tempted just to keep to his own room. In an attempt to placate her favourite son and enliven the atmosphere at the Pavilion Elizabeth invited Lord Francis's current infatuation, Lady Cowper, down to dinner. But within a week Lord Francis was again complaining of boredom and made good his threat to take refuge in his room, telling his mother that he would only come down to dinner if more stimulating guests appeared.[10] Yet he was careful not to let the King know the real reason for his increasing absence as he could ill afford to alienate such a generous benefactor. His sister, Lady Elizabeth, also confessed herself bored with the dull routine at the Pavilion but felt that she had no alternative but to continue as her mother's close companion. As the reward for this compliance her mother promised her that, with the King's help, she would bring about a marriage to an attractive and eligible young man. George, in his unaccustomed role of matchmaker, suggested the wealthy Lord Gower would make an ideal husband for the girl. Gower's reward for agreeing to the match would be a full dukedom. But neither of the young people proved to be very interested in each other. When invited down to the Pavilion Gower paid little attention to his prospective fiancée and spent most of the evening flirting with the older but far more fascinating Princess Lieven.[11]

Life at the Pavilion continued in the same changeless pattern with everyone but the King becoming increasingly bored and discontented. Then one morning after a sleepless night George was mortified to find that a mysterious prophecy of doom had been inscribed on a downstairs window. Always a superstitious man, he took it at face value and announced to the household that they must all now consider moving to one of the other royal residences. Elizabeth was delighted by the news for she had always felt uncomfortable in Brighton because of its association with its most celebrated resident, Maria Fitzherbert. Even though she had been separated from the King for decades, according to Thomas Croker Mrs Fitzherbert continued to be treated by the Brighton citizens as the rightful Queen of England. 'They don't quite *Highness* her in her domestic circle,' he wrote, 'but they *Madam* her prodigiously, and stand up longer for her arrival than for ordinary folk.'[12] Naturally the great majority of the local people looked on her successor Lady Conyngham with disdain.

When the King informed the Duke of Wellington that he intended to leave Brighton and move to St James's Palace in London the Duke, conscious of George's morbid fear of the mob, advised strongly against it. St James's was right in the middle of London and was 'overlooked on all sides to such a degree as that every movement in the apartments can be seen by the opposite neighbours; and the avenues to it are through the most frequented parts of the town and park'.[13] When the King proposed using Kensington Palace instead the Duke reminded him that it too suffered from a woeful lack of security. It was a convincing argument to a man who had endured the contempt and insults of the crowd for over three decades, beginning with his fatal decision to allow the public into Carlton House in 1811. That occasion was a celebration of his Regency, and on the first day that it opened over 30,000 excited visitors swarmed through the rooms leaving chaos and damage in their wake. At one point the Duke of Clarence felt obliged to climb on the garden wall and harangue the crowd to keep order. George was so horrified by this experience that he never again opened this or any other of his residences to the public. Fear of the mob became a phantom that constantly returned to haunt him. This fear was further exacerbated a few months later by the panic that swept London when a series of brutal and unsolved murders occurred in the London streets. George was panicked into ordering that no one be admitted to Carlton House after eight o'clock at night. Scarcely had he recovered from that fright than the Prime Minister of the day, Spencer Perceval, was assassinated at the Houses of Parliament in broad daylight by a madman. Fearing that this was not an isolated event but an omen of things to come George, who had been staying at Windsor, ordered that all the London armouries be instantly checked and secured and that the public road that ran through Windsor Great Park be closed to the public and a new highway constructed well away from the Royal Lodge.[14]

By 1819 this paranoia had led him to be wary of even his own household staff and he often complained that they were spying on him and the maidservants were looking at him as he went from room to room. If this practice continued, he threatened, he would sack the lot of them. A year later his fear of public violence was renewed when at the time of the Queen's divorce hearing the London mob attacked the London homes of the King's supporters including Lord Castlereagh and Lady Hertford. It was because of this fear that George had decided to stay at Westminster the following July on the night before his coronation so as to avoid running the gauntlet the following day. Again, when driving in Windsor Great Park with Elizabeth one morning he passed two men riding quietly along. Convinced that they were the prelude to an assassination attempt he ordered that the whole park be closed to the public forthwith. Even when assured that the riders were two perfectly respectable neighbours he refused to rescind the order and commanded that the park gate locks not only be changed but that new and more substantial gate lodges also be constructed.[15]

At the time none of the London palaces offered any assured protection from the unpredictable mob so after much discussion it was agreed that the only safe alternative to Brighton must be Windsor. As it was a good thirty miles from London, and far safer than any London palace, the Duke of Wellington suggested that the Court move there. If the King agreed, he was confident that he could persuade the government to spend money on improving both the castle and the Royal Lodge in Windsor Great Park. The government would even allow the King complete artistic control of the project, and for the first time in his life George would be able to try his hand at landscape gardening. He and the Conynghams could then live together in rural bliss safe from the jeering London mob.

George thought it an admirable suggestion and accepted at once, soon becoming more interested in the modest Royal Lodge than in

172

the vast and decrepit castle itself. In 1812 the architect John Nash had given the Lodge, at that time little more than a large cottage, a makeover and had also renovated nearby Cumberland Lodge in order to provide overspill accommodation for royal guests. Nash's initial work had been costly to the nation, a conservatory resulting in a bill for £2,429 and new furniture a staggering £17,000. But price had never proved a deterrent to a man who had already lavished vast sums on Carlton House and the Brighton Pavilion. George ordered the urbane but uninspiring architect Sir Jeffry Wyatville to continue the good work and the result soon provoked embarrassing questions in Parliament. The minister concerned, Lord Londonderry, attempted to explain to indignant members that the word 'Cottage' was a misnomer for the Lodge was not, in reality, a modest thatched house but 'a very comfortable residence for a family, and the only one the Prince could make use of when he went to Windsor'.[16]

Work also began on the more challenging renovation of Windsor Castle itself but by 1826 the Duke of Wellington must have come to regret encouraging the King to move to Windsor in the first place as work on both projects had already cost the nation over a million pounds. Wyatville used every trick of the new gothicism, including Tudor chimneys, arched windows and stuccoed walls, to complement the original medieval framework of the Lodge. Purists such as the young Augustus Pugin thought the result an eclectic mess that had produced little more than a 'thatched palace'. The only feature that all visitors praised was the conservatory, 'a lovely Greenhouse' where George and Elizabeth would listen to the King's German band in the evenings. Sir Walter Scott, visiting the Lodge in October 1826, thought it ridiculously large for a cottage and disliked the way the trees had been planted too close to the house. His main criticism, however, was the lack of interesting guests as most of the King's more colourful friends were now either dead of drink or no longer invited by Lady Conyngham. Scott had not seen the King since his visit to Edinburgh four years earlier and found him a changed man, sad and reclusive. 'A sort of reserve', he wrote, 'creeps upon him daily, and prevents his going to places of public resort, it is a disadvantage, and prevents his being so generally popular as is earnestly to be desired.'[17]

Yet the King seemed content with his new home. He had taken up permanent residence in 1826 and was enjoying the quiet life surrounded by his surrogate family, the Conynghams. He took a particular pleasure in just pottering about the house or tending the garden, a pastime gently mocked by William Heath in his cartoon entitled *Rusticating*. It depicts the King digging a vegetable patch while Elizabeth pumps water and Lord Francis pushes a wheelbarrow. But George's greatest pleasure was driving his favourite pony carriage through the Great Park with Elizabeth at his side. Another cartoon by William Heath shows just such an outing with the unfortunate ponies almost sinking to their fetlocks from dragging the combined weight of the two corpulent passengers. Their cosy domesticity was also mocked by an anonymous poem where Elizabeth is compared to Mistress Quickly and George to Falstaff:

> And who so sweet as Mistress Q
> To do what should be done,
> To give the R——l George his due,
> And cheer his setting sun?
>
> And gratitude now makes her bend
> On G——e the debonnaire.
> His aged face with rouge to mend
> And curl his wig with care.

To mark this new phase of their rural domesticity, the King had given his mistress a bedroom with the finest views over the Park, its walls lined with blue damask and gilt and dominated by a vast polonaise bed decorated with classical helmets. Predictably Henry Conyngham was provided with a more modest apartment on the floor below them. Thomas Creevey, visiting the renovated Lodge for the first time in the summer of 1826, thought it far more manageable than the over-decorated Pavilion, although he lamented the King's continuing obsession with the low ceilings that had always spoilt the fine proportions of his previous houses. Princess Lieven also preferred the modest lodge to the Brighton Pavilion, considering it 'the reunion of comfort, elegance, and unspoilt magnificence'. She particularly admired its visual deception in looking like a modest cottage from outside but with a surprisingly magnificent interior.[18] But the real charm of the Royal Lodge, commented upon by every guest, was its fine setting among the magnificent trees of Windsor Great Park. From its windows could be seen spectacular views of Windsor Castle and Virginia Water, a small ornamental lake that was to give the King so much pleasure in his declining years.

It was on an island in Virginia Water that George's uncle, the old Duke of Cumberland, had built a Chinese temple forty years earlier. Near it the King now placed a group of classical remains purloined from a neglected corner of the British Museum together with a small classical fishing temple. The King loved to drive Elizabeth to this charming folly on winter afternoons to watch the last rays of the setting sun. In summer when the Lodge was full of guests needing to be entertained the King handed the reins of the pony carriage to his favourite coachman, Hudson, who led a line of more cumbersome horse-drawn landaus along the woodland tracks to the lake. At the landing stage the whole party would embark and be rowed out to the centre of the lake where they drifted throughout the afternoon fishing for trout. Alongside them and always to windward floated a larger boat with the King's musicians on board to entertain the guests.

Now that the days of sumptuous entertaining were over George confined his invitations to a smaller circle of personal friends. When duty demanded that visiting foreign dignitaries and government officials be entertained they were put up at the old Cumberland Lodge nearby and driven over to the Royal Lodge for dinner. The most frequent visitor continued to be the Duke of Wellington who confessed himself perplexed by these constant summonses to Windsor. They always came, he complained, when he was already committed to some other social engagement. Yet he was loath to refuse for when he once declined a royal invitation because it clashed with the annual shoot at his house, Stratfield Saye, Lady Conyngham was reported to have flown into a rage, thumping the table and complaining to the King that Wellington treated them both in the most impertinent manner. In future, she said, he must learn that 'he should not choose his own days for going there'.[19] Yet the King never tired of the Duke's company, even once suggesting that the

Wellingtons and their friends the Arbuthnots should join him and Elizabeth on an excursion to the Continent. This prospect held little appeal for the Duke, however, who continued to profess, in private, that he still found Lady Conyngham a most annoying and unsympathetic woman. Once, after spending Ascot week at the Lodge, Wellington complained to Harriet Arbuthnot of the growing insolence of the whole Conyngham family. He said that their conduct to the King disgusted him and he detested the very sight of them. His fellow guest that week had been Thomas Creevey, who was surprised to see the King dressed as soberly as he now lived, travelling to the races in a plain brown coat, black cravat and brown wig, with his hat cocked over one eye. 'There he sits in the corner of the stand,' Creevey wrote, 'Lady C rather behind him, hardly visible but by her feathers.'[20] The Duke attributed Elizabeth's reticence to show herself in public to her growing disenchantment with the relationship. Creevey thought her 'bored to death, disgusted and miserable, and the King more in love than ever'. In his opinion Lady Conyngham, having got what she wanted, was now quite prepared to end the affair altogether. The more perceptive Harriet Arbuthnot, however, was convinced a separation would never happen, reminding Wellington that if Elizabeth decided to leave she would walk away with little more than 'a few jewels and pieces of furniture'. Then the King, Harriet assured him, would swiftly find a replacement for Lady Conygham as he could never live alone again. This new mistress would then turn her and her family 'out of their places as she had turned out the Seymours'.[21]

Harriet later had the opportunity to judge for herself the state of the royal affair when she attended a reception at St James's Palace. But to her disgust it was not an intimate dinner where she would have been able to talk privately to either Elizabeth or the King but 'a standing up supper, which is not very royal'. Harriet was shocked to see that even the King had to eat standing up. It was all part, she told the Duke, of Elizabeth's vulgar economy drive. She had even forced the King to cancel a formal breakfast he had arranged for her own son, Lord Albert Conyngham. She had done it, claimed Harriet, to make sure that more money was available for her own use; this proved beyond doubt that Lady Conyngham was indeed 'the most avaricious woman in the world'.[22]

# TWELVE

## *Who Rules the Roost?*

Elizabeth's economies at Windsor may well have been the result of the more rigorous control of royal finances being exerted by the King's latest secretary Sir William Knighton – a very different character from his predecessor. Whereas Benjamin Bloomfield, whatever his faults, had been affable and gregarious Knighton appeared cold and austere. Industrious and conscientious and above all discreet, he could also be infuriatingly affected and petulant. Like Bloomfield he had risen from humble origins. William Knighton had enjoyed a successful career as a naval doctor before setting up practice in Hanover Square as a fashionable gynaecologist or *accoucheur*. As Bloomfield had made himself indispensable by providing mistresses to the aristocracy so Knighton dealt with their unwanted pregnancies. Among his impressive list of clients was the celebrated actress Moll Raffles, one of the many mistresses of Lord Wellesley, the Duke of Wellington's elder brother. Richard Wellesley, once amusingly described by George IV as 'a Spanish grandee grafted on an Irish potato', was a highly able politician who had come close to being Prime Minister twenty years earlier. In 1809 he was sent to head the diplomatic mission in Spain, discreetly accompanied by Moll Raffles who insisted on bringing along William Knighton as well. Wellesley seems not to have questioned the need for a full-time gynaecologist on the military campaign but agreed to Knighton's colossal demand for £5,000 as compensation, so he claimed, for two years lost earnings in London.

When Lord Wellesley was unexpectedly recalled after only a year in Spain, Knighton complained that his contract had not been honoured. Like Bloomfield, he was not a man to be crossed lightly, knowing as he did the most compromising secrets of his clients, so instead of compensating him financially Wellesley agreed to recommend him personally to the Prince of Wales, suggesting that he be added to George's growing retinue of doctors.[1] Knighton found George intelligent, proud and overbearing but with a most fascinating 'complacency of manner'. When George complained of a persistent lameness in one hand Knighton, although careful not to offend medical ethics by treating him personally, gave him such good advice that George promptly invited him to become one of his physicians-in-ordinary. Knighton's personal manner was as impressive as his medical skills and George was soon treating him as a trusted confidant. A baronetcy followed as Knighton became increasingly indispensable.[2] Some of the King's companions, knowing how he relished scandal, attributed his fascination with Knighton to the doctor's unrivalled knowledge of society sex life. His experience as London's leading 'man-midwife', as the contemptuous Princess Lieven always described him, had meant that he knew 'all the complaints of all the ladies that consult him'.[3] Knighton's practical skills in this area, as well as his discretion, may well have been useful to the King given his own intimate relationship with Elizabeth Conyngham.

Soon Knighton's duties extended far beyond the medical and he was known to be undertaking delicate personal missions on his sovereign's behalf. One of the first involved dealing with one of his predecessors, the King's blackmailing ex-secretary Colonel John McMahon. Throughout his time as Comptroller of the Prince's Privy Purse McMahon had never lost an opportunity to enrich himself by selling sinecures or contracts in the royal gift. His wife, the lovely woman at the cottage window long ago, joined him in the enterprise so successfully that after her death £14,000 in cash was found hidden in a kitchen drawer. 'They all came to her for places,' Knighton told a friend disapprovingly, and it was common knowledge, according to Thomas Creevey, that Lady Beauchamp had paid McMahon £10,000 for getting her husband advanced from baron to earl.[4] Word of McMahon's corrupt activities eventually reached Parliament after he had left his position and questions were asked as to why he continued to be paid by the Crown when he was no longer in the Prince's service. When the radical MP Samuel Whitbread questioned one such demand for £2,000, McMahon explained that it was for the upkeep of 1,600 war widows who had remained his personal responsibility. Whitbread, in a witty reference to McMahon's notorious reputation as a libertine, replied 'that if the gallant Colonel would produce a voucher from the ladies that he had performed his duties to their entire satisfaction he should think him well entitled to the salary'.[5]

Throughout his years in royal service the Secretary had been careful to retain copies of any documents or letters that might prove embarrassing to his clients in the event of a dispute. This was a form of insurance, a procedure still apparently practised by some royal servants. Among his secret hoard were many compromising letters from George to numerous lovers including some of a highly salacious nature written to him by Lady Conyngham. McMahon looked upon these as his retirement pension and now, old and enfeebled, he decided to sell the cache. He wrote to the King inviting an offer, hinting that if George did not come up with a generous one he would sell off the whole lot to the highest bidder. The King, panic-stricken as always in such situations, called in Knighton and asked him to conduct the negotiations on his behalf and to ensure that the documents were either recovered or destroyed at any cost. Knowing that the old man was now a hopeless alcoholic Knighton arrived alone at the McMahons' cottage in Kent clutching a bottle of his favourite brandy. Knighton insisted they down a measure together before getting down to business then, as they bargained, Knighton persistently topped up McMahon's glass until the atmosphere had so mellowed that the old man was happy enough to hand over the entire collection in return for a large, but realistic, fee. Knighton was delighted with his success and returned to London in triumph, assuring the King unctuously that nothing could have been handled more secretly or satisfactorily than his retrieval of the 'desirable objects'.[6]

When McMahon died two years later in 1817, leaving a fortune of £90,000, the newspapers were outraged, claiming it was yet another example of the corruption that permeated the Prince Regent's household. *The Times* described the will as 'a large fortune, which never could possibly have been obtained from the income of his several places'. But Knighton was to prove no better than his predecessor for the King was later to confide to Charles Arbuthnot that he suspected Knighton was up to McMahon's old tricks and had stolen some of his personal letters, pretending disingenuously they were mislaid but that he might know who had them. The King claimed that Knighton demanded £50,000 to buy them back and a fee of £12,000 for himself as compensation for the disappointment of not getting a sinecure post that the King, he alleged, had recently promised him.[7] These were huge sums at the time and it is hard to see what unknown secrets the letters contained or why George tolerated such behaviour other than that he was desperate to avoid new scandal.

In his early days of royal service Knighton made himself indispensable by taking over most of Benjamin Bloomfield's duties as secretary and financial controller and performing them, as his wife wrote sanctimoniously in her memoir, 'with the unshrinking firmness which its embarrassments required'.[8] Elizabeth had supported Knighton's demand that he be made Keeper of the Privy Purse with a salary doubled to £4,000 a year. His repeated justification for this promotion was that he had given up a lucrative medical practice to serve the King and was now losing a small fortune. Knighton also insisted that the King agree to relinquish financial control of his own household, allowing Knighton to inform all royal suppliers that in future only purchase orders signed personally by himself would receive payment. Knighton's boundless ambition continued and although he had now accrued to himself the offices of Auditor of the Duchy of Cornwall, Secretary and Keeper of his Royal Highness's Privy and Council Seals, he still felt them insufficient reward for his many talents. In 1821 he demanded that he be made a Privy Councillor. The King, unwilling to contest the issue, passed on his request to Lord Liverpool, who angrily refused outright to sanction the elevation of such a relative nonentity to one of the most important councils of state. Knighton responded to this rebuff with such a display of anger and petulance that Elizabeth, if not the King, was convinced that he might well turn out to be an even greater irritant than his predecessor.

To many observers Elizabeth Conyngham and Sir William Knighton seemed natural allies at Court, as both were outsiders who had wormed their way into the King's favour and depended entirely on his friendship for advancement. Avarice was also a vice they had in common, according to the diarist Henry Hobhouse, who thought both equally 'fond of lucre'.[9] Lord Lauderdale voiced similar doubts, considering Knighton 'a damned clever fellow', but found it odd that of the four conversations he had with him 'each one of them ended with his asking me what I thought of the price of stocks'.[10] But Knighton's demands for greater rewards were only possible because of the King's curious dependence upon him. As he had done for years with Elizabeth, George had even started discussing matters of state with his new secretary before taking any decision. An invitation from the Austrian Emperor to visit Vienna in 1823 required Knighton's immediate presence at Brighton before the King could make up his mind to accept. Knighton was urged to come down to Brighton 'be it only for an hour . . . See you I must'.[11]

As the King became increasingly ill and depressed he grew to rely on Knighton, not just as secretary and adviser but as a male confidant too. It was a role William Knighton was perfectly suited to play, for his years as a practising doctor had given him a canny grasp of the psychology of dependency as well as a polished bedside manner.

Knighton was thus able to offer George credible reassurance about his many physical ailments as easily as he gave his opinions on the King's increasingly fraught relationship with his ministers. In return for his comprehensive support Knighton demanded not only material rewards but insisted that the King recognise his literary talents, too for the doctor considered himself a poet of no mean ability. It is hard to see how the King, a man renowned for his literary and aesthetic good taste who had recognised and promoted the genius of Jane Austen, could respond as he did in March 1821 to Knighton's latest banal composition:

It was a very, very, very wonderful poem . . . a most beautiful production of the human mind, perhaps, if not the most grand one certainly of the very grandest and most elegant at the same time that any pen produced, either in our language or any other.[12]

Hyperbole does not come any greater.

With great skill and persistence Sir William Knighton became almost as important to the King as Elizabeth Conyngham herself, and in the last few years of George's life they shared the arduous task of comforting and supporting this most demanding of monarchs.

As Elizabeth went out one door, Knighton would physically and metaphorically come in at another. A master at creating an atmosphere of intrigue in the most innocent of daily transactions, Knighton would send the King sealed notes proposing clandestine rendezvous at unlikely hours. One such read 'I hope to be in your Majesty's bedroom by half past twelve to-night . . . let no one know I am coming with the exception of the one' (a reference to Elizabeth).[13] Perhaps Knighton was simply coming to say evening prayers, for much of the King's sudden and unexpected interest in religion could be attributed to the influence of the pious secretary. Certainly his letters to the King are written with a cloying tone of piety, pomposity and sanctimony worthy of Uriah Heep. One of the most ingratiating reads:

> I trust that the Almighty will give you peace, and that your afflicted mind will cease to be tortured by the overwhelming inquietudes which have of late made such painful inroads on your health . . . your Majesty would scarcely believe the extent of my anxiety and misery respecting you. Burn this if you please . . . I have the honour to be, Sir, your Majesty's most dutiful and most affectionate attached devoted servant.[14]

Knighton was well aware that his fawning on the King had made him well nigh indispensable, for as he boasted to Charles Arbuthnot, 'the King perhaps, ought not to have a favourite, but he cannot do without me . . . The King is the most helpless creature in the world, he cannot write a letter for himself and he must have a person like me about.'[15] When Knighton foolishly repeated these sentiments to Wellington, the Duke in his usual blunt manner advised him to confine his activities to the King's private matters and to keep his nose out of politics – advice for which Knighton characteristically thanked him profusely. Wellington would have been even more outraged had he known that the King, at the time, was actually asking Knighton's advice as to whether he should sack his Tory ministry and bring in the Whig opposition. Whatever Knighton decided on this matter, the King told him, would be done.

But the Secretary had become dangerously complacent and, thinking himself invulnerable, had begun to voice his private contempt for his royal master, complaining ill-advisedly to Charles Arbuthnot that the King was 'a great beast who liked nothing so much as indecent conversation and that, in that respect Lady C managed him well for he dared not do it in her presence'.[16] When this was reported to him, George's attitude to his secretary began to change. Knighton's enemies, and there were many, were quick to seize on his sudden and unsuspected vulnerability. One of the King's oldest friends, Sir Thomas Tyrwhitt, declared that he had no doubt that Knighton was 'the greatest villain as well as the lowest black-guard that ever lived'.[17] Princess Lieven also confessed her dislike of the 'man-midwife' and was convinced that beneath his agreeable and polished exterior Sir William Knighton was a scheming villain. There were even rumours in London, she claimed, that 'the doctor's chief exploit is having poisoned his wife twenty years ago. The King's household', she continued, 'is really the most extraordinary thing in the world. He is head over heels in love [but] the doctor's influence rules him in the first place.'[18]

Elizabeth must have welcomed this unexpected reversal in Knighton's fortunes for she had become increasingly overshadowed by the presence of the egregious doctor. A royal page told Charles Greville in confidence that although Lady Conyngham had once been all-powerful she was now in total subservience to Sir William Knighton and that she did not dare to have anyone dine 'without previously ascertaining that Knighton would not disprove of it'.[19] But Elizabeth was always careful not to openly challenge his position with the King and an unspoken mutual understanding appeared to exist that neither would encroach on the other's terri-tory. Moreover Elizabeth was fully aware that she still needed Knighton's support in her continuing feud with Lady Hertford and his cooperation in excluding any friend of the Hertfords from the royal circle.

No one could be too careful in observing the rules of this tedious battle, which persisted throughout the 1820s. Even the canny Princess Lieven unwittingly became embroiled when she made the mistake of inviting Lady Hertford to the christening of her son in July 1824. She took the precaution of asking Isabella to arrive well after the King and Lady Conyngham had left but, sensing an opportunity to irritate her successor, Isabella ignored the request and arrived early. As she was about to enter the drawing room where the King and Elizabeth were still talking to the guests the Princess grabbed Isabella's arm and led her gently back into the hall, so avoiding a direct and highly embarrassing confrontation.[20] Later that year, when told that Lord Hertford was to be given the Order of the Garter, Elizabeth was said to have erupted in rage, going immediately to her room and refusing to come out. Only after a furious exchange of notes with the King did she allow herself to be pacified, but it was past nine o'clock before she emerged and they could all sit down to dinner. Still smarting from the loss of this skirmish over the Garter, Elizabeth had a chance to get even the following May when Lord William Gordon, the Deputy Ranger of Windsor Park, died. His widow, who had the misfortune to be Lady Hertford's sister, applied to the King for permission to stay on at their official residence. When she heard of the request Elizabeth marched into the King's study and demanded that Lady William be evicted forthwith. Moreover she told the astonished King that she, Elizabeth Conyngham, should be made the new Deputy Ranger and have the benefit of the Ranger's house herself. Unable to cope with this new imbroglio the King implored Sir William Knighton to intervene. After much wrangling Lady William was allowed, at Knighton's suggestion, to stay on at the house but in return Lady Conyngham was appointed Deputy Ranger.[21] By now George was becoming heartily sick of being drawn into this incessant warfare against his old friends the Hertfords, as well as of his mistress's incessant demands for self-advancement. As he wearily complained to Princess Lieven, 'she certainly understood her own interests better than anybody; that she got everything for herself and her family'.[22] Indeed she had recently secured the appointment of Lord Conyngham's brother, General Burton, to the lucrative post of Governor of Jamaica in place of the retiring Duke of Manchester.

Yet Elizabeth refused to countenance a truce, let alone end the war with the Hertfords, and the King continued to be drawn into the conflict. He was even directed to tell his sister-in-law the Duchess of Gloucester that he was displeased because she had accepted an invitation to dine with the Hertfords. Even the Duke of Wellington did not escape a lecture from Elizabeth when she warned him that she and the King thought he was seeing far too much of the enemy and should curtail his visits to Sudbourne and Manchester House. If he did not mend his ways, Elizabeth told him with a rare touch of humour, she might be forced start her own political party which would be decidedly pro-Canning and pro-Catholic! The Duke's confidante Harriet Arbuthnot also earned a sharp rebuke for daring to continue her Thursday evening visits to Manchester House. Harriet had apparently compounded the offence by being seen to join Isabella Hertford in her box at the opera. Although outraged by Elizabeth's presumption, Harriet told the Duke that she had better oblige 'this nasty woman' if only to keep the peace for the King's sake.[23] The Duke agreed that it was the right thing to do but a few weeks later he had to tick Harriet off for being seen in public with Lady Hertford again:

> It can scarcely be expected that you were not seen in the Box last night. If she goes to the French Play herself tonight, there will not be a Dandy at the play who will not mention to all his acquaintance that he saw you there. She will most probably if not certainly know it, and as certainly reproach the King that those with whom he is most intimate . . . are the constant and Intimate Associates of his and her Enemy.[24]

That the most illustrious political figure in England and the hero of Waterloo was so concerned with placating a woman who had little official standing at Court shows how powerful Elizabeth had now become. In March 1824 the Duke had told Harriet that Lady Conyngham was still meddling in the King's affairs and that she had 'grown wonderfully haughty and high and mighty, which makes her appear even more vulgar than ever'. The Duke had begun to lose patience with the King for aiding and abetting this and for condoning the absurd campaign against the Hertfords. More importantly, he was concerned that he was neglecting official matters and seemed far more interested in the architectural improvements and alterations at Windsor than in his duty to the country.

Sir William Knighton meanwhile continued his slide from grace as Elizabeth's attitude towards him changed from polite acceptance to discreet hostility. Knighton resented this deeply, telling Thomas Creevey that he could not understand why the Duke of Wellington remained so civil to a woman who took every opportunity to condemn him to the King. Why did the Duke waste his time kissing Lady Conyngham's hand and paying court to her when the best way to keep her in order 'was to frighten her'?[25] It was incomprehensible that a man who had triumphed over Napoleon should be so faint-hearted when dealing with a mere upstart woman. But Wellington considered that it was politically essential for him to maintain a good relationship with the sovereign – and if need be, his mistress. He was aware that in recent months a coolness had developed between himself and the King that Wellington attributed to the government's firm refusal to increase the royal Privy Purse.

There were other reasons, too, for the growing tension at the Royal Lodge for Elizabeth had been frustrated in her attempt to marry off her elder daughter Lady Elizabeth to an eligible husband. In 1824 she had been expected to become engaged to Lord Burford, heir to the Duke of St Albans, but the young man proved to be so unmannerly that Lady Elizabeth wrote him a curt note dismissing him. Later when pursued by the high-spirited Fred Lamb, the brother of the future Prime Minister, Lord Melbourne, Lady Elizabeth had taken her mother's advice and refused him out of hand. Elizabeth was convinced that her daughter could do far better than the impecunious younger son of a peer. A far more suitable catch appeared to be the handsome and wealthy future Marquess of Huntley, but the engagement lingered on for months without resolution – perhaps because of Lady Elizabeth's reluctance to leave her mother. Her years as an unofficial chaperone seemed to have conditioned Elizabeth to that role and she appeared to find it difficult to cut the tie. Thomas Creevey was present when Elizabeth, with this in mind, asked her daughter outright if she was scared to leave her mother's side. 'It is so is it not, Tissy?', she asked, and with downcast eyes Lady Elizabeth nodded her agreement.[26] Finally, to her mother's great satisfaction and undisguised relief, Elizabeth eventually married Lord Huntley in July 1826. But her second daughter Lady Maria Conyngham was far less troubled by these considerations and the prospect of marrying her off seemed much easier. Elizabeth went about the business of finding a suitor with determination, inviting, as Princess Lieven put it tartly, 'a parcel of eldest sons and Lords in possession' down to the Royal Lodge for inspection.

These emotional concerns did little to improve the King's low spirits and he became even more peevish and irritable. Although his health had temporarily improved he continued to dose himself liberally with draughts of laudanum and down vast quantities of wine. Yet in spite of more frequent quarrels and disagreements with Elizabeth he steadfastly maintained his love for her. As frequent a guest at Windsor as she had been at Brighton, Princess Lieven thought the King as much in love as ever and 'very comfortable in his love'. Her experience of him had even led her to develop a grudging respect for the way in which the English conducted their love affairs. 'Here's to English love-affairs,' she wrote to Metternich, 'they are the only really convenient kind. How well they are arranged!'[27]

The King's relationship with Sir William Knighton, however, had deteriorated even further. Puffed up with self-importance and considering that he was now indispensable for having put the King's finances in good order, Knighton finally over-reached himself. One evening Elizabeth, who had been confined to her room with a fever, asked him to come and discuss some important household business. Knighton ignored her request and when the King reproached him for it the following day he responded petulantly, 'I should like to know whose servant I am in this house'. This insolence could not be ignored and the King sent him packing to London for a week. That first evening of his absence the King surprised his dinner guests by suddenly shouting out 'I wish to God somebody would assassinate Knighton'.[28] He was utterly determined, he informed his startled guests, to get rid of Knighton once and for all and to replace him with his dear friend the Earl of Mount Charles. He claimed he had offered Francis the position on numerous occasions but the young man had always politely declined, saying that he thought Knighton indispensable to his sovereign.[29] Although George's anger appeared genuine some thought his outburst mere hot air for he relied on Knighton for everything. 'The King's indolence is so great that it is next to impossible to get him to do even the most ordinary business and Knighton is still the only man who can prevail on him to sign papers,' wrote Charles Greville. Without Knighton's vigilance the King would return to his old habit of keeping officials waiting in anterooms 'while he is lounging with Mount Charles or anybody talking of horses or any trivial thing . . . a more contemptible, cowardly, selfish, unfeeling dog does not exist than this King'.[30]

The King's growing irritation with his secretary was partly the result of his own declining health and increasing reclusiveness. After years of public ridicule he was now reluctant to emerge from the safety of the Royal Lodge. Too often had his short brown wig and corpulent stomach been mocked in hundreds of cartoons, causing him to resort to ever tighter and more uncomfortable corsets. Doctors warned that the tight stays he insisted on wearing were damaging his health and must be abandoned. Reluctantly he began leaving them unlaced again. Thus uncorseted he was not an attractive sight, as his vast belly ballooned out over the top of his pantaloons. 'Prinny,' Lord Folkestone confided to Thomas Creevey, 'has let loose his belly which now reaches his knees.'[31] Added to this discomfort was the pain of gout which had plagued him inter-mittently for years and was now persistent. Four months after Canning's death George had written sadly of himself:

> I have little or no use of my poor limbs, for I can neither walk up nor down stairs, and am obliged to be carried and in general to be wheeled about everywhere . . . at the same time that my knees, legs, ankles and feet swell more formidably and terribly than ever.[32]

He was seen to take Elizabeth's arm, rather than she his, when going into dinner. As a concession to his increasing immobility he openly used his Merlin chair, an early form of wheelchair that had been brought up from the Brighton Pavilion. This novel machine stood in the passage behind his bedroom and each day he would lower himself with difficulty into it then set off down the corridors of the Royal Lodge, propelling it along by means of rotating handles, a page following at a discreet distance behind. In later years he would often remain in it even at dinner, finding the Merlin far more comfortable than a formal dining chair. As his health deteriorated so did the King's temper. For the first time in their relationship he even began to find fault with Elizabeth herself. Princess Lieven was convinced that his short temper and authoritative manner would now finally drive her away, even though they continued to clink glasses together at dinner. Perhaps, the Princess thought, Elizabeth now recalled the words of Lady Charlotte Bury who had warned her in the early days of the affair that 'to be anyone's mistress is a miserable lot. To be a royal man's mistress worse still, for how seldom is a Prince constant.'[33] No wonder Elizabeth could now be described as 'looking bored to death' and barely on speaking terms with the King.

By 1827 George's irritation and bad humour began to affect even such old favourites as Francis, Mount Charles, who now thought it safer to keep out of the way leaving his long-suffering father to bear the brunt of the King's bad temper. Sir William Knighton in particular seemed constantly to provoke his wrath. Although most of the King's companions had loathed Knighton from the start – 'this most vindictive man, eternally upon the watch' – George now shared their opinion. One evening when flirting with the King, Princess Lieven noticed Knighton smiling 'in his mysterious way' at several compliments she gave the King. The Princess could not make out whether Knighton was laughing at her or thought he was joining her in mockery of the King.[34] Knighton had become so unpopular that when he took an unaccustomed short holiday the King appeared delighted. Shaking off his lethargy he invited a party of travelling Tyrolean entertainers, hired by the Russian ambassador Prince Esterhazy, to perform at the Lodge. To George's delight the men kissed his hand after the performance and, more agreeably, the women kissed his cheek. Like a naughty schoolboy defying authority he whispered to Princess Lieven that he would give ten guineas at that moment just to see Knighton's face if he happened to walk into the room. He spoke of Knighton, she said, as if he were some absent master who 'should suddenly return and find his family and servants merrymaking in his absence'. [35]

But the Tyrolean dancers did little to lift Elizabeth's spirits. She appeared unmoved by the merrymaking and still looked bored to death, hardly speaking to the King all evening. The Duke of Wellington was another guest who noticed George's growing irritation with all the Conynghams and he told Mrs Arbuthnot that the King was now much more formal with them.

He calls Lord Conyngham 'My Lord' very frequently and gave him a lecture the other day about having bad wine. He calls Lady

Elizabeth 'Lady Strathavon' likewise . . . I am not astonished at it
as I never saw two people shew such evident symptoms of being
bored as Lady Conyngham and Lady Strathavon. It appears to me
that his love for her is at an end altho'. . . he will probably keep
her on in her present situation; and she appears to have no
thoughts of going, tho' always complaining how much she is
bored.[36]

A few days after Knighton returned from his holiday the Duke asked
him if he agreed that the King was now far less obsessed with Lady
Conyngham and she with him. Knighton nodded assent, adding that
the King had become very harsh in his manner towards Elizabeth
and now neglected her a good deal. Significantly, Knighton thought,
Elizabeth no longer threatened to pack her bags and leave as she had
once done on these occasions. The reason was, said Knighton, that
the King would now be only too glad to get rid of her. Many old
faces were missing at dinner, leaving the long evenings to be taken
up with wrangling and quarrelling with each other. The King said
that Lady Conyngham had stopped his most entertaining friends
from visiting the Lodge but she insisted that it was his own bad
temper that had driven them all away.

The friction between Elizabeth and Knighton had also increased
and she made it apparent to her guests how much she detested the
unctuous doctor. When Wellington asked her what was wrong she
told him openly that she was so bored with life at the Lodge that she
would like to just go away and have done with it. To her astonishment the Duke, who she knew had always disapproved of her,
replied that he thought her an invaluable asset to the King and that
without her presence the King would most certainly go into an even
greater decline. The nation too should be grateful to her for all she
had done to make the King happy, he told a dumbfounded
Elizabeth, for she had taken him away from Lady Hertford who
would certainly have trapped him in a disastrous marriage one
day.[37]

Elizabeth was so gratified by the Duke's words that she made a
resolution, albeit short-lived, to pay him more attention in public.
This led the King to comment morosely that he wished she would
treat him as well. Ironically Elizabeth's charm offensive was lost on

the Duke, who told Mrs Arbuthnot that Lady Conyngham continued to treat him 'with the greatest insolence'.[38] A few weeks after this conversation, feeling that his praise had not encouraged her to make an effort, he switched tactics and told her bluntly that she must stop making the King's life 'a desert'. It was her responsibility to make things enjoyable and she should make a more determined effort to please him. If that required a little self-sacrifice then it was the price she must pay. When she again protested to Wellington that she could not endure the boredom of life at the Royal Lodge, the Duke advised her to change the daily routine for as Lady Stewardess of the household she had the authority to invite as many people as she wanted to dinner, be it twenty or 100 each day. Fashionable society would be only too delighted to accept her invitation if only she could be bothered to invite them. When she repeated her old complaint that she had been shunned by London society in the past the Duke, in his forthright manner, told her that she should have thought of that before agreeing to become the King's companion. If she left him now when he so desperately needed her it would bring even greater opprobrium on her head. After all, it was she who had first complained about his old drinking companions and had persuaded him to drop them from the guest list. It was she who was the gatekeeper at the Lodge and the King's friends were in fear of her. Many of the King's long-standing companions who were no longer invited to the Lodge would have agreed with the Duke. Charles Freemantle, once a regular guest, bombastically told his friend the Duke of Buckingham:

This was the policy of the potent and portly Stewardess who literally enthralled him, body and soul. He was but a huge babe, nursed by that human Argus. In his Cicean hermitage – a wreck of all he was, a momento of the nothingness of mundane pomp, the worthlessness of wealth.[39]

In December 1828 the King was persuaded by his ministers to escape the dreary routine at Windsor and to come up to London to open a new session of Parliament. A visitor from Europe, Prince Puckler-Muskau, who watched the ceremony thought him pale and bloated and noted that he was 'obliged to sit on the throne for a considerable time before he could get breath enough to read his speech'. Any semblance of majesty, Muskau thought, was dissipated by his notorious tendency to cast 'friendly glances and condescending bows towards some favoured ladies'. When the King came to read his speech he did so with a nonchalance that Muskau found incompatible with his role of 'the most powerful monarch of the earth'. It was little more than pantomime, made even more ridiculous by the Duke of Wellington who had the greatest difficulty in removing the royal sword from its scabbard for an ennobling ceremony afterwards. When he did eventually manage to extract it and place it in the royal hands the King raised it unsteadily then brought it down with considerable force, completely missing the kneeling man's shoulder and landing on his head so that 'instead of alighting on a new knight, it fell on an old wig, which for a moment enveloped King and subject in a cloud of powder'.[40]

In spite of his infirmity the King's libido appeared to remain impressively unimpaired for when he returned to Windsor that month he conceived a sudden and unexpected passion for Princess Lieven, much as he had done for Lady Hertford decades earlier. For years he had admired her sharp sardonic wit and her impressive intellect but being thin and sharp-featured she was totally unlike his usual choice of buxom woman. Although she had been a constant guest at both Brighton and Windsor the King had never shown the least amorous intent towards her before, although he constantly laughed at her jokes and applauded her acerbic comments. Now he began paying open court to her and appeared consumed by an almost schoolboy infatuation. For her part the Princess was more amused than shocked to be pursued by a man whom she liked but had never admired. Flattered by his sudden advances she responded sufficiently for Elizabeth to become suddenly jealous. As the Princess told Metternich, with some satisfaction:

The King is paying me a great deal of attention. I am filling out, and my arms are getting plump in fact I am developing quite to his taste. He talks to nobody but me. The Marchioness is annoyed; and yesterday she could not contain herself. The King was sitting up later than usual; and I was seated by him at the window. The Marchioness was sulking by the garden door.

Suddenly she got up and went out on to the lawn. I was the first to notice it, and I told the King. He took fright and rose, so did I. We went out to look for her. It was dark. He brought her back and scolded her. She replied that, if the King was busy, she had a right to go out. The evening came to an end suddenly. I withdrew, to give them a chance of an explanation; which, with lovers, means reconciliation. The result is I shall be in her bad books.[41]

This did not deter George from continuing his suit a month later when the Princess was again his guest at the Royal Lodge. As she was dressing in her room one afternoon a footman arrived with a note from the King summoning her to the royal bedroom. When she arrived she found him lying in a dressing gown on his bed:

He began by talking about the affairs of Europe . . . and then went on to his own affairs. His mistress bores him; she is a fool. He has been in love with me for some thirteen years. He has never dared tell me. . . . Today an inner voice told him that I alone could guide him. Our minds are alike; our views; my tastes will be his; 'In a word, Heaven made us for one another'. [42]

She agreed that they were indeed close friends, even cousins, and shared many attitudes and opinions but said that to take their relationship further would, at this stage, be a tragic mistake. Yes, she told the King, she did love him dearly but appropriately 'as a friend'. She then excused herself and made to leave, only for George to jump up out of his bed and rush to the door ahead of her. It appeared he wanted to point out to her his latest acquisition hanging on the corridor wall outside. It was, to her great surprise, her own portrait painted by Sir Thomas Lawrence, which George had acquired at great expense. 'What do you think of this strange scene?' she asked Metternich. 'I intend to avoid a quarrel with my new cousin. It will be easier because he is lying: he is not in love with me at all. Yet the King persists in his wooing.'[43]

Invited again to the Lodge the following week, she was dressing for dinner when she saw in her mirror the reflection of the King creeping across the lawn towards her French windows. As he approached the house he slipped behind some hornbeams in the tree-lined walk as if surprised by a passer-by. The Princess flung open the window and pretended to be conversing with an imaginary servant in the room. Alarmed at the prospect of being discovered on his undignified amatory expedition the King put his finger up to his lips as if warning her to be quiet and not reveal his presence. Almost collapsing with laughter at the sight of her ridiculous suitor, the Princess called out to her maid to bring her hat. When the girl appeared the King fled in terror, running so fast that he almost fell over. Taking a short cut through the park the Princess gleefully arrived at the Lodge before him and entered the crowded drawing room. When George arrived hot and flushed a few minutes later he spotted her immediately and in acknowledgement of her skill in outwitting him made her a deep and formal bow of submission. In spite of the years he still retained his sense of humour. For the rest of the evening, she wrote, he treated her with formal, almost exaggerated respect. That night she wrote in her diary that it been no more than a harmless, amorous game:

> I fancy that he hopes for the trifling emotions of an affair, and that he hardly cared whether he entered my room or not. In the King's composition are general disgust, boredom, and superlative vanity.[44]

Probably nothing would or could have come of this royal passion. Even a man of the King's robust constitution would have found a sexual encounter difficult if not impossible given his massive consumption of drugs and alcohol. Wellington, who was a constant critic of the King's overindulgence, told Mrs Arbuthnot that the quantity of cherry brandy he drank was 'not to be believed'. Nor did the King confine himself to alcohol, being often rendered semi-comatose by frequent doses of the powerful laudanum he took to dull the increasing pain of gout and the ominous and as yet still undiagnosed symptoms of arteriosclerosis. His doctor, Sir Henry Halford, had by 1828 became so alarmed at his prodigious consumption of the drug that he insisted the dose be reduced to a maximum of 30 drops a day. In this debilitated state George now had to face the greatest political challenge of the last years of his reign – the battle for Catholic Emancipation.

# THIRTEEN

## *Justice for the Catholics*

As the young Prince of Wales, George had taken a tolerant attitude towards the Roman Catholic minority in the kingdom. This was partly due to the liberal influence of his friend the Whig leader, Charles James Fox, and partly out of a desire to provoke and infuriate his staunchly Protestant father George III. On meeting the Catholic widow Maria Fitzherbert he became even more convinced of the need to end legal discrimination against her co-religionists. Maria had told him of her tragic experience of religious intolerance when her late husband Thomas Fitzherbert had died prematurely as a result of the injuries he received at the hands of the London mob in the Gordon Riots of 1780. By 1797 George had become so sympathetic to the Catholic cause that, on the eve of the Great Irish Rebellion, he implored William Pitt, then Prime Minister, not only to bring in a Catholic Emancipation Bill but also to mollify Irish opinion by making him Lord Lieutenant of Ireland.[1] Predictably the mere suggestion further enraged his father who refused even to discuss the proposal. Yet George continued to tacitly support the Catholic cause throughout the next decade and, according to Thomas Creevey, in 1805 he delivered a long harangue in favour of the Catholics at a public dinner in London.

After Fox's death in 1806 the Prince appeared to alter his opinion radically, and many observers thought they saw the hand of his latest mistress Isabella Hertford in this. For not only was the entire Hertford family strongly Protestant but Isabella also maintained a passionate loathing of her predecessor, the Catholic Maria Fitzherbert. Soon after taking up with Lady Hertford George mysteriously banned any discussion of the issue in his presence, claiming that as Regent he must now respect his father's wishes for George III had always insisted that any bill for Catholic relief would violate the coronation oath. By 1813 George had moved even further into the anti-emancipation camp, openly declaring that a relief bill of any form would endanger the very safety of the nation. This entrenched position was to be seriously challenged by the advent of Lady Conyngham.

In marked contrast to her immediate predecessor, Elizabeth, in spite of her marriage to a member of the Irish Protestant Ascendancy, was suspected from the start of being a firm supporter of the Catholics. Nor did she hesitate to make her opinion known to the King and to impress upon him her conviction that it was both desirable and inevitable that some form of emancipation occur. She was also convinced that such a measure would in no way conflict with the oath. In 1821, just before the coronation, Princess Lieven found her

> surrounded by large tomes on theology and explanation of the oath that the king has to take at his coronation. He contends that this oath obliges him to maintain the exclusion of the Catholics from all public offices and civil rights. She wants to persuade him of the contrary; and this is now the object towards which her influence is directed. Evidently someone is putting her up to it. Lady C's fear is of being placarded and abused as a Roman.[2]

However, another diarist, Charles Greville, was informed by Francis Mount Charles that although his mother was strongly in favour of emancipation herself she claimed never to have discussed it or any other political issue with the King. This was nonsense, given Elizabeth's known influence on the King's opinions during his disputes with Lord Liverpool's government and the Canning and Londonderry crises. Yet the origins of Elizabeth Conyngham's Catholic sympathies remain a mystery. They certainly did not originate in her upbringing for she was the daughter of a low-church Yorkshireman and the sister of a prominent Nonconformist and strongly Protestant MP. The reason for her commitment to such an unpopular cause may well have been merely pragmatic as befitted the daughter of a successful merchant banker. Her husband was a Protestant aristocrat with over 150,000 acres of land in Ireland but his seat, Slane Castle, had been expropriated from a Catholic family after the Battle of the Boyne. Henry had seen at first hand the violence and destruction of property that could happen if the native Catholic Irish continued to be excluded from the political process. Like his wife he was no bigot and as the commander of his militia regiment had been sent to Tipperary in the unrest that preceded the Rebellion of 1798. There he had dealt firmly with a gang of local Orangemen who were terrorising their Catholic neighbours by ordering them neither to wear their colours nor to assemble in public, an unusual and courageous stand at the time. Although Lord Conyngham voted in the Irish parliament for the Act of Union of 1801 he was undoubtedly in favour of peaceful emancipation. As pragmatic as his wife, he was prepared to accept change as long as he could retain his inheritance. This, after all, was a man who had already demonstrated that he was prepared to tolerate his wife's intimate relationship with another man as long as significant benefits and rewards came from it.

In spite of its traditional opposition to Catholic relief the majority of the Tory party in the 1820s gradually came to accept its inevitability. Not only would emancipation grant justice to a loyal but long disenfranchised minority in England but, more importantly, it might forestall yet another dangerous rebellion in Ireland. The British public was, however, hostile to any concessions for the 'papists' and in 1827, suspecting that the government was contemplating such a measure, the London mob took to the streets again as they had done in the Gordon Riots. The King, who had reluctantly come up to London to open Parliament, dreaded a repeat of the damage caused at the time of the late Queen's trial and ordered that St James's Park be shut to the public. The reason for this, he claimed, was that Lady Conyngham was nervous of driving through the park to join him for dinner, at which the Duke of Wellington was said to have muttered 'why the devil can't she go thro' the streets!'[3] Elizabeth's apprehension was understandable for it was generally known that she supported emancipation. Attacks upon her character became ever more vituperative, given that the satirists were generally radical and anti-Catholic in their sympathies. One cartoon, 'Converts in High Life', has a tonsured monk encouraging her to 'Speak freely, thou *Cunning-one* and by St George, I will give thee Absolution'.

Matters were brought to a head in July 1829 when the Irish Catholic leader, Daniel O'Connell, was elected Member of Parliament for Clare. Wellington realised that he must now act for if such a man as O'Connell, a democrat and one of the natural leaders of Ireland, continued to be disqualified from sitting in a parliament then further rebellion was inevitable. For the Union to survive the Catholic Irish must now be enfranchised. His ministers reluctantly shared his opinion but when the Duke informed the King of his proposal to bring in a bill George flew into a rage, accusing his Prime Minister of going soft on the issue. Like his father, he declared that he could not and would not violate an oath that committed him to defending the supremacy of the Protestant faith.[4] Months of wrangling, tears, protestations and recriminations were to follow.

The Catholic debate polarised the entire nation and throughout the country every local Protestant diehard group urged the monarch to stand firm. George was reminded of his promise to his dying brother, the Duke of York, in 1827 that he would not deviate from the principles in which 'we have gained honour and relief since the year 1688'.[5] As ever, when faced with a difficult issue, the King attempted to ignore it in the hope that it might quietly disappear. Mr Gregory, following the emancipation debate from Ireland, thought him 'like a Giant Pope, he had to content himself with sitting in his cave's mouth, grinning at the Emancipationists and biting his nails because he could not get at them'.[6] Those who knew George best were the most pessimistic about the chances of him making the right decision. John Wilson Croker, an opponent of emancipation, thought the King would come down on the side of the Catholics and wrote, 'the thing is well over, and will make Windsor as Popish as Downing Street'.[7] As ever the satirists made capital of the situation blaming Wellington for championing the Catholic cause and casting doubts on his true motives. One cartoon appeared showing him coaxing the King to sign the Emancipation Act and in another the Duke tries on the crown as George, a monarch-baby, sleeps on the floor among his toys, which include a model of the new Buckingham Palace.

Throughout this entire clamour the King remained silent, refusing to commit himself in any way and refusing point blank to have the matter even mentioned in his presence, although he must have discussed it frequently in private with Elizabeth even though she told her brother William Denison in March 1827 that the King did not permit 'any one whatsoever to speak to him on the matter'.[8] But as the debate continued the public became ever more suspicious that Lady Conyngham, a confirmed Catholic sympathiser, was putting unseen pressure on him to change his mind and support the bill. Articles railing against her 'Popish' interference appeared in the more diehard Protestant newspapers, prompting Elizabeth to complain to Wellington about these unwarranted personal attacks. She was also shocked, she told him, by the violent anti-Catholic sentiments directed towards her by some of his own, more extreme Tory colleagues in the House of Lords, to where the debate had now shifted. But Wellington showed her little sympathy, retorting angrily 'Lady Conyngham what do you mean? Do you suppose that such men as the Dukes of Rutland, Newcastle and Northumberland and Lords Hertford and Lonsdale have any object in opposing the Government but the good of country and the honour of the Crown?'[9] Then, to the delight of the extreme Protestants but to the consternation of Elizabeth and the King, news came from Hanover that his younger brother, the Duke of Cumberland, intended to pay a visit from Germany. His stated intention was to lead the nation in a crusade against emancipation and to go down to Windsor and bully his brother into refusing to endorse any Relief bill whatsoever. George and Elizabeth awaited his arrival with dread.

The object of their apprehension, Ernest, Duke of Cumberland, was a tall, thin martinet with little conversation and a well-deserved reputation for military brutality. His army career had ended in disgrace when he was abruptly recalled from Gibraltar with the garrison in near mutiny after months of the daily floggings and a total ban on alcohol that he had ordered. Cumberland's personal life was no less brutal. He was rumoured to have been the lover of his own sister, Princess Sophia, and also to have attempted to rape the Lord Chancellor's wife, the beautiful Lady Lyndhurst. Furthermore, it was said, he had even attempted to murder his own valet, Joseph Sellis. The reason for this was supposed to have been that the Duke was Mrs Sellis's lover or, even more luridly, that Sellis had been the Duke's homosexual lover. The truth, as it turned out, was that Sellis

199

had gone mad and attempted to assassinate the Duke. A cold, sarcastic man completely dissimilar in character to his sensitive elder brother, Cumberland had for many years terrified his entire family. When news of his impending return was announced Elizabeth asked the Duke of Wellington why the King was so scared of him. The Duke explained that although George was unafraid of anything 'hazardous, perilous or uncertain', he was utterly terrified of ridicule; and Cumberland's ability to mock was, said Wellington, unsurpassed.[10]

Even before his arrival in January 1829 Cumberland had written from Berlin urging his elder brother to 'show publicly, the purity and staunchness of your sentiments on the great question'. In a vain attempt to protect his sovereign Wellington wrote back imploring him not to leave Berlin, but Ernest ignored the letter and continued on his grim mission to London. On arrival he made good his threat and began bombarding the King at Windsor with even more violent exhortations to stand firm, honour his Coronation oath and protect the supremacy of the Protestant church. In the face of this new onslaught, George continued to dither but Elizabeth urged him to totally ignore Cumberland's bluster. She again assured him of her personal conviction that in sanctioning an Emancipation Bill he would be compromising neither his personal honour nor that of the monarchy. A constant visitor to the Royal Lodge at this time, Princess Lieven, who had always considered Elizabeth empty-headed, was astonished to find her one day alone in her drawing room again consulting heavy tomes on theology and constitutional law.

But the Duke of Cumberland's persistence prevailed and within a month of his brother's arrival the King appeared to have caved in to all his demands. Wellington was appalled and said he thought that George had become just as fanatical a Protestant as his bigoted brother. Also, having for months refused to discuss emancipation at all, he now appeared to speak of little else. Francis Mount Charles told Wellington that life at Windsor had become impossible as the King was driving his mother and everyone else in the royal household crazy by endless discussion of the issue. If this obsession continued, thought Francis, the King would probably go mad himself. When told that one of his other brothers, the Duke of Clarence, had decided to speak in support of the Bill in the House of Lords the King told Lord Eldon that this was really the last straw. He was sorely tempted to renounce the throne at once, a threat he had made repeatedly when Prince of Wales, and retire to Hanover leaving the Duke of Clarence to become the new 'Catholic' King of Great Britain.[11]

This threat of resignation was serious enough, for George repeated it formally to Wellington when the Prime Minister went down to Windsor a month later. In an emotional audience that lasted well over five hours the King ranted at the Duke, wept repeatedly and appeared completely overwrought. Much of his distress was caused, he claimed, by the members of his own household, including the entire Conyngham family, who kept urging him to ignore Cumberland and support the government's proposals. Wellington was shocked by the mayhem he had witnessed at the Lodge and even managed to find some unaccustomed sympathy for Elizabeth. 'The Duke of Cumberland keeps the whole house in awe, particularly the Lady,' Wellington told Harriet Arbuthnot. 'She appears to be in perpetual alarm.'[12] Yet Elizabeth put on a brave face in front of Cumberland and continued to behave cordially towards him in spite of the provocation, claiming that his bluster did not scare her in the least.

Refusing to become emotionally involved in the debate, she decided that the King needed a considered and rational argument to put to his brother and turned to her old friend Dr Sumner, now Bishop of Winchester. She urged Sumner, who had become one of the leading Anglican theologists of his day, to write to the King presenting a well-argued case for Catholic Emancipation.[13] But George, always more moved by emotion than reason, took her intervention and the Conynghams' continuing support of Catholic relief as an act of personal betrayal. The situation became even more fraught when Francis Mount Charles spoke in support of the Bill in Parliament, making the King so furious that he demanded to know why such a close friend had thought it necessary to 'get up and expose yourself in the House of Commons'. Mount Charles explained that he had heard that 'there were some doubts about his own and his father's sentiments' and that he wished to explain them. Charles Greville, who witnessed the King's anger at the male Conynghams, wrote, 'the King is very angry with him and his father for voting as they do'. This domestic skirmish seemed to have brought the whole issue to a head. George then summoned the members of his household together and told them bluntly that he expected those with a vote in the House of Lords to cast it against the Bill at the next reading. At this Francis stood up and bravely told the King that in all conscience and as much as he respected his wishes, he could not do as asked.[14]

Predictably, Sir William Knighton played a devious role throughout the turmoil at the Royal Lodge. On 14 May he made the odd suggestion to Charles Arbuthnot that the Duke of Cumberland seemed determined to engineer the reinstatement of Lady Hertford as royal mistress at the expense of Lady Conyngham. But to Elizabeth he remained as polite and helpful as ever, clearly recognising that they both depended for their survival on the King's good opinion. 'Nothing', Greville wrote of this strange domestic pact, 'can be done but by their permission, and they understand one another and play into each other's hands. Knighton opposes every kind of expense, except that which is lavished on her.'[15] Greville was certain that Elizabeth had already accumulated enormous wealth from the King and that he was continuing to heap presents of all kinds on her. Although he accepted that as the royal mistress Elizabeth was entitled to such gifts, Greville was incensed that the royal largesse should extend to the whole Conyngham family. He felt it a scandal that they were all living at the King's expense and that their servants, including Lord Conyngham's valet, were paid for by the King. But what riled him most was the discovery that even the Conynghams' food came from the royal kitchens:

> They dine every day while in London at St James's, and when they give a dinner it is cooked at St James's and brought up to Hamilton Place in Hackney coaches and in machines made expressly for the purpose; there is merely a fire lit in their kitchen for such things as must be heated on the spot.[16]

Disheartened by the incessant bickering, the King spent most of the day in bed trying to avoid Cumberland who prowled the house looking for him. Charles Greville lamented that the Royal Lodge was now a 'despicable scene' and Court life was being ruined by 'selfishness, avarice . . . petty intrigue and mystery'. On 18 March the King's valet de chambre told Greville that his master had still not made up his mind on the Catholic Bill. The valet thought the King was his own man and 'afraid of nobody but Knighton' and 'after him Lady C was all-powerful'. But the valet was convinced that the final arbiter must be Knighton, for he controlled both the house and the King's opinions. So powerful had he become that even Lady Conyngham now had to ask his permission before inviting a new guest to dinner.[17]

These domestic tensions at Windsor were matched by the political turmoil at Westminster as the debate dragged on without resolution. Even the Iron Duke began to wilt under the strain of dealing with the fractious royal brothers at a time when news he received from Ireland made it more imperative than ever that the bill be passed. For Wellington had a secret confidant in Dublin, the Roman Catholic Primate of Ireland, Dr Curtis. The two men had first met decades earlier during the Peninsular War when Wellington had rescued Curtis, then principal of the Irish College at Salamanca, from the French. They became unlikely friends and maintained a secret correspondence in later years with Curtis acting as secret intermediary between Wellington and the Irish nationalist leader, Daniel O'Connell.

Ironically, having once been a staunch defender of the Protestant cause, Wellington was now labelled an unprincipled turncoat and found himself bitterly attacked by its current leaders. The most rabidly anti-Catholic of all was the Earl of Winchelsea who, after a speech in the House of Lords demanding that Catholic priests and monks be deported, ended his tirade with an attack on Wellington's integrity as a politician and his honour as a gentleman. The Duke felt he had no option but to call him out and the duel, the last involving a serving British Prime Minister, took place at dawn in Hyde Park on 21 March 1829. The Duke, a notoriously bad shot, fired first and deliberately missed, then his opponent, with an open target before him, raised his pistol and fired into the air. He had sensibly chosen not to risk national opprobrium by killing the victor of Waterloo. Much relieved, Winchelsea then stepped forward and offered a formal apology to the Duke, which was curtly accepted. When told that his Prime Minister had just fought a duel with a fellow peer the King expressed himself as delighted with the event as he was with the outcome, adding with relish that in the Duke's place he would have done exactly the same.[18]

Having dealt with Lord Winchelsea the Duke could now turn his attentions to the most prominent anti-emancipationist of all, the Duke of Cumberland, who was threatening to march on Windsor at the head of 20,000 supporters to petition the King against the bill. When told of Cumberland's intention Wellington informed him by note that if he did so then as Prime Minister he would order Cumberland to be immediately arrested and taken as a prisoner to the Tower of London. The King must not and would not be bullied by anyone, not even his own brother. Privately Wellington doubted Cumberland's ability to gather such a crowd. The only way he could get such a mob on the road, he told Harriet Arbuthnot, was to promise them all free ale when they arrived in Windsor.[19]

Faced with the inevitable deterioration of law and order Wellington decided to bring the matter to a head and on 26 February he left London at dawn and drove down to the Royal Lodge where he handed Knighton a letter to be handed to the King as soon as he awoke. It stated bluntly that if Cumberland were allowed to remain in the country much longer all would descend into chaos. In his reply to what was a virtual ultimatum George suggested that his infuriating brother be made Governor of Hanover and the present incumbent, the Duke of Cambridge, be recalled and made Commander-in-Chief of the army. Wellington considered this a ridiculous suggestion as Cambridge 'was as mad as Bedlam' himself. Not that he differed from the rest of the family, complained Wellington, who had become convinced that all the Hanoverians were crazy. Why else, he asked Mrs Arbuthnot, did the King persist in claiming that he had taken part in so many battles of the Napoleonic war? Had he not claimed to have fought at Waterloo and to have saved the day at Salamanca when leading a daring cavalry charge disguised as General Bock? The King's self-deception was so complete, thought Wellington, that his eyes filled convincingly with tears when he made these absurd claims, leaving his guests so dumbfounded that they could only nod in agreement.[20]

To maintain his own integrity during these monologues but without openly contradicting the monarch the Duke had devised a cunning stratagem. Whenever the King appealed to him to confirm that he had indeed been present on the field of Waterloo, the Duke replied 'so I have often heard your majesty say'.[21]

Two further visits to Windsor during March by Wellington and the Home Secretary, Robert Peel, seemed to convince the Duke that the King had finally lost his wits. On both occasions George rambled on continuously for over five hours, constantly sipping brandy and water. On both occasions he threatened to retire to Hanover with the Conynghams and seemed even more obsessed by the implications of his Coronation oath, which he appeared to confuse with the Oath of Supremacy. At the end of the second meeting, weeping profusely, he told both ministers that it was they who should resign. They offered their resignation gladly, and made their escape grateful to be released from all this torment. After they had gone Elizabeth and Sir William entered the room to find the King lying on a sofa in a 'deplorable state' of collapse. After much comforting they managed to persuade him to pull himself together and take dinner with them.

Yet still the main issue remained unresolved while Parliament waited, for now, even without Wellington and his ministers, there was a clear majority in the Commons for the Emancipation Bill. That evening the King, realising the full consequences of political life without the steadying hand of the great Duke, wrote him this short letter of total capitulation:

My dear Friend, as I find the country would be left without an administration, I have decided to yield my opinion to that which is considered by the cabinet to be for the immediate interests of the country. Under these circumstances you have my consent to proceed as you propose with the measure. God knows what pain it causes me to write these words. G.R.[22]

Then with a spark of his old wit he told the Conynghams at dinner that evening that although Daniel O'Connell was said to be the King of Ireland it was now Arthur Wellesley who was the new King of England. As for himself, George said, why, he was merely the 'Canon of Windsor'.[23]

Although a decision in favour of emancipation had been made by the Crown, the fraught atmosphere at Windsor could not improve until the Duke of Cumberland was gone. Even the easygoing and good-natured Maria Conyngham found him unbearable. That April the atmosphere was so unpleasant that the King even allowed himself to be persuaded by Elizabeth to escape Windsor and his ranting brother and go up to London with her to attend a series of parties and receptions. When they returned Elizabeth claimed to have devised a new strategy for dealing with Cumberland. Whenever he pestered her for the King's reaction to the 200 anti-Catholic petitions that he had collected to put before his brother, she now told him that the King was so confused by laudanum that he understood nothing. In fact, she told Cumberland, the King could not even remember a word of the speech that he had given at the opening of Parliament a few days earlier.

When the House of Lords debated the Emancipation Bill, the Duke of Cumberland, as anticipated, put the anti-emancipationist case as follows: 'the moment that there are Roman Catholics admitted into this or the other House of Parliament, this House must cease to be a Protestant House of Peers, and the House of Commons must cease to be a Protestant House of Commons'.[24] The government's position was put simply and sincerely by his younger brother, the Duke of Clarence, who said, 'I maintain that that which is asked for is not concession but Justice. It is merely an act of Justice to raise the Roman Catholics from their present state of degradation. And when an Act is passed for that purpose, I will pledge my life that it will have the effect of uniting and quieting eight millions of His Majesty's subjects.' Clarence ended his speech by warning 'my illustrious relative' that he had lived so long abroad that 'he has almost forgotten what is due to the freedom of debate in this country'.[25] Then to everyone's surprise a third royal brother, the mild-mannered Duke of Sussex, stood up and supported Clarence in condemning their older brother's extreme anti-Catholicism. This unexpected intervention surprised even Cumberland, who later told his friends that he was appalled to see three brothers of the highest rank 'disputing publicly in the eyes of the whole country'.

When the vote came on 28 April 1829 the government produced a comfortable majority of 104 for Emancipation. Still grumbling resentfully, the King signed his consent to the Roman Catholic Relief Act. A week later, when the Duke arrived for an audience the King, in retaliation for all the trouble he had suffered, kept the Prime Minister waiting in a freezing cold room for twenty minutes then cut the audience to a mere half hour. After he had returned to London, Wellington reported: 'I saw Lady Conyngham who was very much alarmed at the prospect of having the Duke of Cumberland there so long. But she told me nothing excepting that the King was more easy since he had given the royal consent to the Bill.'[26] A few days later the Duke of Norfolk took his seat in the House of Lords and became the first Catholic to sit there among his peers since the Reformation. Peace again prevailed at Windsor as the Duke of Cumberland was sent packing back to Hanover.

# FOURTEEN

## *A Sad Decline*

For a whole year the King had been caught up in the turmoil of the Emancipation Bill and driven half-mad by his bullying brother and, as he thought, put under unbearable pressure by his ministers. He returned to Windsor a near-broken man and for the remaining year of his life lived quietly in seclusion with the Conynghams. Confined within the precincts of the Royal Lodge he appeared to take little or no interest in either the public or the political affairs of the nation. Only his intimates and ministers were allowed to see him and when he did venture out for a drive in the Park with Elizabeth his favourite coachman, Hudson, was ordered to 'cast his eye into every brake or thicket, to ascertain if some prying, inquisitive intruder lurked there'. The keen eye of Prince Puckler-Muskau noticed when riding in the Great Park that the King had reserved several roads that ran through the most picturesque sections of the park 'for his own special and peculiar use'. It seemed to Muskau that the Park had been deliberately and hermetically sealed to everyone without exception who 'did not belong to his own company'. Noticing that the King's favourite resting spots were screened by trees Muskau mused that for such a reclusive man it must be unpleasant to see a 'strange face, or indeed any human being within his hidden domain'.[1] But George IV's first and most vitriolic biographer, Robert Huish, writing within a year of George's death, was convinced that the monarch hid from his subjects because he did not want them to 'behold the ravages that time had made his fine features'.[2] A later royal biographer, Sir Owen Morshead, was closer to the truth when he said 'the King withdrew because he was unpopular and he was unpopular because he withdrew'.[3]

Huish was one of the few outsiders in that final year to see the King at close quarters when he encountered him one day at Sandpit

Gate Lodge on his way to visit the royal menagerie. Typically George was seated in his pony-chaise with his favourite cockatoo on his arm and enjoying a glass of the cherry-gin that was always kept on board for him. For the cartoonists George's continued absence from public view only confirmed their suspicions that he was little more than a prisoner at the Lodge. They now portrayed him as a huge, fat baby hustled and bustled and kept from the world by the infamous trio of Lady Conyngham, the Duke of Wellington and Sir William Knighton. Much was also made of the Chinese temples and oriental landscaping of Windsor Park and of the King's sole remaining outdoor exercise, fishing on Virginia Water. But out of sight of prying eyes the King was enjoying one of the most contented periods of his life, even though he could still be racked by occasional bouts of jealousy. Even with Lord Ponsonby far away in Buenos Aires he still dreaded that someone else might suddenly appear and lure Elizabeth away from him. His friends found this possessiveness amusing in a man of his age and Thomas Creevey thought it so extreme that 'no strange eyes dare be so bold as to look upon her ladyship with impunity'.[4] In his last year he even became suspicious of harmless strangers. When told that an officer on leave was frequently seen walking in the Home Park and had been seen gazing at Lady Conyngham as she passed, the King immediately ordered that the locks on all the gates be changed. When next they drove out together in his phaeton he insisted that outriders go on ahead to clear any bystanders from the road.[5]

In spite of this paranoia he still managed to enjoy their daily excursions through Windsor Great Park and to the Chinese temple at Virginia Water where, unless the weather was bad, he would insist on going each afternoon. As the royal party arrived at the landing stage the band would strike up 'God Save the King', then they would all climb into small boats and be rowed out into the lake. As the small craft drifted idly George and Elizabeth would bait their hooks and fish over the side. Never one to stint on a hobby, the King spent over £200 on fishing tackle for himself and his guests during his first year at Windsor.

Soon news of these bucolic fishing excursions reached the cartoonists and prints appeared lampooning George as the 'King Fisher', dipping his hook into the Treasury revenues to fund ever more grandiose projects or as 'The Fat Gentleman who Bobs for Eels', boating with Elizabeth and giving her a smacking kiss on her plump cheeks. The sobriquet King Fisher must have been in common use at the time for Thomas Creevey described him as such when he saw him at Virginia Water and driving 'in a little phaeton with Lady Conyngham'.[6] Among the many guests who joined them on these fishing parties was the young Princess Victoria, who remembered staying with her aunt at the neighbouring Cumberland Lodge. One afternoon she was taken to meet her infamous uncle and his mistress at the Chinese Temple:

> The King took me by the hand saying 'Give me your little paw'. He was large and gouty but with a wonderful dignity and charm of manner. He wore the wig that was so much worn in those days. Then he said he would give me something to wear, and that it was his picture set in diamonds . . . I was proud of this – and Lady Conyngham pinned it on my shoulder.[7]

When the fish were not biting, the King's guests would return to the shore and picnic at the temple. Lady Holland, a frequent visitor, remembered admiring the exotic interiors of the three temple rooms with their gilt dragon decorations. When the temple was still under construction the King had entertained his guests outside in Indian tents captured seventy years earlier by Robert Clive. Facing the Temple across the lake stood a picturesque classical ruin, the Temple of Augustus, ingeniously fabricated out of the antique Libyan columns that Wyatville had purloined from a neglected courtyard at the British Museum. Looking in the opposite direction visitors could see Fort Belvedere – a small rococo castle that Wyatville had enlarged dramatically in 1828. A century later it was to become the favourite residence of another controversial Prince of Wales, Edward VIII. Like his successor George IV had always liked playing at soldiers and he found this toy castle an ideal place to indulge his fantasies. Throughout the summer of 1829, whenever they were not boating, he could be found with Elizabeth seated by a window in one of its gothic rooms. But all this came at a price and when he died in 1830 the improvements and maintenance at Windsor Great Park were costing the Treasury over £20,000 a year. Even in his last months, when seriously ill, the King's spending continued unabated and one of his last acts was to purchase an adjoining estate at an excessive price of £21,000.

George had grown so fond of the Royal Lodge that he declared in September 1829 that he had decided not to live at Windsor Castle, now nearing completion, in spite of the money that had been spent on its restoration. Thomas Creevey deplored this appalling waste and predicted that the King would also never live at the new Buckingham Palace, on which equally vast sums were now being spent.[8] Nothing, it appeared, would induce him to go up to London again and since 1823 he had visited the city little more than a dozen times, once to open Parliament in 1826, twice to go to the theatre and five times for meetings of the Privy Council. Even when his favourite brother, the Duke of York, was dying George only managed to visit him three times and then he insisted that wholly unnecessary precautions be taken for his safety. St James's Park was closed to the public for two days so that no one should see their sovereign clambering in and out of his carriage. George remembered the humiliation he had suffered at the State Opening of Parliament in 1822 when, unbalanced by his increasing girth, he had almost fallen out of the coach.

So the King remained contentedly idle at Windsor, only venturing out to attend an occasional local race meeting. As late as August 1828 he had stirred himself to visit the races at Egham while Princess Lieven took Elizabeth off for lunch at nearby Cliveden. The excitement of the day seemed to reinvigorate him for on the way back to Windsor he collected both ladies and took them to an al fresco dinner at Virginia Water. But a year later Francis Mount Charles told Charles Greville that he found the King's indolence so great that it was next to impossible to get him to do even the most ordinary business.[9]

As he began his long withdrawal from the world George's memory of his father's madness haunted him and he would often break into tears without apparent cause. His friends became anxious that he too might go blind and mad like his father although Charles Greville wrote in his journal that he thought the King was 'already a little of both'.[10] The recent death of his favourite brother, the Duke of York, and the similarity of their symptoms also became an almost daily obsession. On 9 January 1828 George had excused himself to Knighton for not replying to a letter, claiming that he did not have the strength to sit up in bed. Two months later a household official noticed that the King now suffered 'dropsy to the most dreadful degree' and surmised that he would probably not last much longer.

For a man who loved colour and symmetry the last years of George IV's life were made a misery by poor eyesight. Blind in one eye and with an advanced cataract in the other, his vision had become severely impaired. To save the one remaining eye his surgeons decided in September 1829 to perform a difficult and painful operation. George bore the agony with remarkable fortitude, fully justifying Wellington's judgement that the King 'neither feared operations nor their possible consequences'. But limited vision made the daily signing of dozens of state papers a miserable ordeal. In desperation he appealed to his chief physician, Sir Henry Halford, to devise a way of relieving him of this burden. Halford replied that if Parliament were consulted it would insist on the King being examined by a panel of doctors to ascertain the full extent of his disability.[11] Such a humiliating prospect was too much for so proud a man, and the King never mentioned the subject again. By March 1830 his eyesight had deteriorated further and he described himself pathetically as being as 'blind as a beetle'. This debility was now so obvious that the government finally agreed that he could sign official papers with an ink stamp of his signature if at least three witnesses were present. Yet a poignant reminder of this visual past now hung on his bedroom wall, a large painting of a female nude on which, in the disapproving words of Robert Huish 'his jaded senses, no longer able to enjoy the reality, tested themselves on the representation'.[12]

There were other signs of the King's increasing decrepitude. His few remaining teeth gave him constant pain and were finally removed by the royal dentist, Samuel Cartwright, who fitted him with a passable set of false ones. Overcharging by medical professionals was a common practice of the day and Cartwright demanded an exorbitant fee of twenty guineas for each of his thirty-seven visits to Windsor. George's breathlessness had also increased and was now combined with mild panic attacks whenever he had to deal with awkward issues. But these vicissitudes were as nothing compared to the problems caused by his weakened heart. According to Knighton it was 'much loaded with fat'.[13] Four years earlier he had witnessed the King wracked by a sudden violent pain in his chest, probably the onset of angina. When Knighton had informed the Prime Minister of the time, George Canning, he replied dismissively that he shared the Duke of Wellington's opinion that the King was merely a notorious hypochondriac. But Knighton, himself a doctor, angrily insisted that this was not play-acting for he had witnessed himself that 'nothing can exceed the pain of such attacks'.[14] However, he misdiagnosed the cause of the pain, considering that it was due to gout, 'principally confined to the neck of the bladder and all along the course of the urethra' rather than to the angina from which George clearly suffered. Knighton then compounded the error by prescribing an ineffectual and irrelevant treatment of leeches to be applied around the King's pelvis.

As she watched him manoeuvring himself along the corridors at the Royal Lodge Elizabeth Conyngham was said to have wept to see her lover reduced to this pitiable condition. In an effort to relieve his gloom she suggested in November 1829 that they go down to Brighton for a holiday at the Pavilion. But she then fell ill herself and the trip was postponed until the following spring. Trapped at Windsor she again despaired of her lot and told those around her that she could stand it no longer and was prepared to leave. One of the royal valets later told Charles Greville that it was Knighton who induced her to stay on. She did nothing, said the valet, but pray from morning to night.[15]

George's infirmity and the gloomy atmosphere at the Royal Lodge now began to affect Elizabeth's health as well. In November 1829 she fell ill with 'a bad bilious fever' that soon developed into such persistent fainting fits, possibly panic attacks, that she became convinced that she was dying herself. Never having seen her this depressed before, George became so alarmed that he temporarily forgot his own problems and became a constant visitor to her sickroom. Illness and a shared contemplation of their own mortality, it seemed, had brought them closer together.

To the astonishment of the servants at the Royal Lodge Lady Conyngham was now frequently seen weeping openly at the King's miserable condition. Each morning she attended prayers for his safe recovery, joining in fervently with the responses. Like Knighton she was convinced that he was not shamming and by the spring of 1830 even the sceptical Duke of Wellington, seeing the sovereign 'wasted and wasting' was forced to admit that he was indeed seriously ill. On 14 April George seemed to recover sufficiently to rouse himself and take a rare excursion by pony-chaise into the grounds of Windsor Great Park. There, as he stopped to look at his pack of hounds, he was seized by a sudden severe pain in his chest and had to be rushed back to the Lodge. At dinner that evening Wellington thought he still looked very unwell but was pleased to see that a heavy dose of laudanum restored him to a 'very good humour'. To the Duke's amazement the King's appetite appeared to be totally unaffected by the trauma of the day. As he told Harriet Arbuthnot:

> He drank two glasses of hot ale and toast, three glasses of claret, some strawberries!! and a glass of brandy. Last night they gave him some physic and, after it, he drank three glasses of port wine and a glass of brandy. No wonder he is likely to die. But they say he will have all these things and nobody can prevent him.[16]

A few days later Wellington was even more astonished to watch the King demolish with relish 'a pigeon and beef steak pie of which he ate two pigeons and three beef-steaks, three parts of a bottle of Mozelle, a glass of dry champagne, two glasses of port [and] a glass of brandy!' Nor was he finished that evening for when the servants were about to go down for their own dinner George called back his page and said to him: 'Go downstairs and cut me off just such a piece of beef as you would like to have yourself, cut from the part you like the best yourself, and bring it me up.' The page duly went and fetched an enormous quantity of roast beef, all of which the King ate, and then slept for five hours.[17]

To the years of gluttony and over-drinking was added the long-established problem of laudanum. George had been taking ever larger doses of the powerful opiate and was now clearly addicted to it. Recently he had graduated from 100 to over 250 drops a day. Combined with a copious intake of alcohol this produced in him depression, violent mood swings and severe lethargy. Yet this massive dose of narcotics never seemed to impede his thought process and Wellington was amazed at how well he maintained a rational conversation in spite of the laudanum.

The morning after the excursion to see the hounds, the royal physician Sir Henry Halford was called and he finally confirmed that the King was suffering from a severe heart condition. Halford ordered that fluid that had accumulated in his swollen legs and belly should be drawn off. This was done a pint at a time. Realising that his royal patron was seriously ill Halford became particularly protective of the King, often refusing to allow other doctors to examine him. When *The Lancet* got to hear of it they published an editorial condemning both Halford's secretive attitude and his supposed reluctance to prescribe anything other than powerful sedatives for the sick monarch.[18] Halford, as self-important in his way as Sir William Knighton, ignored the criticisms. Again, like Knighton, he seemed more concerned with ingratiating himself with members of the King's circle. He had even written to Maria Fitzherbert, without informing George, warning her that the King was 'excessively ill, with embarrassment and difficulty of breathing'.[19] In spite of their long years of separation Maria wrote immediately to her old love, sending the letter to Halford to deliver personally, so bypassing both Knighton and Elizabeth Conyngham. The King, according to Halford, seized it eagerly and read the words:

After so many years of continual silence, my anxiety concerning your Majesty has got the better of my scruples, and I trust your Majesty will believe me most sincere when I assure you how truly I have grieved to hear of your sufferings . . . No one can feel more rejoiced to learn your Majesty is returned to complete convalescence, which I pray you may long enjoy, accompanied by every degree of happiness you may wish for or desire.[20]

With tears in his eyes the King finished reading the letter then hid it under his pillow away from Knighton and Elizabeth.

That same day, 8 June 1830, probably as a result of Maria Fitzherbert's letter, the King asked Halford to confirm that he was, indeed, dying. When Halford nodded his confirmation the King showed no emotion but immediately asked him to leave and summoned Sir William Knighton to his bedchamber. Knighton was informed that after various legacies had been discharged Lady Conyngham was to be the main beneficiary of the King's will. All that he possessed would be hers. Later that evening the King asked his secretary how Elizabeth had received the news. 'She was much affected, Sir, and burst into tears,' Knighton replied.[21]

The following day the King repeated his wishes in front of three witnesses: Halford, Knighton and Sir Matthew Tierney. Everything he possessed, he insisted, should on his death become the property of the lady. Ever eager to ingratiate himself with powerful political figures, Halford felt it his duty to inform the Duke of Wellington of the potentially embarrassing situation if the King's mistress were seen to inherit his property. The Duke immediately drove down to Windsor and asked to see Elizabeth alone. He told her bluntly that for her own sake and that of the nation she must not accept the legacy. Elizabeth protested her complete innocence and insisted to the Duke that it was her right to receive whatever the King intended to give her. Lord Lyndhurst, who was present at the meeting, told his wife that the Duke then became furious and told Elizabeth that he would give her a copy of the memoirs of Madame du Barry as a warning. That woman's greed and profligacy, he said, had led not only to the fall of the French monarchy and the execution of Louis XVI but had also cost Madame du Barry her own head. If Elizabeth was to accept the King's gifts then both she and the monarchy would suffer irreparable damage. What was more, Wellington threatened, he would certainly do everything in his power to overthrow the will legally and make sure that she lost everything she had gained in the past.[22]

Ten days earlier, on the last day of May 1830, John Wilson Croker had gone down to Windsor to have the King stamp a new government bill with his signature. It was the first time he had seen him in months and he was shocked by George's decrepit appearance but forced to admire the monarch's new stoicism. 'The King is aware of his situation,' Croker wrote, 'and contemplates it, as I learn, boldly. He sits bolstered up in bed, or in a chair, incapable of lying down . . . he is very torpid, and evidently fading rapidly away.'[23] No one who saw the King that month could doubt Croker's gloomy prediction. The Duchess of Gloucester reported that he was now 'enormous, like a feather bed' and that his waterlogged legs were as 'hard as stone'.[24] The attacks of pain and breathlessness were ever more frequent yet none of the growing band of doctors that was assembling at the Lodge seemed capable of alleviating the painful symptoms. His only relief came from the ever-larger doses of laudanum that Halford allowed him. Frequently he suffered terrible spasms as a deep gurgling erupted in his throat and he fought desperately for breath. His face then his fingertips would gradually turn black. When the attack had passed he would drag himself wearily up on his pillows and reach out for a large glass of brandy. Occasionally he recovered so rapidly that he would then decide to go out for a drive, and a carriage would be summoned to take him and Elizabeth into the Park.

A notorious hypochondriac and near-hysteric throughout his life, the King prepared for his end with a coolness and courage that deeply impressed all those who witnessed it. Halford, who saw more of him than anyone, admired his fortitude and dignity and was moved by the King's consideration for those around him. Lord Ellenborough too wrote that 'in constitution and mind he is certainly wonderful'.[25] But George still spoke of making a speedy recovery and promised that soon he would take them all to the races at Ascot again. Unable to perform his state duties he still managed in the very month of his death to take an interest in the design of the new uniforms for the Pensioners at Chelsea, a last symbolic gesture to his own frustrated military ambitions. Now a strange calm came upon him and when he cheerfully informed Elizabeth that he might die at any moment the incredulous Duke of Wellington commented that he was merely trying to vex her.

In recent years, supposedly under Elizabeth Conyngham's influence, the King had begun to show an unaccustomed interest in religion. Now they began taking communion together each morning in the presence of Sir William Knighton. Beside the King's bed Sir William had placed a copy of the Bible which the King was frequently seen to refer to. Sleep in the conventional manner was impossible and George spent every night propped up in a chair by his bed. As fatigue overcame him he would lean forward and rest his head on his hands on a table in front of him.

In his last days George showed an unexpected resilience and a determination to do his duty whatever his physical limitations. On 16 June he even cleared the backlog of state papers awaiting his endorsement, stamping all 400 of them himself. A week later he saw the Duke of Wellington for what was to be the last time.[26] During the conversation George appeared unusually optimistic about the future, assuring the Duke that he was feeling much better and would soon be on the move again. That Friday night, 25 June, George retired to his bedroom chair as usual and fell asleep with his head on the table and his hand in that of another physician, Sir Wathen Waller, who had agreed to sit with him. At two a.m. he awoke and took his medicine, together with a sip of tea, before falling asleep again. Then an hour later he awoke in distress and called for a commode and Sir Henry Halford. When Halford arrived he found the King slumped back in his chair with his eyes closed. A moment later a blood vessel burst in his stomach and he lurched up clutching a page by the shoulder. His last words, according to Sir Henry, were 'my dear boy! This is death.' As the page supported him, the King fell forward on to the young man's shoulder and died.[27]

Elizabeth was immediately summoned to the room to see her lover for over ten years laid out on his deathbed. Then an event was said to have occurred that became the foundation for the last of the many scurrilous stories about her. It originated with the Countess Brownlow, who claimed that when she was a lady-in-waiting at William IV's court a page named Whiting told her that Lady Conyngham had frequently asked the King for the key to his private closet where he kept his valuables. This key, according to Whiting, was on a chain round his neck. The King, he said, had always refused to give it to her but within minutes of George's death he had come back into the bedroom to find Lady Conyngham attempting to take the key from the dead man's neck.[28]

What is certain is that now her protector was dead Elizabeth Conyngham could expect little sympathy from his successor. Ever a realist, she knew it was time to go and by noon that same day she and her daughters had packed all their belongings and were ready to leave Windsor. The story of their rapid departure – supposedly with two wagonloads of booty – spread throughout the land and helped to confirm her in the public imagination as a greedy and cynical hypocrite. 'First she packed and then she prayed,' it was said. As an account written twenty years later put it, 'where was she, his constant companion during the years that his huge Herculean frame was crumbling to decay? Packing up jewels, cash and movables in the upper apartments of the castle!' The Countess Brownlow predictably condemned 'the heartlessness of the vile and mercenary woman on whom and her family he had lavished hundreds of thousands of pounds'.[29] The story of the Conynghams' rapid departure spread throughout London. One of the best-known cartoons at the time was titled 'Packing Up!!!' and shows a vast Lady Conyngham desperately trying to lock a treasure chest while her husband ties up a parcel.

The swift exit of the Conyngham ladies was confirmed by such reliable witnesses as Charles Greville and Lady Emily Cowper. The latter was shocked to hear that they left

without even showing the decent respect of appearing in mourning; their carriages loaded with packages of all shapes and sizes covered with matting and containing, as Sir Frederick Watson (Master of the Household) believed, clocks, china, etc., purloined from different rooms, and which disappeared with them.[30]

Lady Emily Cowper was certainly no friend of Elizabeth Conyngham, whom she blamed for the suicide of her adored uncle, Lord Londonderry.[31] She claimed that news of the Conynghams' sudden departure had already leaked out and 'they were obliged to go by the Home Park for it was known that the inhabitants of Windsor intended to hoot them as they passed'.[32] The manner of their departure appeared only to confirm the worst public suspicion of the Conynghams and more caricatures appeared showing Elizabeth pushing a wheelbarrow laden with pots and kettles away from the Lodge and off to Slane Castle. But the Conynghams were not the only ones collecting mementoes of the flamboyant lifestyle of George IV. Sir Henry Halford's coachman was later convicted of stealing items of furniture from Windsor using his own master's carriage, and fined £60. There seems little doubt that the servant

219

took the blame for the master as Halford had earlier told his wife that he had begun collecting little items belonging to the King. He also told her that he had his eye on an unusual section of gilding in the King's sickroom – a swallow's nest executed in the Chinese style. It would, he thought, be a fascinating souvenir of the King's memorable years at the Brighton Pavilion.[33]

The King had told Wellington that he wished to be buried in his nightclothes and 'with whatever ornaments might be upon his person at the time of his death'. From 14 July, George's body lay in state in the Great Drawing Room at Windsor Castle. Fittingly, as Steven Parissien has noted, the room with its over-decorated 'Tudorbethan' style perfectly matched the late King's own flamboyant taste. As he made his final inspection alone on the morning of the funeral Wellington noticed a black ribbon around the King's neck. Driven by curiosity he pulled at it and a diamond locket containing a miniature portrait of Mrs Fitzherbert appeared. The Duke hastily pushed it back into the King's nightshirt but years later he confessed to Mrs Dawson-Damer, Mrs Fitzherbert's daughter, Minny, what his inquisitiveness had revealed. When Minny told her mother that the King had been buried with her picture round his neck, Maria listened without a word. But presently it was seen 'that some large tears fell from her eyes'.[34]

But the same John Whiting, the royal page who claimed to have seen Elizabeth attempting to take the key from around the late King's neck, told a different story. He assured Queen Victoria many years later that the portrait in the locket was not that of Mrs Fitzherbert but of the King's last and most constant companion, Lady Conyngham.[35]

# FIFTEEN

## *End of an Era*

As the Conyngham ladies prepared for their hasty departure from Windsor the Duke of Wellington and Sir William Knighton returned to the King's private rooms and searched through all his possessions for anything that might blemish his posthumous reputation even more. Their main concern was the huge bundle of correspondence from various women that the King was known to have kept all his life, together with the copies of his replies. The letters were soon discovered hidden in a cupboard and those from Lady Conyngham in particular were seen to be of 'an ardent nature' and so libidinous that they clearly confirmed the existence of a strong sexual relationship between herself and the late King. The Duke, no prude himself, later claimed to have been shocked by their content.[1] Gathering them up he took them over to the fireplace and carefully burnt them all in an act of historical desecration. This was fast becoming an age of respectability and only a bowdlerised version of a man's life could be permitted to survive. Even such a past roué as the Duke of Wellington now had to accommodate the pious mores of a man like Sir William Knighton.

With all this compromising material reduced to ashes the Duke and Knighton then examined the royal wardrobes and chests of drawers. All were crammed to bursting with articles and souvenirs that George had been reluctant to throw away. Naturally there was an immense collection of clothes including coats, suits, waistcoats and shirts, boots and breeches, gloves and hats and walking sticks and wigs. There were 300 riding whips, 'canes without number, every sort of uniform, the costumes of all the orders in Europe, splendid furs, pelisses, etc.'[2] George's fascination with clothes had continued to the end and there were a dozen pairs of new corduroy riding breeches ordered long after he could ever have mounted a horse again. The King appeared never to have parted with anything and among the more intimate possessions were faded nosegays, women's gloves retaining the perspiration from some long-forgotten ball and locks of women's hair 'of all colours and lengths, some having the powder and pomatum yet sticking to them'.[3]

The levity with which the King had treated financial matters was revealed by the 'five hundred pocketbooks, of different dates, and in every one of them money' as Wellington later told Charles Greville. In all they collected over £10,000 from the pocketbooks, trinket boxes and bundles of banknotes lying about. The discovery of so much cash was ironic for throughout his life George was never once out of debt, owing large sums of money to his father, to the state, to his jewellers and tradesmen, to his architects and his builders. Even as he lay dying Knighton had thought it prudent to write to the King's creditors declining any personal responsibility for the royal debts. Later he faced the ignominy of having to hand over to the London jewellers Rundell, Bridge & Co. the magnificent jewelled Order of the Holy Spirit that Louis XVIII had awarded the King in 1814 in part payment of the huge sum they were still owed.

There was little mourning in Britain for the King, for he had long since withdrawn himself from public life. At Brook's, in the last week of his life, the members had cynically placed bets on how long the monarch would live and were more concerned that race meetings might be cancelled than with his survival. While some like Thomas Creevey recalled his past kindness and genuinely mourned 'poor Prinny', public opinion was far less generous. *The Times* criticised his 'most reckless, unceasing and unbounded prodigality', and his 'indifference to the feelings of others'. In a ruthless and splenetic article condemning both the late King and his mistress it set the mood by which he would be judged for the rest of the century:

What heart has heaved one throb of unmercenary sorrow . . . for that Leviathan of the haut ton, George IV. . . . Nothing more remains to be said about him but to pay – as pay we must – for his profusion; and to turn his bad conduct to some account by tying up the hands of those who come after him in what concerns the public money.[4]

One positive quality that George IV had shared with Elizabeth Conyngham and that was not mentioned in the obituaries was human compassion. She was said to have often pleaded with him to persuade the government to end the barbaric practice of executing women criminals. He in turn would scour the lists of the condemned 'who had no other advocate' to find reasons to justify a remission of sentence. He was particularly horrified by the large number of multiple executions that had become commonplace in the late 1820s, often writing to the Home Secretary, Sir Robert Peel, insisting on the Crown's right to exercise the prerogative of mercy. Once when Peel was a guest at the Pavilion he was summoned in the middle of the night and begged to pardon a particular criminal awaiting death. When Peel eventually gave in the King kissed him on the cheek then, noticing his ill-favoured dressing gown said, 'Peel, where did you get your dressing gown? I'll show you what a dressing gown ought to be.' With that he took off his own gown and gave it to Peel.[5]

George had left meticulous orders for his own funeral but these were largely ignored and a simple and inexpensive ceremony was arranged for the burial on Thursday 15 July instead. At the last moment, when the cortège was about to leave Windsor Castle, his enormous lead coffin was seen to have bulged ominously and the undertaker had to puncture it to release the gases. When it was carried inside the over-decorated St George's Chapel the Guardsmen's flaming torches soon obscured the scene with smoke. *The Times* correspondent could not discern 'a single mark of sympathy' in a congregation that, apart from the new King and his party, consisted mainly of servants from the royal household and their friends. The other mourners appeared to be local carpenters, upholsterers and the petty tradesmen of the town who, *The Times* lamented, had been admitted to the exclusion of more respectable public servants. Those who arrived first had not only seized the best places but also stopped others from sitting, by reserving places for their friends. 'Never', *The Times* went on, 'have we seen so motley, so rude, so ill-managed a body of persons.'[6] Robert Huish was equally shocked by 'the screams of the females and the rude and indecent jokes of the blackguards that gave the whole scene more the appearance of a crowd hastening to some raree-show than to the chamber of death'.[7]

Chaos followed George to the very last, for as the choir began a pealing anthem a large section of wooden carving above the stalls crashed down on to the head of Sir Ashley Cooper, who clamped a large pocket-handkerchief on the wound and remained stoically in his place.

Perhaps the only genuine mourners were Elizabeth Conyngham, who had returned for the occasion, and her son Francis Mount Charles, who stood alone and wept for the old man who had been his benefactor. They had shared much in common, a predilection for love affairs, a weakness for gossip and a love in very different ways for the same woman – both libertines but both with kind hearts.

A few weeks after the funeral Princess Lieven, who had for so long chronicled the late King's misdemeanours, wrote to Metternich that 'the late King is completely forgotten, and, if remembered, it is only to criticise his morals. It is among the middle and lower classes especially that he left a very unfavourable impression.'[8] As the historian Sir Owen Morshead memorably observed, George 'had melted like a snowman: only the clothes remained'.[9] Soon these too disappeared as the King's entire wardrobe was publicly auctioned in a three-day sale of 438 lots. The notorious Coronation outfit that had cost the nation so much was knocked down for a mere 127 guineas.[10]

That autumn Elizabeth Conyngham returned to London and from her house in Hamilton Place wrote to the Duke of Wellington offering, to his surprise, to return much of the jewellery that George had bestowed upon her in later years. 'It appears', she wrote, 'doubtful whether His late Majesty ought to have given it away.'[11] Wellington, as Prime Minister, accepted her offer with alacrity and John Bridge of Rundell, Bridge & Co. was sent round to collect a large paper parcel marked 'diamonds and pearls'. Delighted with the return of gifts that he considered the property of the crown Wellington passed them immediately on to King William IV. When opened at Buckingham Palace the parcel revealed a treasure trove including over 400 pearls and diamonds that had belonged to the late King's mother, Queen Charlotte, King George III's personal insignia of the Order of the Bath, hundreds of brilliants and, significantly, the much discussed Stuart sapphire that Elizabeth had worn as a brooch.

Delighted to have the jewels back in royal possession Wellington wrote to Elizabeth thanking her for her prompt action and conveying King William IV's assurance that it was not he who had expressed any doubts about the ownership of the gifts. However Wellington was astonished when he received a letter the following day, 2 December 1830, from the new King himself, stating that William was not convinced that the Stuart sapphire was legal crown property after all and believed that it had belonged to his brother personally:

No Question can therefore exist or arise as to the right of Disposal being vested in the late King, as to its being exercised when He gave it to the Marchioness of Conyngham.[12]

To his chagrin, Wellington therefore saw no alternative but to return the sapphire and its brilliant clasp to Elizabeth, but before doing so he again wrote to the King suggesting that as Prince Leopold had returned the sapphire on his wife's death it might yet be Crown property. William was having none of this and replied firmly that he saw no reason 'for departing from His Determination to return it to the Marchioness of Conyngham'.[13] The following day the sapphire and clasp were delivered to Elizabeth at Hamilton Place.

The episode had demonstrated William's blunt, good-natured honesty but in other respects, particularly in matters of taste, he was a disappointing contrast to his late brother. When shown a picture of which George had been particularly fond William remarked: 'Ay, it seems pretty – I daresay it is – my brother was very fond of this sort of nicknackery. Damned expensive taste though.'[14] The new King had little interest in any of the architectural innovations at Brighton or Windsor and allowed his wife, Queen Adelaide, to pull down that part of the Royal Lodge where she imagined the King and Lady Conyngham had indulged in their profligate and adulterous lechery. Most of the old King's servants were summarily dismissed including the famous French chefs – William preferred good plain British food. New-fangled devices which had so fascinated George, such as the recently installed gas lighting at the Pavilion, were immediately ripped out and thrown away. Even the menagerie in Windsor Park that had given George and Elizabeth so much enjoyment was closed down and the animals sent off to the new London Zoo. Finally the German band that had so entertained the King and his guests for almost a decade was dismissed.

This destruction was tangible proof that the indulgences of Regency Britain were finally over and the moral climate of the nation was moving towards the new conservatism that was to characterise Victorian Britain. Yet even Queen Adelaide could not bring herself to order the destruction of the charming little fishing temple at Virginia Water that had given the late King and his mistress such pleasure in his last years. It was simply left to decay so that when the Prince Consort visited it in 1840 it was little more than a ruin and about to be demolished. With his characteristic good sense Albert ordered that it be preserved but soon after his death in 1861 his widow, in spite of her happy childhood memories of fishing there with her uncle and Lady Conyngham, ordered that it be finally demolished. One of the last to see the little temple still standing was the Duke of Wellington. Riding out with Sir John Cope's hounds in 1833, he galloped past it and the sight of the ruins made him feel 'quite unhappy. Alas!'[15] Never slow to criticise George IV when he was alive, the Duke was one of the very few who retained a good word for the late King. He told his friend Thomas Raikes that George had indeed been 'the most extraordinary compound of talent, wit, buffoonery, obstinacy and good feeling – in short, a medley of the most opposite qualities with a great preponderance of good that I ever saw in any character in my life'. The nation, the Duke thought, would always have cause to be grateful to the man who had been 'a most magnificent patron of the arts in this country, and in the world'.[16]

European opinion was certainly more favourable to a man who had displayed such Continental tastes and had ruled Britain at a time of great social and political change. That arch-survivor Prince Talleyrand wrote that, 'When today monarchs continually court popularity, a pointless task, King George IV remained almost uniquely *un roi grand seigneur*.' To the British public the new King and Queen were a welcome contrast to his late brother and his mistress. When Miss Margaretta Brown, sister-in-law of one of the Windsor canons, heard of the departure of Lady Conyngham she wrote in her diary, underlining each word with heavy strokes,

'GOOD RIDDANCE. I am glad we are going to have a QUEEN. Lady C will probably never be thought or heard of more. The King left no will wishing to die intestate so that everything falls to the Crown except what he has already given to the Lady, no doubt *plenty*.'[17]

Elizabeth Conyngham now passed from her position as one of the most scandalous and celebrated women in Britain to a forgotten relic of the age. Two years after the King's death her husband Henry, the first Marquess of Conyngham, also died. Elizabeth, a near-pariah in London, sought privacy in foreign travel and lived for a time in Paris where her looks and grace were reported to be still much admired. Lady Harriet Granville wrote to a friend in England that Lady Conyngham is 'as fresh as a daisy, *bouche comme une rose*, in a light blue gauze hat with white feathers, a salmon-coloured gown made extremely high with long sleeves; she looked infinitely handsomer than when in a satin frock, swaddled in jewels'.[18] A year later Elizabeth had made her way to Rome from where Lord Houghton wrote in 1834 that 'one of the latest converts to Protestant monasticism is no less person than Lady Conyngham who has been living here the whole winter in such absolute seclusion that hardly ten people are aware of her existence'.[19] Yet her family remained in England. Lord Francis retained his office in the government and in 1836 he was acting as King William's emissary to Princess Victoria, offering her an establishment independent of her domineering mother. The following year, as Lord Chamberlain, he accompanied the Archbishop of Canterbury to tell the eighteen-year-old Victoria that her uncle was dead and that she was now Queen of England. Francis retained his post as Lord Chamberlain and that October found himself dining with the young Queen at the Brighton Pavilion when she visited it for the first time in her reign.

With Elizabeth's encouragement, both daughters had married into the British aristocracy and her younger sister had long been married to Sir Robert Lawley, later created Lord Wenlock. Only her brother William Denison had constantly refused royal patronage and when he died in 1849 his enormous fortune, which he had more than doubled since the death of his own father, was left to Elizabeth's third son Albert but only on condition that he change his surname to Denison. This proved to be a timely legacy for Lord Albert, who had lost his fortune in speculating with George Hudson on the railway boom of the early 1840s and was living abroad out of reach of his many creditors. A year later in 1850, fortunes restored, Albert was created the first Baron Londesborough. He lived on to become one of the greatest collectors of art and antiques of the Victorian era, never quite escaping the whispered rumours that he was, in reality, King George IV's natural son.

The destruction that Queen Adelaide had begun at Windsor, Queen Victoria completed in a final eradication of a 'shameful memory of a different age'. The last traces of George IV and Lady Conyngham were finally swept away when she ordered the Brighton Pavilion to be gutted and the contents distributed between Buckingham Palace and Windsor Castle. Between 1847 and 1848 over 140 vans took away most of the furniture, carpets, clocks and porcelain that George had so loved. It would be almost a century before Brighton Council, realising that a unique treasure lay at the centre of its town, bought the dilapidated building and began the long process of its careful restoration.

As for Lady Conyngham, once mistress of this unique building, she became increasingly pious and lived out her life as a widow continuing to travel on the Continent before finally settling at Bifrons, the Conyngham estate in Kent. Then in July 1844 came a strange and poignant reminder of the past when Tsar Nicholas of Russia, now a married and middle-aged man, made a state visit to England to meet the young Queen Victoria four years after her marriage to Prince Albert. The Tsar had retained fond memories of England and after attending a grand military review insisted on being taken to the races at Ascot. To his courtiers' surprise he then expressed a great desire to meet his old friend Lady Conyngham again, having been 'well received by her twenty seven years ago during her splendour'. Lady Holland thought his request 'very pretty' but wondered if he was aware that the lady was still under such a cloud that she would be considered a near-pariah at court. When Elizabeth, now seventy-four years old, was told of Nicholas' request she agreed to come up from Kent and meet him in London. Predictably, the passage of the years had taken its toll and the Tsar confessed to his aides, according to Lady Holland, that he was shocked by her aged appearance.[20]

Elizabeth Conyngham returned to her estate at Bifrons and lived out her last years, a relic of a more lively and scandalous age. There she died peacefully in 1861 at the age of ninety-one. Shortly before her death when staying at a bitterly cold country house she had complained of the draught. A servant was sent to bring a screen from the attic to put round her sofa. Returning to the drawing room later her hosts found their elderly guest fast asleep but suddenly noticed, to their horror, that she was surrounded by an old print screen decorated with scurrilous cartoons from forty years earlier showing King George IV and his scandalous mistress Lady Conyngham cavorting together in their prime.[21]

# Notes

## Prologue

1. Brownlow, Countess, *The Eve of Victorianism*, London, John Murray, 1940, p. 138

## 1. The Conyngham Trap

1. Berkeley, i, p. 84
2. Greville Memoirs, i, p. 83
3. *Secrets of the Castle*, p. 12.
4. Quoted in *The Amatory Life of the Marchioness of C—ny—m.*
5. Jackson Diary
6. Parliamentary Debates, xxii, 85 (19 March 1812)
7. *Morning Post*, 18 March 1812
8. Calvert, The Hon. Mrs, *An Irish Beauty of the Regency*, London, John Lane, 1911, p. 96
9. Bury Diary, i, p. 96
10. Greville Memoirs, i, p. 96
11. Jekyll Correspondence, p. 74
12. *The Private Letters of Princess Lieven to Prince Metternich*, ed. Peter Quennell, London, John Murray, 1937, p. 38
13. Ibid.
14. Holland Letters, p. 8
15. *Secrets of the Castle*, p. 13
16. Greville Memoirs, i, p. 103

## 2. A London Heiress

1. Arbuthnot Journal, i, p. 47
2. *Biographia Leodiensis*, p. 228
3. Ibid.
4. Sitwell, p. 56
5. Ibid.
6. Wollstonecraft, Mary, *Vindication of the Rights of Women*, ed. Miriam Kramnick, 2nd edn reprint, London, Harmondsworth, Penguin, 1978, p. 289
7. *The Reminiscences and Recollections of Captain Gronow*, 2 vols, London, 1892, p. 187
8. Ponsonby, p. 75
9. Wilson, Harriette, p. 72
10. Ibid.
11. Ibid., p. 73
12. Sitwell, p. 58
13. *The Amatory Life of the Marchioness of C—ny—m*, p. 4
14. *Sketches of Irish Political Characters of the present day*, H. MacDougall, Dublin, 1799, p. 92
15. Old Drogheda Society, *Drogheda and 1798*, Drogheda, 1998, p. 20
16. *The Amatory Life of the Marchioness of C—ny—m*, p. 5
17. Creevey Papers, ii, p. 29
18. Pakenham, Thomas, *The Year of Liberty*, London, Hodder & Stoughton, 1969, p. 208

19. Carpenter, William, *Peerage for the People*, London, 1837, p. 8
20. Creevey Papers, ii, p. 37
21. *Secrets of the Castle*, p. 14
22. Wilson, Frances, p. 252
23. *Secrets of the Castle*, p. 15
24. Huish, i., pp. 404–8
25. Ibid.
26. *Secrets of the Castle*, p. 15
27. Parissien, Steven, *George IV. The Grand Entertainment*, London, John Murray, 2001, p. 342
28. Huish, i, p. 420
29. *Secrets of the Castle*, p. 18
30. Ibid.
31. Priestley, J.B., *The Prince of Pleasure*, London, Heinemann, 1969, p. 280
32. *Memoirs of the Celebrated Lady C\*\*\*\*\*m*, London, 1825
33. *Secrets of the Castle*, p. 18
34. Creevey Papers, i, p. 58
35. Ibid., p. 157
36. Brownlow, p. 68
37. Creevey Papers, i, p. 75
38. Hibbert, *George IV, King and Regent*, p. 37

## 3. Ménage à Trois

1. Musgrave, Clifford, *Life in Brighton*, London, Faber, 1970, p. 74
2. Greville Memoirs, i, p. 118
3. Arbuthnot Journal, i, pp. 117–18
4. Ibid.
5. Lieven, p. 81
6. Quoted in Brownlow, p. 112
7. Arbuthnot Journal, i, p. 369
8. Ibid., i, p. 130
9. Ibid., i, p. 132
10. Creevey Papers, ii, p. 75
11. Ibid., ii, p. 58
12. Ibid., ii, p. 96

13. James, Francis, *Lords of the Ascendancy. The Irish House of Lords and its Members, 1600–1800*, Dublin, Irish Academic Press, 1995, p. 207
14. *Secrets of the Castle*, p. 22
15. *The Amatory Life of the Marchioness of C—ny—m*, p. 7
16. Berkeley, i, p. 120
17. Greville Memoirs, i, p. 118
18. Huish, i, p. 125
19. Creevey Papers, ii, p. 77
20. Croker Papers, ii, p. 28
21. Greville Memoirs, i, p. 130
22. Croker Papers, i, p. 43
23. Lieven, p. 60
24. Seymour, Robert, 'Great Joss and his Playthings' (cartoon), 1829
25. Fulford, p. 180
26. Heath, William, 'Baise-Mon-Q' (cartoon), 1820
27. Greville Memoirs, i, p. 12
28. *The Reminiscences and Recollections of Captain Gronow*, London, 1892, ii, p. 249
29. RA, Queen Victoria's Journal, August 1838
30. Parissien, p. 148
31. Greville Memoirs, i, p. 132
32. Creevey Papers, i, p. 58
33. Royal Archives, Windsor Castle, Add 3/27 [1822]
34. Ibid., RA 50911–3
35. Hibbert, *George IV, Prince of Wales*, p. 239
36. Royal Archives, Windsor Castle, Add. 3/30 [1822]
37. Holland Letters, p. 10
38. Croker Papers, p. 45

## 4. Divorce and Coronation

1. Royal Archives, RA 21/179/159
2. Wraxall, v, p. 391

3. Bury Diary, i, pp. 38–9
4. *The Diaries and Correspondence of James Harris, First Earl of Malmesbury*, ed. 3rd Earl of Malmesbury, London, 1844, ii, p. 252
5. Leveson Gower Correspondence, ii, p. 206
6. RA. George IV, Box 8, 29 March 1816
7. Brougham Memoirs, ii, p. 298
8. Bury Diary, i, p. 4
9. Creevey Papers, i, p. 212
10. Lieven, p. 178
11. *Report of the Proceedings before the House of Lords on a Bill of Pains and Penalties*, London, 1821, i, pp. 268–83
12. Hobhouse Diary, p. 26
13. Greville Memoirs, i, p. 24
14. Lieven, p. 38
15. Greville Memoirs, i, p. 29
16. Lieven, p. 61
17. Creevey Papers, i, p. 333
18. Ibid., p. 342
19. Parissien, p. 345
20. Wellington Friends, p. 8
21. Greville Memoirs, i, p. 29
22. RA, George IV, Box 11
23. Hawes, Frances, *Henry Brougham*, London, Jonathan Cape, 1957, p. 158
24. Creevey Papers, i, p. 339
25. Brougham, i, p. 259
26. Arbuthnot Journal, i, p. 48
27. Ibid., i, p. 53
28. Ibid., i, p. 108
29. Lieven, p. 68
30. New, Chester W., *The Life of Henry Brougham to 1830*, Oxford, Clarendon Press, 1961, p. 260
31. Hibbert, *George IV, Regent and King*, p. 195

32. Lever, p. 184
33. Greville Memoirs, ii, p. 44
34. RA, Coutts Papers, 56/40
35. Article in *Edinburgh Weekly Journal*, 20 July 1821
36. Parissien, p. 304
37. RA Accounts, Asp/K.iii.499
38. Aspinall, *The Letters of King George IV*, p. 323
39. Lever, p. 185
40. Scott Letters, v, p. 38
41. Matthews, Anne, *A Continuation of the Memories of Charles Matthews*, London, 1839, pp. 138–45
42. Lieven, p. 145
43. Lyttleton Correspondence, p. 236
44. Hibbert, *George IV, Regent and King*, p. 193
45. Taylor, Thomas, *Life of Benjamin Robert Haydon*, London, Longmans, Green & Co, 1853, p. 339
46. Huish, i, p. 198
47. Lever, p. 220
48. Anglesea, Marquess of, *One-Leg*, pp. 164–5
49. Arbuthnot Journal, i, p. 108
50. *The Times*, 20 July 1821
51. Taylor, p. 314
52. *The Diary of Benjamin Robert Haydon*, ed. Willard Pope, Harvard University Press, 1960, p. 179
53. Huish, i, p. 166
54. Reported in *The Courier*, 19 July 1821
55. Jermingham Letters, ii, pp. 99–200

## 5. A Trip to Ireland

1. Letters of Harriette, Lady Granville, i, 183
2. Jermingham Letters, ii, p. 203
3. Croker Papers, p. 60

4. Barnard Letters, p. 292
5. Creevey Papers, i, p. 363
6. RA, George IV, Box 8, Envelope 14
7. Jermingham Letters, ii, p. 203
8. Buckingham and Chandos, ii, p. 197
9. Ibid., ii, p. 199
10. Fitzgerald, Percy, *The Life of George IV*, London, 1881, ii, p. 286
11. *The Royal Visit*, p. 8
12. Creevey Papers, ii, p. 30
13. Gregory Memoir, p. 57
14. *The Royal Visit*, p. 9
15. Creevey Papers, ii, p. 30
16. Barnard Letters, p. 294
17. *The Royal Visit*, p. 9
18. Castlereagh Correspondence, p. 279
19. RA, 39319–23
20. Cloncurry, p. 227
21. Arbuthnot Journal, ii, p. 389
22. Croker Papers, p. 61
23. *The Royal Visit*, p. 12
24. Ibid., p. 15
25. Gregory Memoir, p. 63
26. Fulford, p. 238
27. Hardinge, George, *Miscellaneous Works in Prose and Verse*, London, 1827, p. 134
28. Gregory Memoir, p. 64
29. Ibid., p. 66
30. Ibid., pp. 67–8
31. Lieven, p. 155
32. Gregory Memoir, p. 69
33. Creevey Papers, ii, p. 33
34. Ibid., pp. 69–70
35. Ibid., p. 72
36. Croker Papers, p. 61
37. Ibid.
38. Creevey Papers, ii, p. 30
39. *The Royal Visit*, p. 15
40. Creevey Papers, ii, p. 31
41. Ibid.
42. Castlereagh Correspondence, p. 388
43. Buckingham and Chandos, ii, p. 207

## 6. Trading Places

1. Yonge, C.D., *Life and Administration of Robert Banks Jenkinson, 2nd Earl of Liverpool*, London, Collins, 1972, iii, p. 91
2. Lieven, p. 131
3. Arbuthnot Journal, i, p. 9
4. RA, 22577
5. Lieven, pp. 104–5
6. Ibid., p. 145
7. RA, 22574–5
8. RA, 22588
9. Yonge, iii, p. 104
10. RA, 22590
11. Huish, i, p. 223
12. Arbuthnot Journal, i, p. 9
13. Greville Memoirs, ii, p. 71
14. Lieven, p. 167
15. Arbuthnot Journal, i, p. 12
16. Greville Memoirs, ii, p. 30
17. RA, 22687
18. RA, 22689
19. RA, 22690
20. Hibbert, *George IV, Regent and King*, p. 206
21. Hobhouse Diary, p. 53
22. Castlereagh Correspondence, p. 259
23. Hobhouse Diary, p. 72
24. RA, 22691
25. Arbuthnot Journal, i, pp. 17–18
26. Ibid.
27. Lieven, p. 110
28. Hibbert, *George IV, Regent and King*, p. 228
29. Jesse, Captain, *The Life of Beau Brummel*, London, 1854, p. 96
30. Jermingham Letters, ii, p. 213
31. *The Diary of Frances, Lady Shelley*, ed. Richard Edgcumbe, London, 1912–13, ii, p. 110

32. Huish, ii, p. 257
33. Lieven, p. 154
34. Ibid., p. 142
35. BM *Sat, x*, 14254

## 7. *Battle of the Drawing Rooms*

1. Lieven, p.115
2. New, Chester W., *The Life of Henry Brougham to 1830*, Oxford, Clarendon Press, 1961, p. 107
3. Lieven, p. 116
4. Castlereagh Correspondence, p. 179
5. Ibid., p. 289
6. Lieven, p. 150
7. Ibid., p. 152
8. Ibid., p. 157
9. Ibid., p. 159
10. Ibid., p. 160
11. Ibid., p. 171
12. Creevey Papers, ii, p. 38
13. Arbuthnot Journal, i, p. 91
14. Holland Letters, p. 12
15. Lieven, p. 173
16. Ibid., p. 174
17. Ibid., p. 176
18. Ibid., p. 179
19. Ibid.
20. Ibid., p. 180
21. Ibid.
22. Ibid., p. 181
23. Ibid.
24. Ibid., p. 183
25. Ibid., p. 189
26. Hobhouse Diary, p. 89
27. Ibid.
28. Buckingham and Chandos, p. 107
29. Ibid., 108
30. RA, 29551–600
31. Lockhart, iii, p. 92
32. Ibid., iii. p. 101
33. Lieven, p. 191

34. Ibid., p. 194
35. Croker Papers, p. 71
36. Creevey Papers, ii, p. 43
37. Byron, ed. Peter Quennell, *Collected Poems (Vision of Judgement)*, London, Nonesuch Press, 1949, p. 189
38. Croker Papers, p. 218

## 8. *Spending It*

1. Greville Memoirs, i, p. 94
2. Ibid., ii, p. 47
3. *The Correspondence of George, Prince of Wales, 1770–1812*, London, Cassell, 1963–71, i, p. 164
4. Ward, p. 123
5. Stroud, Dorothy, *Henry Holland*, London, Country Life, 1966, p. 84
6. *Morning Chronicle*, 21 June 1811
7. RA, 32696, 26161
8. Lever, p. 91
9. Lieven, p. 130
10. Ibid., p. 137
11. Arbuthnot Journal, i, p. 138
12. Hobhouse Diary, p. 82
13. George, Dorothy M., *English Political Caricature 1793–1832*, Oxford, Clarendon Press, 1959, i, p. 162
14. Creevey Papers, ii, p. 26
15. Greville Memoirs, ii, p. 51
16. Ibid., ii, p. 52
17. Creevey Papers, ii, p. 47
18. Buckingham and Chandos, ii, p. 218
19. Ibid.
20. Creevey Papers, ii, p. 447
21. RA, 22804
22. RA, 22866–8
23. Creevey Papers, ii, p. 449
24. Croker Papers, p. 70

25. Buckingham and Chandos, ii, p. 266

## 9. *Playing Politics*

1. RA, George IV, p. 219
2. RA, 22740–3
3. Lieven, p. 200
4. Hobhouse Diary, p. 61
5. Quoted by Longford in *Wellington*, p. 99
6. Ibid.
7. Yonge, p. 172
8. Lieven, p. 176
9. Longford, p. 112
10. Lieven, p. 182
11. Lever, p. 156
12. Lieven, pp. 219–20
13. Ibid., p. 281
14. Ibid.
15. Creevey Papers, ii, p. 431
16. Hobhouse Diary, p. 98
17. Creevey Papers, ii, p. 440
18. Ibid.
19. Lieven, p. 315
20. Lieven, p. 317
21. Ibid., p. 324
22. Ibid.
23. Bury Diary, p. 182
24. Greville Memoirs, ii, p. 59
25. Ibid., p. 324
26. Lieven, p. 317
27. Ibid.
28. Greville Memoirs, ii, p. 201
29. Stapleton, A.G., *Political Life of George Canning*, London, 1831, p. 438
30. Ibid., p. 470
31. Creevey Papers, i, pp. 450–1
32. Petrie, Sir Charles, *Canning*, revised edition, London, Eyre & Spottiswoode, 1946, p. 228
33. Arbuthnot Journal, i, p. 378

## 10. *A Nasty Scandal*

1. Arbuthnot Journal, ii, p. 142
2. Aspinall, *Politics Politics and the Press, c. 1780–1850*, London, Home and Van Thal, 1949, p. 195
3. Aspinall, *George IV and Sir William Knighton*, London, English Historic Review, 1940, p. 110
4. Berry, Paul, *Mary Ann Clarke*, p.42
5. Wilson, Harriette, p. 269
6. Wilson, Frances, p. 223
7. Greville Memoirs, ii, p. 120
8. Brougham Memoirs, ii, p. 93
9. Wilson, Frances, p. 230
10. Wilson, Harriette, i, p. 7
11. Brougham, ii, p. 535
12. Wilson, Frances, p. 252
13. Ibid., p. 267
14. Aspinall, *George IV and Sir William Knighton*, p. 112
15. Aspinall, *The Letters of King George IV*, p. 501
16. Ibid.
17. Brougham, ii, p. 523
18. Wilson, Frances, p. 260
19. RA, 24755–6

## 11. *Off to Windsor*

1. Lieven, pp. 169–70
2. Ibid., p. 121
3. Greville Memoirs, i, p. 497
4. Holland Letters, p. 35
5. Lieven, p. 172
6. Ibid., p. 177
7. Ibid., p. 182
8. Croker Papers, p. 91
9. Croker Papers, p. 104
10. Lieven, p. 122
11. Ibid., p.143
12. Croker Papers, p. 130
13. Arbuthnot Journal, i, p. 295

14. Gray, Denis, *Spencer Perceval*, Manchester, Manchester University Press, 1963, p. 459
15. Huish, i, p. 178
16. Morshead, Owen, *George IV and the Royal Lodge*, Regency Society of Brighton and Hove, 1965, pp. 12–13
17. Ibid., p. 32
18. Lieven, p. 277
19. Arbuthnot Journal, ii, p. 7
20. Creevey Papers, i, p. 430
21. Arbuthnot Journal, ii, p. 8
22. Ibid., p. 15

## 12. Who Rules the Roost?

1. RA, 19045–6
2. Knighton Memoir, p. 384
3. Lieven, p. 178
4. Creevey Papers, ii, p. 105
5. Ibid.
6. RA, George IV, Box 8
7. Arbuthnot Journal, ii, p. 12
8. Knighton Memoir, p. 458
9. Hobhouse Diary, p. 75
10. Ibid., p. 76
11. RA, Knighton Papers, p. 48
12. Hibbert, *George IV, Regent and King*, p. 225
13. RA, Knighton Papers, p. 56
14. RA, 22820
15. Arbuthnot Journal, ii, p. 23
16. Ibid., p. 3
17. Creevey Papers, ii, p. 236
18. Lieven, p. 326
19. Ibid., p. 135
20. Ibid., p. 137
21. Arbuthnot Journal, i, p. 232
22. Lieven, p. 297
23. Arbuthnot Journal, i, p. 268
24. Ibid., i, p.279
25. Creevey Papers, ii. p. 324
26. Ibid., p. 380
27. Ibid., p. 391
28. Lieven, p. 358
29. Greville Memoirs, i, p. 236
30. Ibid.
31. Ibid., p.244
32. Creevey Papers, ii, p. 425
33. RA, 22965
34. Lieven, p. 329
35. Ibid., p. 352
36. Ibid., p. 380
37. Arbuthnot Journal, i, p. 332
38. Ibid., p. 299
39. Ibid., p. 304
40. Buckingham and Chandos, p. 287
41. Butler, pp. 95–6
42. Lieven, p. 329
43. Ibid., p. 371
44. Ibid.

## 13. Justice for the Catholics

1. Mitchell, L.B.G., *Charles James Fox and the Disintegration of the Whig Party, 1782–1794*, Oxford, Oxford University Press, 1970, p. 206
2. Lieven, p. 131
3. Arbuthnot Journal, ii, p. 246
4. Ibid., ii, p. 250
5. Ibid., ii, p. 245
6. Gregory Memoir, p. 83
7. Croker Papers, p. 115
8. Greville Memoirs, i, p. 236
9. Arbuthnot Journal, ii, p. 263
10. Ibid., p. 259
11. Ellenborough Diary, i, p. 370
12. Arbuthnot Journal, ii, p. 269
13. Fulford, p. 264
14. Greville Memoirs, i, p. 236
15. Ibid., p. 184
16. Ibid., p. 156
17. Ibid., p. 257
18. Creevey Papers, i, p. 542

19. Arbuthnot Journal, ii, p. 254
20. *Wellington Despatches*, viii, p. 95
21. Ibid.
22. RA, 24673–6
23. Lieven, p. 240
24. Parker, Charles Stuart, *Sir Robert Peel, from his Private Papers*, 3 vols, London, John Murray, 1899, ii, p. 18
25. Ibid.
26. Arbuthnot Journal, ii, p. 268

## 14. A Sad Decline

1. Butler, p. 120
2. Huish, p. 392
3. Morshead, p. 42
4. Creevey Papers, i, p. 549
5. Leveson Gower Correspondence, i, p. 172
6. Creevey Papers, i, p. 556
7. Queen Victoria, *Letters*, 1st series, London, 1889, p. 172
8. Gore, John, *Creevey's Life and Times*, London, John Murray, 1934, p. 307
9. Greville Memoirs, i, p. 346
10. Ibid.
11. RA, Add. 18/30
12. Huish, p. 402
13. Knighton Memoir, p. 98
14. Ibid.
15. Greville Memoirs, i, p. 380
16. Arbuthnot Journal, ii, p. 352
17. Ibid., p. 357
18. *The Lancet*, 12 June 1830
19. Wilkins, W.H., *Mrs Fitzherbert and George IV*, i, p.214
20. RA, 50227
21. Oman, p. 176
22. Dover Papers, 17 July 1830
23. Croker Papers, p. 127

24. Hibbert, *George IV, Regent and King*, p. 332
25. Ellenborough Diary, i, pp. 257–8
26. RA, Add. 18/124–130
27. Waller of Woodcote, Mss (Warwick), CR 341/207
28. Brownlow, p. 137
29. Ibid.
30. Lever, p. 195
31. Ibid., p. 102
32. Ibid., p. 195
33. RA, Add.18/86–100
34. Wilkins, p. 296
35. Queen Victoria, *Letters*, 1st series, p. 244

## 15. End of an Era

1. Creevey Papers, i, p. 368
2. Greville Memoirs, ii, p. 23
3. Ibid.
4. *The Times*, 16 July 1830
5. Fulford, p. 226
6. *The Times*, 16 July 1830
7. Huish, p. 452
8. Lieven, p. 283
9. Morshead, p. 93
10. Greville Diary, ii, p. 26
11. Arbuthnot Journal, ii, p. 443
12. Ibid.,, p. 444
13. Ibid.
14. Hibbert, *George IV, Regent and King*, p. 343
15. Wellington Friends, p. 105
16. Oman, p. 93
17. Hibbert, *George IV, Regent and King*, p. 344
18. Leveson Gower Correspondence, i, p. 220
19. Sitwell, p. 72
20. Holland Letters, p. 107
21. Sitwell, p. 73

# Bibliography

*The Amatory Life of the Marchioness of C—ny—m, first Lady of the Royal Bedchamber, and private companion of the late King George IV*, London, 1835

Anglesea, Marquess of, *One-Leg: The Life and Letters of Henry William Paget, 1st Marquess of Anglesea*, London, Jonathan Cape, 1961

Arbuthnot Journal: Wellington, Duke of, and Bamford, Francis, eds., *The Journal of Mrs Arbuthnot*, 2 vols, London, Macmillan, 1950

Aspinall, A., *The Letters of King George IV, 1812–1830*, 3 vols, Cambridge, Cambridge University Press, 1938

—— *The Correspondence of George, Prince of Wales, 1770–1812*, 8 vols, London, Cassell, 1963–71

—— *George IV and Sir William Knighton*, London, English Historic Review, 1940

—— *Politics and the Press, c. 1780–1850*, London, Home and Van Thal, 1949

Barnard Letters: Powell, Anthony, ed., *Barnard Letters 1778–1824*, London, Duckworth, 1928

Bartlett, C.J., *Castlereagh*, London, Macmillan, 1966

Berry, Paul, *Mary Ann Clarke*, London, Femina, 1970

Berkeley, The Hon. Grantley F., *My Life and Recollections*, 4 vols, London, Hurst & Blackett, 1866

*Biographia Leodiensis, or biographical sketches of the Worthies of Leeds and Neighbourhood from the Norman conquest to the present time*. R.V. Taylor, ed., Leeds, 1865

Bloomfield, Georgina, Lady, *Memoir of Benjamin, Lord Bloomfield*, 2 vols, London, 1884

Brougham Memoirs: *The Life and Times of Henry Lord Brougham Written by Himself*, 3 vols, London, 1871

Brownlow, Countess, *The Eve of Victorianism*, London, John Murray, 1940

Buckingham and Chandos, Duke of, *Memoirs of the Court of George IV*, London 1859

Burke, S. Hubert, *Ireland Sixty Years Ago*, Dublin, 1885

Bury Diary: ed., Francis Steuart, *The Diary of a Lady in Waiting by Lady Charlotte Bury*, 2 vols, London, 1808

# Bibliography

Butler, E.M., ed., *A Regency Visitor, The English Tour of Prince Puckler-Muskau Described in his Letters, 1826–1828*, London, Collins, 1957

Byron, Lord, Peter Quennell, ed., *Collected Poems (Vision of Judgement)*, London, Nonesuch Press, 1949

Calvert, The Hon. Mrs, *An Irish Beauty of the Regency*, London, John Lane, 1911

Carpenter, William, *Peerage for the People*, London, 1837

Castlereagh Correspondence: Londonderry, 3rd Marquess of, *Memoirs and Correspondence of Viscount Castlereagh*, London, 1848–53

Cloncurry, Lord, *Personal Recollections*, Dublin, 1849

Cobbett, William, *History of the Regency and the Reign of King George IV*, London, 1830

Conyngham Memoirs: *Memoirs of the Celebrated Lady C\*\*\*\*\*m*, London [1825?]

Creevey Papers: Creevey, Thomas, *The Creevey Papers*, 2 vols. London, John Murray, 1904

Croker Papers: Jennings, Louis, ed., *The Croker Papers*, 3 vols, London, 1884

Dover Papers (Delapre Abbey), Lord Dover's MS Journal

Ellenborough Diary: Colchester, Lord, ed., *A Political Diary 1828–50 by Edward Law, Lord Ellenborough*, London, 2 vols, 1881

Erredge, John Ackerson, *History of Brighthelmston*, Brighton, 1862

Farrington Diaries: ed. James Grieg, *The Farrington Diaries by Joseph Farrington R.A*, 8 vols, London, Hutchinson, 1922–28

Fitzgerald, Percy, *The Life of George IV*, 2 vols, London, 1881

Fulford, Roger, *George IV*, London, Duckworth, 1935

George, Dorothy M., *Catalogue of Personal and Political Satires, vols. v-xi*, London, British Museum, 1935-54

George, Dorothy M., *English Political Caricature 1793-1832*, Oxford, 2 vols, Clarendon Press, 1959

Glenbervie Journals: Bickley, Francis, ed., *The Diaries of Sylvester Douglas, Lord Glenbervie*, London, Constable, 1928

Gore, John, *Creevey's Life and Times*, London, John Murray, 1934

Gray, Denis, *Spencer Perceval*, Manchester, Manchester University Press, 1963

Gregory Memoir, ed. Lady Gregory, *Mr. Gregory's Letter-Box, 1813–1830*, London, Smith, Elder, 1898

Greville Memoirs: Strachey, Lytton and Fulford, Roger, *The Greville Memoirs 1814–1860*, 4 vols, London, Macmillan, 1938

Gronow Reminiscences: *The Reminiscences and Recollections of Captain Gronow*, 2 vols, London, 1892

Hardinge, George, *Miscellaneous Works in Prose and Verse*, London, 1827

Hawes, Frances, *Henry Brougham*, London, Jonathan Cape, 1957

Haydon Diary: Pope, Willard, ed., *The Diary of Benjamin Robert Haydon*, Harvard, Harvard University Press, 1960

# Bibliography

Hibbert, Christopher, *George IV, Prince of Wales*, London, Longman, 1972

Hibbert, Christopher, *George IV, Regent and King*, London, Allen Lane, 1975

Hobhouse Diary: ed. A. Aspinall, *The Diary of Henry Hobhouse 1820–1827*, London, Home & Van Thal, 1947

Holland Letters, ed. Earl of Ilchester, *Elizabeth, Lady Holland to her Son*, London, John Murray, 1946

Huish, Robert, *Memoirs of George the Fourth*, 2 vols, London, T. Kelly, 1830

Jackson Diary: ed. Lady Jackson, *Diaries and Letters of Sir George Jackson*, London, Bentley, 1873

James, Francis, *Lords of the Ascendancy. The Irish House of Lords and its Members, 1600–1800*, Dublin, Irish Academic Press, 1995

Jekyll Correspondence: Bourke, Algernon, ed., *Correspondence of Mr Joseph Jekyll 1818–1838*, London, 1894

Jermingham Letters: ed. Egerton Castle, *The Jermingham Letters: Being Excerpts from the Correspondence and Diaries of the Hon. Lady Jermingham and her Daughter Lady Bedingfield*, 2 vols, London 1896

Jesse, Captain, *The Life of Beau Brummel*, London, 1854

Jones, Wilbur Devereux, *Prosperity Robinson: The Life of Viscount Goderich*, London, Macmillan, 1967

Knighton Memoir: ed. Lady Knighton, *Memoirs of Sir William Knighton*, 2 vols, London, 1838

Leslie, Shane, *George the Fourth*, London, Ernest Benn, 1926

Lever, Sir Tresham, *The Letters of Lady Palmerston*, London, John Murray, 1957

Leveson Gower Correspondence: ed. Granville, Countess Castelia, *Letters of Harriette, Lady Granville, 1810–1845*, 2 vols, London, 1894

Lieven Letters: ed. Peter Quennell, *The Private Letters of Princess Lieven to Prince Metternich*, London, John Murray, 1937

Lockhart, J. G., *Memoirs of the Life of Sir Walter Scott*, Edinburgh, 1837

Longford, Elizabeth, *Victoria RI*, London, Weidenfeld & Nicolson, 1964

—— *Wellington: Pillar of State*, London, Weidenfeld & Nicolson, 1972

Lyttleton Correspondence: Wyndham, Hon. Mrs. Hugh, ed., *Correspondence of Sarah Spencer Lady Lyttleton, 1787–1870*, London, 1912

MacDougall, H., *Sketches of Irish Political Characters of the present day*, Dublin, 1799

Malmesbury Diaries: 3rd Earl of Malmesbury, ed., *The Diaries and Correspondence of James Harris, First Earl of Malmesbury*, 4 vols, London, Bentley, 1844

Matthews, Anne, *A Continuation of the Memories of Charles Matthews*, London, 1839

Mitchell, L.B.G., *Charles James Fox and the Disintegration of the Whig Party, 1782–1794*, Oxford, Oxford University Press, 1970

Morshead, Owen, *George IV and the Royal Lodge*, Regency Society of Brighton and Hove, 1965

# Bibliography

Munk, William, *Life of Sir Henry Halford, Bt.*, London, 1865

Musgrave, Clifford, *Life in Brighton*, London, Faber, 1970

New, Chester W., *The Life of Henry Brougham to 1830*, Oxford, Clarendon Press, 1961

Old Drogheda Society, *Drogheda and 1798*, Drogheda, 1998

Oman, Carola, *The Gascoigne Heiress*, London, Hodder & Stoughton, 1968

Pakenham, Thomas, *The Year of Liberty*, London, Hodder & Stoughton, 1969

Parissien, Steven, *George IV. The Grand Entertainment*, London, John Murray, 2001

Parker, Charles Stuart, *Sir Robert Peel, from his Private Papers*, 3 vols, London, John Murray, 1899

Petrie, Sir Charles, *Canning*, revised edition, London, Eyre & Spottiswoode, 1946

Ponsonby, Sir John, KCB, *The Ponsonby Family 1771–1855*, London, Medici Society, 1929

Priestley, J.B., *The Prince of Pleasure*, London, Heinemann, 1969

Puckler-Muskau, Prince, *Tour in England, Ireland and France 1826–8,* London, 1832

Victoria, Queen, *Letters*, 1st series, London, 1889

Raikes, Thomas, *A Portion of the Journal Kept by Thomas Raikes Esq. from 1831 to 1847*, 4 vols, London, 1856–7

Report of the Proceedings, ed. J. Nightingale, *Report of the Proceedings before the House of Lords on a Bill of Pains and Penalties,* 3 vols, London, 1821

Royal Archives, Windsor Castle

Royal Archive Accounts

Royal Archives, Coutts Papers

Royal Archives, Knighton Papers

*Royal Visit, The*, Burke, Thomas, ed., Dublin, 1821

Scott Letters: ed. H.C. Grierson, *The Letters of Sir Walter Scott,* London, Constable, 1923–37

*Secrets of the Castle!!, The Life of the Marchioness of Co—y—n—h—m*, London, [1835?]

Shelley Diary: ed. Richard Edgcumbe, *The Diary of Frances, Lady Shelley*, 2 vols, London, 1912–13

Sitwell, Osbert, *Left Hand Right Hand!*, London, Macmillan, 1945

Stapleton, A.G., *Political Life of George Canning*, 2 vols, London, 1831

Steuart, Francis, A., *The Diary of a Lady in Waiting by Lady Charlotte Bury*, 2 vols, London, 1808

Stroud, Dorothy, *Henry Holland,* London, Country Life, 1966

Taylor, Thomas, *Life of Benjamin Robert Haydon*, 2 vols, London, Longman, Green & Co., 1853

Waller of Woodcote, MSS (Warwick), CR 341/207

Ward, Marion, *Forth*, London, Phillimore, 1982

# Bibliography

*Wellington Despatches,* ed. Duke of Wellington, *Supplementary Despatches 1794–1818,* 15 vols, London, John Murray, 1858–72

Wellington Friends: ed. 7th Duke of Wellington, *Wellington and his Friends, Letters of the 1st Duke of Wellington,* London, Macmillan, 1965

Wilkins, W.H., *Mrs Fitzherbert and George IV,* 2 vols, London, Longman, Green & Co., 1905

Wilson, Frances, *The Courtesan's Revenge,* London, Faber & Faber, 2003

Wilson, Harriette, *Memoirs of Harriette Wilson Written by Herself,* 4 vols, London, 1825

Wraxall Memoirs: ed. Henry B. Wraxall, *The Historical and Posthumous Memoirs of Sir Nathaniel William Wraxall 1772–1789,* 5 vols, London, 1884

Yonge, C.D., *Life and Administration of Robert Banks Jenkinson, 2nd Earl of Liverpool,* 3 vols, London, Collins, 1972

# Index

# Index